Muriel James

Cambridge IGCSE® and O Level
Additional Mathematics

Practice Book

Second edition

CAMBRIDGE
UNIVERSITY PRESS

CAMBRIDGE
UNIVERSITY PRESS

University Printing House, Cambridge CB2 8BS, United Kingdom

One Liberty Plaza, 20th Floor, New York, NY 10006, USA

477 Williamstown Road, Port Melbourne, VIC 3207, Australia

314–321, 3rd Floor, Plot 3, Splendor Forum, Jasola District Centre, New Delhi – 110025, India

79 Anson Road, 06–04/06, Singapore 079906

Cambridge University Press is part of the University of Cambridge.

It furthers the University's mission by disseminating knowledge in the pursuit of education, learning and research at the highest international levels of excellence.

www.cambridge.org
Information on this title: education.cambridge.org

© Cambridge University Press 2018

First edition published 2016
Second edition published 2018

20 19 18 17 16 15 14 13 12 11 10 9 8 7 6 5 4 3

Printed in Spain by GraphyCems

A catalogue record for this publication is available from the British Library

ISBN 978-1-108-41285-8 Paperback

....

Cover artwork: shestakovych/Shutterstock

Contents

iii

Contents

v

Introduction

This practice book offers full coverage of the *Cambridge IGCSE®* and *O Level Additional Mathematics* syllabuses (0606 and 4037). It has been written by a highly experienced author, who is very familiar with the syllabus and the examinations. The course is aimed at students who are currently studying or have previously studied *Cambridge IGCSE® Mathematics* (0580) or *Cambridge O Level Mathematics* (4024).

The practice book has been written to closely follow the chapters and topics of the coursebook offering additional exercises to help students to consolidate concepts learnt.

At the start of each chapter, there is a list of objectives that are covered in the chapter. These objectives have been taken directly from the syllabus.

Worked examples are used throughout to demonstrate the methods for selected topics using typical workings and thought processes. These present the methods to the students in a practical and easy-to-follow way that minimises the need for lengthy explanations.

The exercises are carefully graded. They offer plenty of practice via 'drill' questions at the start of each exercise, which allow the student to practice methods that have just been introduced. The exercises then progress to questions that typically reflect the kinds of questions that the student may encounter in their examinations.

Towards the end of each chapter, there is a summary of the key concepts to help students consolidate what they have just learnt. This is followed by an 'exam-style' questions section to assess their learning after each chapter.

The answers to all questions are supplied at the back of the book, allowing self- and/or class-assessment. A student can assess their progress as they go along, choosing to do more or less practice as required. The answers given in this book are concise and it is important for students to appreciate that in an examination they should show as many steps in their working as possible.

A Coursebook is available in the *Additional Mathematics* series, which offers comprehensive coverage of the syllabuses. This book includes class discussion activities, worked examples for every method, exercises and a 'Past paper' questions section, which contains real questions taken from past examination papers. A digital Teacher's Resource, to offer support and advice, is available on the Cambridge Elevate platform.

How to use this book

Chapter

Each chapter begins with a set of learning objectives to explain what you will learn in the chapter.

Chapter 1:
Functions

This section will show you how to:

- understand and use the terms: function, domain, range (image set), one-one function, inverse function and composition of functions
- use the notation $f(x) = 2x^3 + 5$, $f : x \mapsto 5x - 3$, $f^{-1}(x)$ and $f^2(x)$
- understand the relationship between $y = f(x)$ and $y = |f(x)|$
- explain in words why a given function is a function or why it does not have an inverse
- find the inverse of a one-one function and form composite functions
- use sketch graphs to show the relationship between a function and its inverse.

Reminder

At the start of each chapter, a Reminder box reminds you of key concepts from the corresponding chapter in the Coursebook. If you are unsure of any of these concepts, look back at the chapter in the Coursebook.

 REMINDER

- When one function is followed by another function, the resulting function is called a **composite function.**

- $fg(x)$ means the function g acts on x first, then f acts on the result.

- $f^2(x)$ means $ff(x)$, so you apply the function f twice.

Remember

Remember boxes contain equations or formulae that you need to know.

REMEMBER

$$\left(x - \sqrt{y}\right)\left(x + \sqrt{y}\right) = x^2 - y$$

Worked Example

Detailed step-by-step approaches to help you solve problems.

WORKED EXAMPLE 1

Solve the simultaneous equations.

$x + 2y = 4$

$x^2 + 4y^2 = 10$

Answers

$x + 2y = 4$ -------------(1)

$x^2 + 4y^2 = 10$ ---------(2)

From (1), $x = 4 - 2y$.

Substitute for x in (2):

$(4 - 2y)^2 + 4y^2 = 10$ expand brackets

$16 - 16y + 4y^2 + 4y^2 = 10$ rearrange

$8y^2 - 16y + 6 = 0$ simplify

$4y^2 - 8y + 3 = 0$ factorise

$(2y - 1)(2y - 3) = 0$

$y = \dfrac{1}{2}$ or $y = 1\dfrac{1}{2}$

Substituting $y = \dfrac{1}{2}$ into (1) gives $x = 3$.

Substituting $y = 1\dfrac{1}{2}$ into (1) gives $x = 1$.

The solutions are: $x = 1$, $y = 1\dfrac{1}{2}$ and $x = 3$, $y = \dfrac{1}{2}$.

Tip

Tip boxes contain helpful hints for working through questions.

TIP

Squaring is not a reversible step. Notice that $x = 16$ does **not** satisfy the original equation.

Summary

At the end of each chapter to review what you have learned.

Summary

One radian (1^c) is the size of the angle subtended at the centre of a circle, radius r, by an arc of length r.

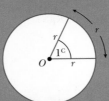

When θ is measured in radians:

- the length of arc $AB = r\theta$

- the area of sector $AOB = \dfrac{1}{2}r^2\theta$

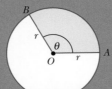

Chapter 1:
Functions

This section will show you how to:

- understand and use the terms: function, domain, range (image set), one-one function, inverse function and composition of functions
- use the notation $f(x) = 2x^3 + 5$, $f : x \mapsto 5x - 3$, $f^{-1}(x)$ and $f^2(x)$
- understand the relationship between $y = f(x)$ and $y = |f(x)|$
- solve graphically or algebraically equations of the type $|ax + b| = c$ and $|ax + b| = cx + d$
- explain in words why a given function is a function or why it does not have an inverse
- find the inverse of a one-one function and form composite functions
- use sketch graphs to show the relationship between a function and its inverse.

1.1 Mappings

« REMINDER

The table below shows one-one, many-one and one-many mappings.

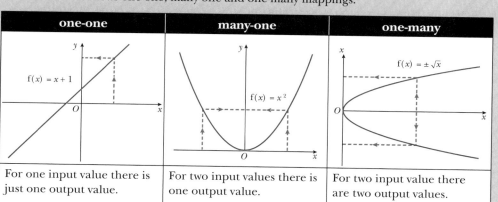

one-one	many-one	one-many
For one input value there is just one output value.	For two input values there is one output value.	For two input value there are two output values.

Exercise 1.1

Determine whether each of these mappings is one-one, many-one or one-many.

1 $x \mapsto 2x + 3$ $x \in \mathbb{R}$

2 $x \mapsto x^2 + 4$ $x \in \mathbb{R}$

3 $x \mapsto 2x^3$ $x \in \mathbb{R}$

4 $x \mapsto 3^x$ $x \in \mathbb{R}$

5 $x \mapsto \dfrac{-1}{x}$ $x \in \mathbb{R}, \ x > 0$

6 $x \mapsto x^2 + 1$ $x \in \mathbb{R}, \ x \geqslant 0$

7 $x \mapsto \dfrac{2}{x}$ $x \in \mathbb{R}, \ x > 0$

8 $x \mapsto \pm\sqrt{x}$ $x \in \mathbb{R}, \ x \geqslant 0$

1.2 Definition of a function

《 REMINDER

A function is a rule that maps each x value to just one y value for a defined set of input values.

This means that mappings that are either $\left\{ \begin{array}{l} \text{one-one} \\ \text{many-one} \end{array} \right.$ are called functions.

The mapping $x \mapsto x + 1$ where $x \in \mathbb{R}$, is a one-one function.

The function can be defined as $f : x \mapsto x + 1, \quad x \in \mathbb{R}$ or $f(x) = x + 1, \quad x \in \mathbb{R}$.

The set of input values for a function is called the **domain** of the function.

The set of output values for a function is called the **range** (or image set) of the function.

WORKED EXAMPLE 1

The function f is defined by $f(x) = (x - 1)^2 + 4$ for $0 \leqslant x \leqslant 5$.

Find the range of f.

Answers

$f(x) = (x - 1)^2 + 4$ is a positive quadratic function so the graph will be of the form

 $(x - 1)^2 + 4$

> This part of the expression is a square so it will always be $\geqslant 0$.
> The smallest value it can be is 0. This occurs when $x = 1$.

The minimum value of the expression is $0 + 4 = 4$ and this minimum occurs when $x = 1$.

So the function $f(x) = (x - 1)^2 + 4$ will have a minimum point at the point $(1, 4)$.

When $x = 0$, $y = (0 - 1)^2 + 4 = 5$.

When $x = 5$, $y = (5 - 1)^2 + 4 = 20$.

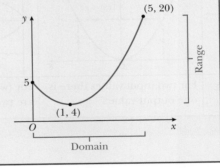

The range is $1 \leqslant f(x) \leqslant 20$.

Exercise 1.2

1 Which of the mappings in **Exercise 2.1** are functions?

2 Find the range for each of these functions.

    a $f(x) = x - 9, \quad -2 \leqslant x \leqslant 8$ **b** $f(x) = 2x - 2, \quad 0 \leqslant x \leqslant 6$

    c $f(x) = 7 - 2x, \quad -3 \leqslant x \leqslant 5$ **d** $f(x) = 2x^2, \quad -4 \leqslant x \leqslant 3$

    e $f(x) = 3^x, \quad -4 \leqslant x \leqslant 3$ **f** $f(x) = \dfrac{-1}{x}, \quad 1 \leqslant x \leqslant 6$

3 The function g is defined as $g(x) = x^2 - 5$ for $x \geqslant 0$.

    Find the range of g.

4 The function f is defined by $f(x) = 4 - x^2$ for $x \in \mathbb{R}$.

    Find the range of f.

5 The function f is defined by $f(x) = 3 - (x-1)^2$ for $x \geqslant 1$.
Find the range of f.

6 The function f is defined by $f(x) = (4x+1)^2 - 2$ for $x \geqslant -\dfrac{1}{4}$.
Find the range of f.

7 The function f is defined by $f : x \mapsto 8 - (x-3)^2$ for $2 \leqslant x \leqslant 7$.
Find the range of f.

8 The function f is defined by $f(x) = 3 - \sqrt{x-1}$ for $x \geqslant 1$.
Find the range of f.

9 Find the largest possible domain for the following functions.

a $f(x) = \dfrac{1}{x+3}$ **b** $f(x) = \dfrac{3}{x-2}$ **c** $\dfrac{4}{(x-3)(x+2)}$

d $f(x) = \dfrac{1}{x^2-4}$ **e** $f : x \mapsto \sqrt{x^3-4}$ **f** $f : x \mapsto \sqrt{x+5}$

g $g : x \mapsto \dfrac{1}{\sqrt{x-2}}$ **h** $f : x \mapsto \dfrac{x}{\sqrt{3-3x}}$ **i** $f : x \mapsto 1-x^2$

1.3 Composite functions

REMINDER

- When one function is followed by another function, the resulting function is called a **composite function.**
- $fg(x)$ means the function g acts on x first, then f acts on the result.
- $f^2(x)$ means $ff(x)$, so you apply the function f twice.

WORKED EXAMPLE 2

$f : x \mapsto 4x+3$ for $x \in \mathbb{R}$
$g : x \mapsto 2x^2 - 5$ for $x \in \mathbb{R}$
Find $fg(3)$.

Answer

$fg(3)$ g acts on 3 first and $g(3) = 2 \times 3^2 - 5 = 13$.
$= f(13)$
$= 4 \times 13 + 3$
$= 55$

WORKED EXAMPLE 3

$g(x) = 2x^2 - 2$ for $x \in \mathbb{R}$
$h(x) = 4 - 3x$ for $x \in \mathbb{R}$
Solve the equation $hg(x) = -14$.

Answers

$hg(x)$	g acts on x first and $g(x) = 2x^2 - 2$.
$= h(2x^2 - 2)$	h is the function 'triple and take from 4'.
$= 4 - 3(2x^2 - 2)$	Expand the brackets.
$= 4 - 6x^2 + 6$	
$= 10 - 6x^2$	
$hg(x) = -14$	
$-14 = 10 - 6x^2$	Set up and solve the equation.
$24 = 6x^2$	
$4 = x^2$	
$x = \pm 2$	

Exercise 1.3

1 $f(x) = 2 - x^2$ for $x \in \mathbb{R}$

$g(x) = \dfrac{x}{2} + 3$ for $x \in \mathbb{R}$

Find the value of $gf(4)$.

2 $f(x) = (x - 2)^2 - 2$ for $x \in \mathbb{R}$

Find $f^2(3)$.

3 The function f is defined by $f(x) = 1 + \sqrt{x - 3}$ for $x \geqslant 3$.

The function g is defined by $g(x) = \dfrac{-3}{x} - 1$ for $x > 0$.

Find $gf(7)$.

4 The function f is defined by $f(x) = (x - 2)^2 + 3$ for $x > -2$.

The function g is defined by $g(x) = \dfrac{3x + 4}{x + 2}$ for $x > 2$.

Find $fg(6)$.

5 $f : x \mapsto 3x - 1$ for $x > 0$

$g : x \mapsto \sqrt{x}$ for $x > 0$

Express each of the following in terms of f and g.

  a $x \mapsto 3\sqrt{x} - 1$ **b** $x \mapsto \sqrt{3x - 1}$

6 The function f is defined by $f : x \mapsto 2x - 1$ for $x \in \mathbb{R}$.

The function g is defined by $g : x \mapsto \dfrac{8}{4 - x}$ for $x \neq 4$.

Solve the equation $gf(x) = 5$.

7 $f(x) = 2x^2 + 3$ for $x > 0$

$g(x) = \dfrac{5}{x}$ for $x > 0$

Solve the equation $fg(x) = 4$.

8 The function f is defined, for $x \in \mathbb{R}$, by $f : x \mapsto \dfrac{2x - 1}{x - 3}, x \neq 3$.

The function g is defined, for $x \in \mathbb{R}$, by $g : x \mapsto \dfrac{x + 1}{2}, x \neq 1$.

Solve the equation $fg(x) = 4$.

TIP

Before writing your final answers, compare your solutions with the domains of the original functions.

9 The function g is defined by $g(x) = 1 - 2x^2$ for $x \geqslant 0$.

The function h is defined by $h(x) = 3x - 1$ for $x \geqslant 0$.

Solve the equation $gh(x) = -3$ giving your answer(s) as exact value(s).

10 The function f is defined by $f : x \mapsto x^2$ for $x \in \mathbb{R}$.

The function g is defined by $g : x \mapsto x + 2$ for $x \in \mathbb{R}$.

Express each of the following as a composite function, using only f and g.

a $x \mapsto (x + 2)^2$ **b** $x \mapsto x^2 + 2$ **c** $x \mapsto x + 4$ **d** $x \mapsto x^4$

11 The functions f and g are defined for $x > 0$ by $f : x \mapsto x + 3$ and $g : x \mapsto \sqrt{x}$

Express in terms of f and g

a $x \mapsto \sqrt{x + 3}$ **b** $x \mapsto x + 6$ **c** $x \mapsto \sqrt{x} + 3$

12 Given the functions $f(x) = \sqrt{x}$ and $g(x) = \dfrac{x - 5}{2x + 1}$,

a Find the domain and range of g.

b Solve the equation $g(x) = 0$.

c Find the domain and range of fg.

1.4 Modulus functions

REMINDER

- The **modulus** (or **absolute value**) of a number is the magnitude of the number without a sign attached.
- **The modulus of** x, written as $|x|$, is defined as
$$|x| = \begin{cases} x & \text{if } x > 0 \\ 0 & \text{if } x = 0 \\ -x & \text{if } x < 0 \end{cases}$$
- **The statement** $|x|, = k$, where $\geqslant 0$, means that $x = k$ or $x = -k$.

WORKED EXAMPLE 4

a $|4x + 3| = x + 18$ **b** $|2x^2 - 9| = 7$

Answers

a $|4x + 3| = x + 18$

$4x + 3 = x + 18$ or $4x + 3 = -x - 18$

$\quad 3x = 15 \qquad\qquad\qquad 5x = -21$

$\quad\quad x = 5 \qquad\qquad\qquad\quad x = -\dfrac{21}{5}$

Solution is : $x = 5$ or $-\dfrac{21}{5}$

b $|2x^2 - 7| = 9$

$2x^2 - 7 = 9$ or $2x^2 - 7 = -9$

$\quad 2x^2 = 16 \qquad\qquad\quad 2x^2 = -2$

$\quad\quad x^2 = 8 \qquad\qquad\qquad x^2 = -1$

$\quad\quad x = \pm 2\sqrt{2}$

Solution is : $x = \pm 2\sqrt{2}$

Exercise 1.4

1 Solve.

a $|2x - 1| = 11$

b $|2x + 4| = 8$

c $|6 - 3x| = 4$

d $\left|\dfrac{x - 2}{5}\right| = 6$

e $\left|\dfrac{3x + 4}{3}\right| = 4$

f $\left|\dfrac{9 - 2x}{3}\right| = 4$

g $\left|\dfrac{x}{3} - 6\right| = 1$

h $\left|\dfrac{2x + 5}{3} + \dfrac{2x}{5}\right| = 3$

i $|2x - 6| = x$

TIP
Remember to check your answers to make sure that they satisfy the original equation.

2 Solve.

a $\left|\dfrac{2x - 5}{x + 4}\right| = 3$

b $\left|\dfrac{4x + 2}{x + 3}\right| = 3$

c $\left|1 + \dfrac{2x + 5}{x + 3}\right| = 4$

d $|2x - 3| = 3x$

e $2x + |3x - 4| = 5$

f $7 - |1 - 2x| = 3x$

3 Solve giving your answers as exact values if appropriate.

a $\left|x^2 - 4\right| = 5$

b $\left|x^2 + 5\right| = 11$

c $\left|9 - x^2\right| = 3 - x$

d $\left|x^2 - 3x\right| = 2x$

e $\left|x^2 - 16\right| = 2x + 1$

f $\left|2x^2 - 1\right| = x + 2$

g $\left|3 - 2x^2\right| = x$

h $\left|x^2 - 4x\right| = 3 - 2x$

i $\left|2x^2 - 2x + 5\right| = 1 - x$

4 Solve each of the following pairs of simultaneous equations.

a $y = x + 4$
$y = \left|x^2 - 2\right|$

b $y = 1 - x$
$y = \left|4x^2 - 4x\right|$

1.5 Graphs of $y = |f(x)|$ where $f(x)$ is linear

Exercise 1.5

1 Sketch the graphs of each of the following functions showing the coordinates of the points where the graph meets the axes.

a $y = |x - 2|$

b $y = |3x - 3|$

c $y = |3 - x|$

d $y = \left|\dfrac{1}{3}x - 3\right|$

e $y = |6 - 3x|$

f $y = \left|5 - \dfrac{1}{2}x\right|$

2 a Complete the table of values for $y = 3 - |x - 1|$.

x	−2	−1	0	1	2	3	4
y		1		3			

b Draw the graph of $y = 3 - |x - 1|$ for $-2 \le x \le 4$.

3 Draw the graphs of each of the following functions.

a $y = |2x| + 2$

b $y = |x| - 2$

c $y = 4 - |3x|$

d $y = |x - 1| + 3$

e $y = |3x - 6| - 2$

f $y = 4 - \left|\dfrac{1}{2}x\right|$

4 Given that each of these functions is defined for the domain $-3 \le x \le 4$, find the range of

a $f : x \mapsto 6 - 3x$

b $g : x \mapsto |6 - 3x|$

c $h : x \mapsto 6 - |3x|$.

5 a $f : x \mapsto 2 - 2x$ for $-1 \leqslant x \leqslant 5$

b $g : x \mapsto |2 - 2x|$ for $-1 \leqslant x \leqslant 5$

c $h : x \mapsto 2 - |2x|$ for $-1 \leqslant x \leqslant 5$

Find the range of each function for $-1 \leqslant x \leqslant 5$.

6 a Sketch the graph of $y = |3x - 2|$ for $-4 < x < 4$, showing the coordinates of the points where the graph meets the axes.

b On the same diagram, sketch the graph of $y = x + 3$.

c Solve the equation $|3x - 2| = x + 3$.

7 A function f is defined by $f(x) = 2 - |3x - 1|$, for $-1 \leqslant x \leqslant 3$.

a Sketch the graph of $y = f(x)$.

b State the range of f.

c Solve the equation $f(x) = -2$.

8 a Sketch on a single diagram, the graphs of $x + 3y = 6$ and $y = |x + 2|$.

b Solve the inequality $|x + 2| < \dfrac{1}{3}(6 - x)$.

1.6 Inverse functions

REMINDER

- **The inverse of the function** $f(x)$ is written as $f^{-1}(x)$.
- The domain of $f^{-1}(x)$ is the range of $f(x)$.
- The range of $f^{-1}(x)$ is the domain of $f(x)$.
- It is important to remember that not every function has an inverse.
- An inverse function $f^{-1}(x)$ can exist if, and only if, the function $f(x)$ is a one-one mapping.

WORKED EXAMPLE 5

$f(x) = (x + 3)^2 - 1$ for $x > -3$

a Find an expression for $f^{-1}(x)$.

b Solve the equation $f^{-1}(x) = 3$.

Answers

a $f(x) = (x + 3)^2 - 1$ for $x > -3$

Step 1: Write the function as $y =$ ⟶ $y = (x + 3)^2 - 1$

Step 2: Interchange the x and y variables. ⟶ $x = (y + 3)^2 - 1$

Step 3: Rearrange to make y the subject. ⟶ $x + 1 = (y + 3)^2$

$$\sqrt{x + 1} = y + 3$$
$$y = \sqrt{x + 1} - 3$$

$f^{-1}(x) = \sqrt{x + 1} - 3$

b $f^{-1}(x) = 3$.

$\sqrt{x + 1} - 3 = 3$

$\sqrt{x + 1} = 6$

$x + 1 = 36$

$x = 35$

Exercise 1.6

1 $f(x) = (x + 2)^2 - 3$ for $x \geqslant -2$.
Find an expression for $f^{-1}(x)$.

2 $f(x) = \dfrac{5}{x - 2}$ for $x \geqslant 0$.
Find an expression for $f^{-1}(x)$.

3 $f(x) = (3x - 2)^2 + 3$ for $x \geqslant \dfrac{2}{3}$.

Find an expression for $f^{-1}(x)$.

4 $f(x) = 4 - \sqrt{x - 2}$ for $x \geqslant 2$.
Find an expression for $f^{-1}(x)$.

5 $f : x \mapsto 3x - 4$ for $x > 0$ 　　　　　　　$g : x \mapsto \dfrac{4}{4 - x}$ for $x \neq 4$.

Express $f^{-1}(x)$ and $g^{-1}(x)$ in terms of x.

6 $f(x) = (x - 2)^2 + 3$ for $x > 2$
 a Find an expression for $f^{-1}(x)$.
 b Solve the equation $f^{-1}(x) = f(4)$.

7 $g(x) = \dfrac{3x + 1}{x - 3}$ for $x > 3$
 a Find an expressions for $g^{-1}(x)$ and comment on your result.
 b Solve the equation $g^{-1}(x) = 6$.

8 $f(x) = \dfrac{x}{2} - 2$ for $x \in \mathbb{R}$ 　　　　　　　$g(x) = x^2 - 4x$ for $x \in \mathbb{R}$
 a Find $f^{-1}(x)$.
 b Solve $fg(x) = f^{-1}(x)$ leaving answers as exact values.

9 $f : x \mapsto \dfrac{3x + 1}{x - 1}$ for $x \neq 1$ 　　　　　　$g : x \mapsto \dfrac{x - 2}{3}$ for $x > -2$
Solve the equation $f(x) = g^{-1}(x)$.

10 If $f(x) = \dfrac{x^2 - 9}{x^2 + 4}$ $x \in \mathbb{R}$ find an expression for $f^{-1}(x)$.

11 If $f(x) = 2\sqrt{x}$ and $g(x) = 5x$, solve the equation $f^{-1}g(x) = 0.01$.

12 Find the value of the constant k such that $f(x) = \dfrac{2x - 4}{x + k}$
 is a self-inverse function.

13 The function f is defined by $f(x) = x^3$. Find an expression for $g(x)$ in terms of x
 for each of the following:
 a $fg(x) = 3x + 2$
 b $gf(x) = 3x + 2$

TIP
A self-inverse function is one for which $f(x) = f^{-1}(x)$, for all values of x in the domain.

8

14 Given $f(x) = 2x + 1$ and $g(x) = \dfrac{x+1}{2}$ find the following.

    a f^{-1} **b** g^{-1} **c** $(fg)^{-1}$ **d** $(gf)^{-1}$ **e** $f^{-1}g^{-1}$ **f** $g^{-1}f^{-1}$

    Write down any observations from your results.

15 Given that $fg(x) = \dfrac{x+2}{3}$ and $g(x) = 2x + 5$ find $f(x)$.

16 Functions f and g are defined for all real numbers.

    $g(x) = x^2 + 7$ and $gf(x) = 9x^2 + 6x + 8$. Find $f(x)$.

1.7 The graph of a function and its inverse

« REMINDER

The graphs of f and f^{-1} are reflections of each other in the line $y = x$.

This is true for all one-one functions and their inverse functions.

This is because: $ff^{-1}(x) = x = f^{-1}f(x)$.

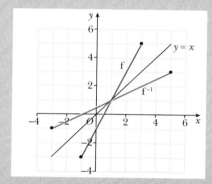

Some functions are called **self-inverse functions** because f and its inverse f^{-1} are the same.

If $f(x) = \dfrac{1}{x}$ for $x \neq 0$, then $f^{-1}(x) = \dfrac{1}{x}$ for $x \neq 0$.

So $f(x) = \dfrac{1}{x}$ for $x \neq 0$ is an example of a self-inverse function.

When a function f is self-inverse, the graph of f will be symmetrical about the line $y = x$.

Exercise 1.7

1 On a copy of the grid, draw the graph of the inverse of the function $y = 2^{-x}$.

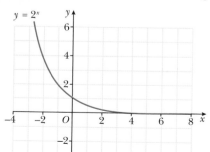

2 $f(x) = x^2 + 5, x \geq 0$.

On the same axes, sketch the graphs of $y = f(x)$ and $y = f^{-1}(x)$, showing the coordinates of any points where the curves meet the coordinate axes.

3 $g(x) = \dfrac{1}{2}x^2 - 4$ for $x \geq 0$.

Sketch, on a single diagram, the graphs of $y = g(x)$ and $y = g^{-1}(x)$, showing the coordinates of any points where the curves meet the coordinate axes.

4 The function f is defined by $f(x) = 3x - 6$ for all real values of x

a Find the inverse function $f^{-1}(x)$.

b Sketch the graphs of $f(x)$ and $f^{-1}(x)$ on the same axes.

c Write down the point of intersection of the graphs $f(x)$ and $f^{-1}(x)$.

5 Given the function $f(x) = x^2 - 2x$ for $x \geq 1$.

a Explain why $f^{-1}(x)$ exists and find $f^{-1}(x)$.

b State the range of the function $f^{-1}(x)$.

c Sketch the graphs of $f(x)$ and $f^{-1}(x)$ on the same axes.

d Write down where $f^{-1}(x)$ crosses the y axis.

6 a By finding $f^{-1}(x)$ show that $f(x) = \dfrac{3x - 1}{2x - 3}$ $x \in \mathbb{R},\ x \neq \dfrac{3}{2}$ is a self-inverse function.

b Sketch the graphs of $f(x)$ and $f^{-1}(x)$ on the same axes.

c Write down the coordinates of the intersection of the graphs with the coordinate axes.

Summary

Functions

A function is a rule that maps each x-value to just one y-value for a defined set of input values.

Mappings that are either $\begin{cases} \text{one-one} \\ \text{many-one} \end{cases}$ are called functions.

The set of input values for a function is called the **domain** of the function.

The set of output values for a function is called the **range** (or image set) of the function.

Modulus function

The modulus of x, written as $|x|$, is defined as

$$|x| = \begin{cases} x & \text{if } x > 0 \\ 0 & \text{if } x = 0 \\ -x & \text{if } x < 0 \end{cases}$$

Composite functions

$fg(x)$ means the function g acts on x first, then f acts on the result.

$f^2(x)$ means $ff(x)$.

Inverse functions

The inverse of a function $f(x)$ is the function that undoes what $f(x)$ has done.

The inverse of the function $f(x)$ is written as $f^{-1}(x)$.

The domain of $f^{-1}(x)$ is the range of $f(x)$.

The range of $f^{-1}(x)$ is the domain of $f(x)$.

An inverse function $f^{-1}(x)$ can exist if, and only if, the function $f(x)$ is a one-one mapping.

The graphs of f and f^{-1} are reflections of each other in the line $y = x$.

Exercise 1.8

1 A one-one function f is defined by $f(x) = (x - 2)^2 - 3$ for $x \geqslant k$.

  a State the least value that x can take.

  b For this least value of k, write down the range of f.

2 The function $f(x) = x^2 - 4ax$ (where a is a positive constant) is defined for all real values of x.

  Given that the range is $\geqslant -8$, find the exact value of a.

3 $f(x) = (2x - 1)^2 + 3$ for $x > 0$

  $g(x) = \dfrac{5}{2x}$ for $x > 0$

  Solve the equation $fg(x) = 7$.

4 The function f is defined by $f(x) = 1 - x^2$ for $x \in \mathbb{R}$.

  The function g is defined by $g(x) = 2x - 1$ for $x \in \mathbb{R}$.

  Find the values of x (in exact form) which solve the equation $fg(x) = gf(x)$.

5 Solve these simultaneous equations.

  $y = 2x + 5$ $y = \left|3 - x^2\right|$

6 **a** Sketch the graph of $y = |2x + 1|$ for $-3 < x < 3$, showing the coordinates of the points where the graph meets the axes.

  b On the same diagram, sketch the graph of $y = 3x$.

  c Solve the equation $3x = |2x + 1|$.

7 **a** Sketch the graph of $y = |x + 3|$.

  b Solve the inequality $|x + 3| > 2x + 1$.

8 $f(x) = x^2 - 3$ for $x \in \mathbb{R}$ $g(x) = 3x + 2$ for $x \in \mathbb{R}$

  Solve the equation $gf(x) = g^{-1}(8)$.

9 Given the functions $f(x) = 2x + 3$ and $g(x) = \dfrac{1}{x + 1}$ $x \in \mathbb{R}$ $x \neq 1$.

  a Find an expression for the inverse function $f^{-1}(x)$.

  b Find an expression for the composite function $gf(x)$.

  c Solve the equation $f^{-1}(x) = gf(x) - 1$.

10 Given the function $f(x) = \dfrac{2x + 1}{x + 2}$ $x \neq -2$.

  a Find $f^{-1}(x)$.

  b Find the points of intersection of the graphs of $f(x)$ and $f^{-1}(x)$.

Chapter 2:
Simultaneous equations and quadratics

This section will show you how to:

- solve simple simultaneous equations in two unknowns by elimination or substitution
- find the maximum and minimum values of a quadratic function
- sketch graphs of quadratic functions and find their range for a given domain
- sketch graphs of the function $y = |f(x)|$, where $f(x)$ is quadratic and solve associated equations
- determine the number of roots of a quadratic equation and the related conditions for a line to intersect, be a tangent or not intersect a given curve
- solve quadratic equations for real roots and find the solution set for quadratic inequalities.

2.1 Simultaneous equations (one linear and one non-linear)

WORKED EXAMPLE 1

Solve the simultaneous equations.

$x + 2y = 4$

$x^2 + 4y^2 = 10$

Answers

$x + 2y = 4$ --------------(1)

$x^2 + 4y^2 = 10$ ---------(2)

From (1), $x = 4 - 2y$.

Substitute for x in (2):

$$(4 - 2y)^2 + 4y^2 = 10 \qquad \text{expand brackets}$$

$$16 - 16y + 4y^2 + 4y^2 = 10 \qquad \text{rearrange}$$

$$8y^2 - 16y + 6 = 0 \qquad \text{simplify}$$

$$4y^2 - 8y + 3 = 0 \qquad \text{factorise}$$

$$(2y - 1)(2y - 3) = 0$$

$$y = \frac{1}{2} \text{ or } y = 1\frac{1}{2}$$

Substituting $y = \frac{1}{2}$ into (1) gives $x = 3$.

Substituting $y = 1\frac{1}{2}$ into (1) gives $x = 1$.

The solutions are: $x = 1$, $y = 1\frac{1}{2}$ and $x = 3$, $y = \frac{1}{2}$.

Exercise 2.1

Solve the following simultaneous equations.

1 a $y = x^2 + 3x + 2$
$y = 2x + 8$

b $y = 3x^2 - 8x$
$y = 3x + 4$

c $x + y = 5$
$xy = 6$

d $y = x - 3$
$y^2 + xy + 4x = 7$

e $x^2 + y^2 = 5$
$y = \dfrac{2}{x}$

f $3y - 2x = 11$
$xy = 2$

g $y^2 + xy + 16x - 13 = 0$

  $y = 3 - 2x$

h $2x^2 - xy + y^2 - 32 = 0$

  $y = \dfrac{-5}{x}$

2 A rectangle is x cm long and y cm wide. Its area is $48\,\text{cm}^2$ and its perimeter is $32\,\text{cm}$.

  a Use the above to form two equations.

  b Find the dimensions of the rectangle.

3 A farmer uses $50\,\text{m}$ of fencing to enclose a rectangular area against a long straight wall. What must be the dimensions of the enclosure if its area is to be $300\,\text{m}^2$.

4 I think of two positive numbers. If the difference between them is 12 and the sum of their squares is 314, find the numbers.

5 The straight line $y - 2x + 3 = 0$ intersects a curve with equation $y = x^2 - 2x$ at the points A and B. Find the coordinates of A and B.

6 The line $y = x + 5$ cuts the curve $y = x^2 - 3x$ at two points A and B. Find the coordinates of A and B and the exact value of the length of the straight line joining these points.

7 The line $y = ax - 1$ and the curve $y = x^2 + bx - 5$ intersect at the points $A(4, -5)$ and B. Find the values of a and b and the coordinates of B.

8 The straight line $2y - x = 5$ intersects with the circle $x^2 + y^2 = 25$ at A and B.

  a Find the coordinates of A and B.

  b Find the exact length of the line AB.

  c Find the equation of the perpendicular line which passes through the midpoint of the line AB.

2.2 Maximum and minimum values of a quadratic function

« REMINDER

The general rule is:

For a quadratic function $\text{f}(x) = ax^2 + bx + c$ that is written in the form:

$$\text{f}(x) = a(x - h)^2 + k$$

i if $a > 0$, the minimum point is (h, k)

ii if $a < 0$, the maximum point is (h, k).

Completing the square for a quadratic expression or function enables you to:

- write down the maximum or minimum value of the expression
- write down the coordinates of the maximum or minimum point of the function
- sketch the graph of the function
- write down the line of symmetry of the function
- state the range of the function.

13

WORKED EXAMPLE 2

$f(x) = 5 + 6x - 3x^2 \quad x \in \mathbb{R}$

a Find the value of a, the value of b and the value of c for which $f(x) = a - b(x + c)^2$.

b Write down the coordinates of the maximum point on the curve $y = f(x)$.

c Write down the equation of the axis of symmetry of the curve $y = f(x)$.

d State the range of the function $f(x)$.

Answers

a $5 + 6x - 3x^2 = a - b(x + c)^2$

$5 + 6x - 3x^2 = a - b(x^2 + 2cx + c^2)$

$5 + 6x - 3x^2 = a - bx^2 - 2bcx - bc^2$

Comparing coefficients of x^2, coefficients of x and the constant gives:

$-3 = -b$ --------(1) $6 = -2bc$ -------(2) $5 = a - bc^2$ -------(3)

Substituting $b = 3$ in equation (2) gives $c = -1$.

Substituting $b = 3$ and $c = -1$ in equation (3) gives $a = 8$.

So $a = 8$, $b = 3$ and $c = -1$.

b $y = 8 - 3(x - 1)^2$

> This part of the expression is a square so it will always be $\geqslant 0$.
> The smallest value it can be is 0.

The maximum value of the expression is $8 - 3 \times 0 = 8$ and this maximum occurs when $x = 1$.

So the function $y = 5 + 6x - 3x^2$ will have a maximum point at the point $(1, 8)$.

c The axis of symmetry is $x = 1$.

d The range is $f(x) \leqslant 8$.

Exercise 2.2

1 Express each of the following in the form $(x - m)^2 + n$

   a $x^2 + 6x - 1$ **b** $x^2 - 2x - 1$ **c** $x^2 - 3x + 1$ **d** $x^2 - x - 3$

2 Express each of the following in the form $a(x - h)^2 + k$

   a $2x^2 + 6x + 2$ **b** $2x^2 + 8x + 5$ **c** $3x^2 - 6x + 1$ **d** $2x^2 - x - 2$

3 Express each of the following in the form $m - (x - n)^2$.

   a $10x - x^2$ **b** $12x - x^2$ **c** $5x - x^2$ **d** $7x - x^2$

4 Express each of the following in the form $a - (x + b)^2$.

   a $5 - 4x - x^2$ **b** $8 - 6x - x^2$ **c** $12 - 5x - x^2$ **d** $9 - 3x - x^2$

5 Express each of the following in the form $a - p(x + q)^2$.

   a $9 - 6x - 3x^2$ **b** $3 - 4x - 2x^2$ **c** $12 - 8x - 2x^2$ **d** $4 - 5x - 15x^2$

6 Given the function $f(x) = x^2 - 8x + 18, \ x \in \mathbb{R}$

   a Write it in the form $f(x) = (x - p)^2 + q$ where p and q are integers to be found.

   b Write down the equation of the axis of symmetry of the graph.

   c Write down the coordinates of the minimum point of the graph of $f(x) = x^2 - 8x + 18$.

> **TIP**
> A quadratic function written in the form $f(x) = a(x - p)^2 + q$ with $a \neq 0$ has an axis of symmetry $x = p$ and a vertex (p, q).

7 Given the function $f(x) = -2x^2 - 12x + 7, \ x \in \mathbb{R}$.

   a Express the function in the form $f(x) = a(x + p)^2 + q$ where p and q are integers to be found.

   b Sketch the graph of the function.

   c Write down the equation of its line of symmetry.

   d Write down the maximum value of the function $f(x) = -2x^2 - 12x + 7$.

> **TIP: BE CAREFUL!**
> You need to distinguish between the maximum **value** of the function and the **coordinates** of the maximum value.

8 Given the function $f(x) = x^2 - 6x + 11, \ x \in \mathbb{R}$:

   a Express the function in the form $f(x) = a(x - p)^2 + q$ where p and q are integers to be found.

   b Write down the coordinates of the stationary point on the graph of $y = f(x)$.

   c State whether this stationary point is a maximum or a minimum.

   d Does the function meet the x axis?

   e Sketch the function.

9 If $f(x) = 2x^2 - 12x + 23, \ x \in \mathbb{R}$

   a Express the function in the form $f(x) = a(x - p)^2 + q$.

   b Find the least value of $f(x)$ and the corresponding value of x.

   c Write down the range of $f(x)$.

   d Write down a suitable domain for $f(x)$ in order that $f^{-1}(x)$ exists.

10 Given that $5x^2 - ax + 14 \equiv b(x + 2)^2 + c$, find the values of a, b and c.

11 Express $f(x) = 2x^2 + 8x + 5$ in the form $f(x) = a(x + p)^2 + q$ stating the values of a, p and q.

12 a Express $f(x) = x^2 + 6x - 1$ in the form $f(x) = (x + p)^2 + q$.

   b Hence solve the equation $x^2 + 6x - 1 = 0$ leaving your answers in exact form.

13 If $f(x) = 4x^2 + 6x - 12$ where $x \geqslant m$, find the smallest value of m for which f has an inverse.

14 $f(x) = 5x^2 - 3x + 7, \ 0 \leqslant x \leqslant 5$

   a Express $5x^2 - 3x + 7$ in the form $a(x - b)^2 + c$ where a, b and c are constants.

   b Find the coordinates of the turning point of the function $f(x)$, stating whether it is a maximum or minimum point.

   c Find the range of f.

   d State, giving a reason, whether or not f has an inverse.

15

2.3 Graphs of $y = |f(x)|$ where $f(x)$ is quadratic

WORKED EXAMPLE 3

a Find the coordinates of the stationary point on the curve $y = |(x+2)(x-2)|$.

b Sketch the graph of $y = |(x+2)(x-2)|$.

c Find the set of values of k for which $|(x+2)(x-2)| = k$ has four solutions.

Answers

a The x-coordinate of the stationary point is equidistant from the x-intercepts.

$|(x+2)(x-2)| = 0$

$x = -2$ or $x = 2$

The x-coordinate of the stationary point $= \dfrac{-2+2}{2} = 0$.

The y-coordinate of the stationary point $= |(0+2)(0-2)| = |-4| = 4$.

The minimum point is $(0, 4)$.

b

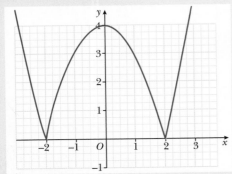

c $0 < k < 4$

Exercise 2.3

1 Sketch the graphs of each of the following functions.

a $y = |x^2 - x - 12|$ **b** $y = |x^2 + 3x - 4|$

c $y = |2x^2 - 5x - 3|$ **d** $y = |x^2 - 2x|$

2 $f(x) = 4 - 4x - x^2$

a Write $f(x)$ in the form $a - (x+b)^2$, where a, b and c are constants.

b Sketch the graph of $y = f(x)$.

c Sketch the graph of $y = |f(x)|$.

16

3 $f(x) = 3x^2 - 6x + 1$

   a Write f(x) in the form $a(x + b)^2 + c$, where a, b and c are constants.

   b Sketch the graph of $y = |f(x)|$.

4 Find the points of intersection of the curve $y = |x^2 - 4|$ and the line $y = 2x + 1$.

5 **a** Find the coordinates of the stationary point on the curve $y = |(x - 3)(x - 1)|$.

   b Find the set of values of k for which $|(x - 3)(x - 1)| = k$ has two solutions.

6 **a** Find the coordinates of the stationary point on the curve $y = |(x - 6)(x - 2)|$.

   b Find the value of k for which $|(x - 6)(x - 2)| = k$ has three solutions.

7 Solve these equations.

   a $|x^2 - 4| = 10$ **b** $|x^2 - 1| = 2$ **c** $|x^2 - x| = 2$

   d $|x^2 + 4x| = 3$ **e** $|2x^2 - 4x + 1| = 6$ **f** $|3 + 2x - x^2| = 6$

8 **a** Sketch the graph of $y = |x^2 - 12|$.

   b Hence solve the equation $|x^2 - 12| > x$.

9 Solve these simultaneous equations.

   a $y = 2x + 1$ **b** $3 = x + y$ **c** $y = 2 - x$

      $y = |x^2 - 2x - 4|$ $y = |-x^2 + 2x + 3|$ $y = |x^2 + 4x - 12|$

2.4 Quadratic inequalities

REMINDER

Solving linear inequalities

Solve $4(x + 5) > 8$ expand brackets

     $4x + 20 > 8$ subtract 20 from both sides

       $4x > -12$ divide both sides by 4

        $x > -3$

Solve $6 - 2x \leqslant 13$ subtract 6 from both sides

     $-2x \leqslant 7$ *divide both sides by –2

      $x \geqslant -3.5$

TIP

*Remember: when you multiply or divide both sides of an inequality by a negative number then the inequality sign must be reversed.

Solving quadratic inequalities

Quadratic inequalities can be solved by sketching a graph and considering when the graph is above or below the x-axis.

WORKED EXAMPLE 4

Solve $x^2 < 3 + 2x$.

Answers

Rearrange the inequality to give $x^2 - 2x - 3 < 0$.

Sketch the graph of $y = x^2 - 2x - 3$.

When $y = 0$, $x^2 - 2x - 3 = 0$

$$(x + 1)(x - 3) = 0$$

$$x = -1 \text{ or } x = 3$$

So the x-axis crossing points are -1 and 3.

For $x^2 - 2x - 3 < 0$, find the values of x for which the curve is negative (below the x-axis).

The solution is $-1 < x < 3$.

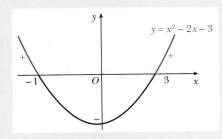

WORKED EXAMPLE 5

Solve $-3x^2 + 2x \leqslant -8$.

Answers

Rearranging: $-3x^2 + 2x + 8 \leqslant 0$.

Multiplying by -1: $3x^2 - 2x - 8 \geqslant 0$.

Sketch the graph of $y = 3x^2 - 2x - 8$.

When $y = 0$, $3x^2 - 2x - 8 = 0$

$$(3x + 4)(x - 2) = 0$$

$$x = \frac{-4}{3} \text{ or } x = 2$$

So the x-axis crossing points are $\frac{-4}{3}$ and 2.

For $3x^2 - 2x - 8 \geqslant 0$, find the values of x for which the curve is either zero or positive (above the x-axis).

The solution is $x \leqslant -\frac{4}{3}$ and $x \geqslant 2$.

Exercise 2.4

1 Solve.

   a $(x + 6)(x - 3) > 0$ **b** $x(x + 6) < 0$ **c** $(3x - 1)(x + 4) \geqslant 0$

   d $(3 - 2x)(2x + 1) \leqslant 0$ **e** $x(3 - 4x) \geqslant 0$ **f** $(2x - 1)(x + 3) \leqslant x(3x - 9)$

2 Solve.

   a $2x^2 - x - 6 < 0$ **b** $2x^2 - 7x - 4 \geqslant 0$ **c** $3x^2 + 5x - 12 \leqslant 0$

   d $x(x + 5) > 6$ **e** $4x^2 - 9x \leqslant -3 - x$ **f** $(6 - x)(3 - x) \leqslant 4$

3 Solve the following inequalities by completing the square. Leave your answers in surd form.

   a $x^2 + 6x < 1$ **b** $x^2 - x \geqslant 1$ **c** $x^2 + 2x < 3(x + 1)$

   d $(x - 2)(1 - x) > x^2 - 3x$

18

4 Find the set of values of x for which

    a $x^2 + 4x + 3 \leqslant 0$ and $2x + 3 \leqslant 1$

    b $(x - 5)(x + 3) \geqslant 0$ and $(x + 1)(x - 2) \geqslant 0$

    c $x^2 + 6 < 5x$ and $2x + 1 > 6$

    d $x^2 - 3x - 18 < 0$ and $x^2 + 3x - 28 < 0$

5 Solve.

    a $\left| x^2 - x - 4 \right| < 2$ **b** $\left| (x - 2)(x - 4) \right| \geqslant 8$ **c** $\left| 3x - \dfrac{1}{2}x^2 \right| < 4$

6   **a**   Find the constants p and q such that for all values of x,

         $x^2 + 8x + 21 = (x + p)^2 + q$.

     b   State the least value of $x^2 + 8x + 21$ and the value of x for which this occurs.

     c   Write down the greatest value of $\dfrac{1}{x^2 + 8x + 21}$.

2.5 Roots of quadratic equations

 REMINDER

- The quadratic formula $x = \dfrac{-b \pm \sqrt{b^2 - 4ac}}{2a}$.

- The discriminant is the value of $b^2 - 4ac$.

- The sign (positive, zero or negative) of the discriminant tells you how many roots there are for a particular quadratic equation.

19

$b^2 - 4ac$	Nature of roots of $ax^2 + bx + c = 0$	Shape of curve $y = ax^2 + bx + c$
> 0	2 real distinct roots	$a > 0$ or $a < 0$ The curve cuts the x-axis at 2 distinct points.
$= 0$	2 real equal roots	$a > 0$ or $a < 0$ The curve touches the x-axis at 1 point.
< 0	0 real roots	$a > 0$ or $a < 0$ The curve is entirely above or entirely below the x-axis.

WORKED EXAMPLE 6

Find the values of k if $2x^2 - kx + 8 = 0$ has equal roots.

Answers

For two equal roots:

$$b^2 - 4ac = 0$$
$$(-k)^2 - 4 \times 2 \times 8 = 0$$
$$k^2 - 64 = 0$$
$$(k-8)(k+8) = 0$$
$$k = \pm 8$$

Exercise 2.5

1 State whether these equations have two distinct roots, two equal roots or no roots.

    a $x^2 + 3x + 3 = 0$ **b** $x^2 + 2x - 11 = 0$ **c** $x^2 + 2x + 1 = 0$

    d $x^2 - 3x + 4 = 0$ **e** $2x^2 - 7x + 3 = 0$ **f** $5x^2 + 9x + 4 = 0$

    g $3x^2 + 42x + 147 = 0$ **h** $5x^2 - 3x + 9 = 0$ **i** $4x^2 - 20x + 25 = 0$

2 These equations have no roots. Find the value of k in each case.

    a $x^2 + kx + 9 = 0$ **b** $kx^2 - 3x + 5 = 0$ **c** $kx^2 - 5x + 7 = 0$

> **TIP**
> For real roots $b^2 - 4ac \geqslant 0$
> (Notice the inequality sign).

3 The following equations have 2 (real) roots. Deduce what you can about the value of k in each case.

    a $x^2 + 3x + k = 0$ **b** $kx^2 - 2x - 7 = 0$ **c** $2x^2 - kx + 6 = 0$

4 For what values of k is $9x^2 + kx + 16 = 0$ a perfect square?

5 Find a relationship between a and b if the roots of $ax^2 + bx + 1 = 0$ are equal.

6 The equation $3x^2 + 2x + k = 0$ has repeated (that is two equal) roots. Find the value of k.

7 Find the values of the constant k given that the equation $(5k + 1)x^2 - 8kx + 3k = 0$ has two equal roots. Find the value of k.

8 Given that the roots of the equation $x^2 + ax + (a + 2) = 0$ differ by 2, find the possible values of the constant a and state the values of the roots of the equation.

2.6 Intersection of a line and a curve

 REMINDER

You have already learnt that to find the points of intersection of a line with a parabola you solve the two equations simultaneously giving $ax^2 + bx + c = 0$.

The roots of the resulting equation can be found using the quadratic formula:

$$x = \frac{-b \pm \sqrt{b^2 - 4ac}}{2a}$$

The condition for this quadratic equation to have real roots is $b^2 - 4ac \geq 0$.

$b^2 - 4ac$	Nature of roots	Line and curve
> 0	2 real distinct roots	2 distinct points of intersection
$= 0$	2 real equal roots	1 point of intersection (line is a tangent)
< 0	0 real roots	no points of intersection

WORKED EXAMPLE 7

Find the values of k for which $y = kx + 2$ is a tangent to the curve $y = 3x^2 + x + 5$.

Answer

$3x^2 + x + 5 = kx + 2$

$3x^2 + (1 - k)x + 3 = 0$

Since the line is a tangent to the curve,

$b^2 - 4ac = 0$

$(1 - k)^2 - 4 \times 3 \times 3 = 0$

$1 - 2k + k^2 - 36 = 0$

$k^2 - 2k - 35 = 0$

$(k + 5)(k - 7) = 0$

$k = -5$ and $k = 7$.

Exercise 2.6

1 Show that the line $y = 3x - 3$ and the curve $y = 3x^2 + 7x + 2$ do not meet.

2 a Find in exact form, the coordinates of the points where the curve $y = x^2 - 4x + 2$ crosses the x axis.

b Find the value of the constant k for which the straight line $y = 2x + k$ is a tangent to the curve $y = x^2 - 4x + 2$.

3 Find the values of k for which the x axis is a tangent to the curve $y = x^2 + (2 - k)x - (2k - 1)$.

4 Find the values of the constant c for which the line $y = x + c$ is a tangent to the curve, $y = 2x + \dfrac{4}{x}$.

5 Find the set of values of k for which $y = 2x + 1$ cuts the curve $y = x^2 + kx + 3$.

21

6 The line $y = x + k$ is a tangent to the curve $x^2 + 3xy + 9 = 0$.

   a Find the possible values of k.

   b For each of these values of k, find the coordinates of the point of contact of the tangent with the curve.

7 Find the set of values for k for which the line $y = k - 2x$ cuts the curve $y = x^2 - 8x + 4$ at two distinct points.

8 Find the set of values of m for which the line $y = mx - 3$ does not meet the curve $y = x^2 - 5x + 6$.

9 The line $y = mx + 4$ is a tangent to the curve $= x^2 - 3x + 5$.
Find the possible values of m.

Summary

Completing the square

For a quadratic function $f(x) = ax^2 + bx + c$ that is written in the form $f(x) = a(x - h)^2 + k$,

i if $a > 0$, the minimum point is (h, k) **ii** if $a < 0$, the maximum point is (h, k).

Quadratic equation ($ax^2 + bx + c = 0$) and corresponding curve ($y = ax^2 + bx + c$)

$b^2 - 4ac$	Nature of roots $ax^2 + bx + c = 0$	Shape of curve $y = ax^2 + bx + c$
> 0	2 real distinct roots	The curve cuts the x-axis at 2 distinct points.
$= 0$	2 real equal roots	The curve touches the x-axis at 1 point.
< 0	0 real roots	The curve is entirely above or entirely below the x-axis.

Quadratic curve and straight line

Situation 1	Situation 2	Situation 3
2 points of intersection	1 point of intersection	0 points of intersection
The line cuts the curve at two distinct points.	The line touches the curve at one point. This means that the line is a **tangent** to the curve.	The line does not intersect the curve.

Solving simultaneously the equation of the curve with the equation of the line will give a quadratic equation of the form $ax^2 + bx + c = 0$. The discriminant $b^2 - 4ac$, gives information about the roots of the equation and also about the intersection of the curve with the line.

$b^2 - 4ac$	Nature of roots	Line and curve
> 0	2 real distinct roots	2 distinct points of intersection
$= 0$	2 real equal roots	1 point of intersection (line is a tangent)
< 0	no real roots	no points of intersection

The condition for a quadratic equation to have real roots is $b^2 - 4ac \geq 0$.

Exercise 2.7

1 **a** Solve the inequality $(2x + 1)(3x - 1) < 14$.

    b Solve the inequality $\left| x^2 - 3x + 6 \right| > 10$.

2 Find the set of values of x for which $2x^2 + 14x + 20 \leq (x - 3)(x + 2)$.

3 Given $f(x) = 2x^2 + 8x + 2$.

    a Express $f(x)$ in the form $A(x + B)^2 + C$, where A, B and C are positive constants.

    b Find the minimum value of $f(x)$.

    c Find the solutions of the equation $f(x) = 0$, giving your solutions in the form $p \pm \sqrt{q}$, where p and q are integers.

4 A one-to-one function is defined by $f(x) = (x - 2)^2 - 4$ for $x \geq k$.

    a State the minimum possible value of k.

    b For this least value, write down the range of f.

    c Find $f^{-1}(x)$.

5 The line $x + y = 23$ intersects the curve $y = 25 - (x - 4)^2$ at the points A and B.

    The x coordinate of A is less than that of B.

    Find the coordinates of A and B.

6 Find the set of values of k for which the roots of the equation $x^2 - 4kx + (5 + k) = 0$ are real and distinct.

7 **a** Write $y = 9 + 6x - x^2$ in the form $y = P - (x + Q)^2$.

b State the maximum value of $y = 9 + 6x - x^2$.

c Find the coordinates of the points of intersection of the curve $y = 9 + 6x - x^2$. with the x axis. Give your answers in the form $a + b\sqrt{2}$ where a and b are integers.

d Sketch the curve $y = 9 + 6x - x^2$.

8 Find the set of values of x for which $2x(x + 3) > (x + 2)(x + 3)$.

9 $f(x) = 4x^2 + 6x + 7 \quad x \in \mathbb{R}$

a Write $f(x)$ in the form $a(x + b)^2 + c$ stating the values of a, b and c.

b Write down the value of x for which $f(x)$ is a minimum and state the minimum value of $f(x)$.

c Find the set of values of x for which $f(x) < 17$.

10 Find the set of values of x for which $2(x + 1)(x - 4) - (x - 2)^2 > 0$. Give your answers as exact values in the form $a + b\sqrt{c}$ where a, b and c are integers.

11 The figure shows part of the curve with equation $y = p + 10x - x^2$ (where p is a constant) and a straight line with equation $y = qx + 25$ (where q is a constant). The x coordinates of A and B are 4 and 8 respectively.

Find the values of p and q.

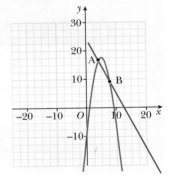

12 The equation $4x^2 - kx + (k - 3) = 0$ where k is a constant, has real roots.

a Find the set of possible values of k.

b If the roots to the equation are equal, state the smallest value of k.

c Solve the equation $4x^2 - kx + (k - 3) = 0$ using this value of k.

13 The function f is defined by $f(x) = x^2 - 2x - 1$ for the domain $-2 \leqslant x \leqslant 5$.

a Write $f(x) = x^2 - 2x - 1$ in completed square form.

b Find the range of $f(x)$.

c Explain why $f(x)$ does not have an inverse.

14 It is given that $f(x) = 6 + 8x - x^2$.

a Find the value of a and of b for which $f(x) = a - (x - b)^2$ and hence write down the coordinates of the stationary point of the curve $y = f(x)$.

b On a copy of the axes below, sketch the graph of $y = f(x)$, showing the coordinates (written in an exact form if necessary) of the points where the graph intersects each axis.

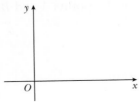

Chapter 3:
Indices and surds

This section will show you how to:

- understand what is meant by negative, zero and fractional indices and surds
- simplify expressions using indices and surds
- solve equations containing indices and surds.

3.1 Simplifying expressions involving indices

  REMINDER

You should already know the meaning of the words index, power, exponent and base:

$$2 \times 2 \times 2 \times 2 = 2^4$$

index, exponent or power

base

The plural of the word index is indices.

You should also know and be able to apply the following rules of indices:

In order to practise questions in this chapter, you should be familiar with the rules of indices.

Rule 1: $a^m \times a^n = a^{m+n}$

Rule 2: $a^m \div a^n = a^{m-n}$ or $\dfrac{a^m}{a^n} = a^{m-n}$

Rule 3: $\left(a^m\right)^n = a^{mn}$

Rule 4: $a^n \times b^n = (ab)^n$

Rule 5: $\dfrac{a^n}{b^n} = \left(\dfrac{a}{b}\right)^n$

Rule 6: $a^0 = 1$

Rule 7: $a^{-n} = \dfrac{1}{a^n}$

Rule 8: $a^{\frac{1}{n}} = \sqrt[n]{a}$

Rule 9: $a^{\frac{m}{n}} = \left(\sqrt[n]{a}\right)^m = \sqrt[n]{a^m}$

- These rules are always true if the bases a and b are positive real numbers and the indices m and n are real numbers.
- If the bases a and b are negative then the indices m and n must be integers for Rules 1–5 to be always true.
- Rules 6 and 7 are also true if base a is negative.

WORKED EXAMPLE 1

Simplify $3a^2b \times (3ab^2)^{-3}$

Answers

Method 1:

$3a^2b \times (3ab^2)^{-3} = 3a^2b \times \dfrac{1}{\left(3ab^2\right)^3}$

$\qquad\qquad\qquad\quad = 3a^2b \times \dfrac{1}{27a^3b^6}$

$\qquad\qquad\qquad\quad = \dfrac{3a^2b}{27a^3b^6}$

$\qquad\qquad\qquad\quad = \dfrac{1}{9\,ab^5}$

> **!**
> **TIP**
> Always write complete lines of working at each stage.

write the question with positive indices

> **!**
> **TIP**
> It is good practice to write $9ab^5$ rather than $9b^5a$.

Method 2:

$3a^2b \times (3ab^2)^{-3} = 3a^2b \times (3ab^2)^{-3}$ expand the brackets

$\qquad\qquad\qquad\quad = 3a^2b \times 3^{-3}a^{-3}b^{-6}$ add the indices

$\qquad\qquad\qquad\quad = 3^{(1-3)}a^{(2-3)}b^{(1-6)}$ simplify

$\qquad\qquad\qquad\quad = 3^{-2}a^{-1}b^{-5}$

$\qquad\qquad\qquad\quad = \dfrac{1}{9\,ab^5}$

Exercise 3.1 (In the following exercise, you may assume that all bases are positive real numbers).

1 Simplify each of the following.

   a $x^6 \times x^3$

   b $\left(x^4\right)^7$

   c $\left(2x^3\right)^4$

   d $x^6 \div x^2$

   e $\sqrt{x^4}$

   f $\sqrt[3]{27x^9}$

   g $(x^{-2})^5$

   h $\left(x^{-3}\right)^{-5}$

   i $\sqrt{36x^{-4}}$

   j $\left(2x^{-3}\right)^{-3}$

   k $\left(\sqrt{36x^{-6}}\right)^2$

   l $\left(2\dfrac{1}{2}x\right)^{-1}$

   m $(4x)^{\frac{1}{2}}$

   n $2x^{\frac{1}{3}} \times (27x^3)^{-\frac{2}{3}}$

   o $(4y^{-6})^{-\frac{1}{2}}$

   p $\dfrac{1}{4}\left[\dfrac{4a^6}{b^{-3}}\right]^{-2}$

   q $\dfrac{x^2}{x^{-3}} + \dfrac{x^3}{x^{-2}}$

   r $\dfrac{(2xy^6)^2}{\sqrt{36x^{-4}}}$

   s $(1+2x)^{\frac{5}{2}} + (1+2x)^{\frac{1}{2}}$

   t $\left(64x^6\right)^{-\frac{2}{3}}$

   u $\dfrac{(9x^2y^4)^{-\frac{1}{2}}}{(4x^2y^{-4})^{-\frac{3}{2}}}$

2 Given that $\dfrac{(25x^4)^2}{5x^2} = 5^a x^b$ evaluate a and b.

3 Given that $\dfrac{\sqrt{x^{-2}} \times \sqrt[3]{y^4}}{\sqrt{x^4 y^{-\frac{1}{3}}}} = x^a y^b$, find the value of a and the value of b.

4 Given that $\dfrac{\left(a^2\right)^x}{b^{4-x}} \times \dfrac{b^{y-5}}{a^y} = a^2 b^4$, find the value of x and the value of y.

5 Simplify $(1+2x)^{-\frac{1}{2}} + (1+2x)^{\frac{1}{2}}$.

3.2 Solving equations using indices

WORKED EXAMPLE 2

Solve $\dfrac{27^{3y}}{3^{5-y}} = \dfrac{3^{4y-1}}{9^{y-2}}$

> **TIP**
> Remember to use brackets when subtracting the indices.

Answer

$\dfrac{\left(3^3\right)^{3y}}{3^{5-y}} = \dfrac{3^{4y-1}}{\left(3^2\right)^{y-2}}$ write 27 and 9 as powers of 3

$\dfrac{3^{9y}}{3^{5-y}} = \dfrac{3^{4y-1}}{3^{2y-4}}$ expand the brackets

$3^{9y-(5-y)} = 3^{4y-1-(2y-4)}$

$3^{9y-5+y} = 3^{4y-1-2y+4}$ remove brackets

$9y - 5 + y = 4y - 1 - 2y + 4$ equate the indices

$10y - 5 = 2y + 3$

$8y = 8$

$y = 1$

WORKED EXAMPLE 3

Solve the equation $x^{\frac{1}{3}} - 2x^{\frac{-1}{3}} = 1$

> **TIP**
> Let $y = x^{\frac{1}{3}}$.

Answers

$y - \dfrac{2}{y} = 1$ multiply each term by y

$y^2 - 2 = y$ rearrange equation

$y^2 - y - 2 = 0$ factorise

$(y - 2)(y + 1) = 0$ solve

$(y - 2) = 0$ or $(y + 1) = 0$

$y = 2$ or $y = -1$

So $x^{\frac{1}{3}} = 2$, which gives $x = 8$, or $x^{\frac{1}{3}} = -1$, which gives $x = -1$.

Exercise 3.2

1 Solve each of the following equations.

  a $4^x = 4^{2x-1}$ **b** $6^{2y-3} = 6^{\frac{1}{3}}$ **c** $5^x = \dfrac{1}{5}$ **d** $2^{\frac{2}{x}} = 2^{x-1}$

2 Solve each of the following equations.

  a $8^{x+2} = 2^x$ **b** $4^x = 8^{2x-3}$ **c** $4^{\frac{n}{2}} = 64$ **d** $x^{\frac{2}{3}} = 4$

  e $16^{-x} = \dfrac{1}{8}$ **f** $2x^4 = 0.0032$ **g** $9^y = \left(\sqrt{3}\right)^6$ **h** $x^{-\frac{2}{3}} = \dfrac{1}{4}$

  i $x^{\frac{3}{2}} = x\sqrt{2}$ **j** $x^{\frac{3}{2}} = 2\sqrt{x}$ **k** $27^{-\frac{1}{3}} = 3x^2$ **l** $x^{-\frac{1}{4}} = \dfrac{1}{3}$

  m $4^{2x} = 64^{x-3}$ **n** $4^{x^2} = 16^{4-3x}$ **o** $3^{y+2} = 27^{5-y}$ **p** $4^{t-5} = \left(\dfrac{1}{2}\right)^{t+1}$

3 Solve each of the following equations.

  a $8^{3x} \times 16^{x+1} = 64$ **b** $\left(2^x\right)^3 \times 4^{x-1} = 16$ **c** $\dfrac{9^y}{27^{3y+1}} = 81$

4 Solve each of the following equations.

  a $2^{2x} \times 3^x = 144$ **b** $2^y \times 3^{y-2} = 24$ **c** $\dfrac{5^x}{3^{1-x}} = \dfrac{1}{45}$

5 Solve each of the following pairs of simultaneous equations.

  a $2^x \times 2^y = 16$ **b** $16^x = 4\left(2^y\right)$

     $3^{2x} \div \left(\dfrac{1}{3}\right)^{y-1} = 81$ $8^x \div 16^y = \dfrac{1}{32}$

6 **a** Solve the equation $y^2 - 2y - 8 = 0$.

    b Use your answer to part **a** to solve $x - 2\sqrt{x} - 8 = 0$.

7 **a** Solve the equation $y^2 - 8y + 15 = 0$.

    b Use your answer to part **a** to solve $x + 15 = 8\sqrt{x}$.

8 **a** Solve the equation $x = 3 + \dfrac{10}{x}$.

    b Use your answer to part **a** to solve the following equation $x^2 = 3 + \dfrac{10}{x^2}$.

3.3 Surds

REMINDER

Rules of surds

Rule 1: $\sqrt{ab} = \sqrt{a} \times \sqrt{b}$

Rule 2: $\sqrt{\dfrac{a}{b}} = \dfrac{\sqrt{a}}{\sqrt{b}}$

Rule 3: $\sqrt{a} \times \sqrt{a} = a$

The product of conjugate surds $a + b\sqrt{c}$ and $a - b\sqrt{c}$ is a rational number.

Simplifying Surds

Exercise 3.3

1 Simplify:

  a $5\sqrt{3} + 2\sqrt{3} - \sqrt{3}$ **b** $4\sqrt{2} + 2\sqrt{3} - 5\sqrt{2}$ **c** $3(2\sqrt{2} - 6) - 4\left(3\sqrt{2} - 5\right)$

2 What must be added to $6 - 3\sqrt{5}$ to give an answer of $12 + 4\sqrt{5}$?

3 Simplify $3\sqrt{2} + 4\sqrt{3} - 5 + 5\sqrt{2} - 5\sqrt{3}$.

4 Match up the following pairs of surds.

a $2\left(2\sqrt{2}+\sqrt{3}\right)$

A $3\sqrt{3}+3\sqrt{2}$

b $2\left(3-2\sqrt{2}\right)+2$

B $\sqrt{3}+\sqrt{3}+\sqrt{3}-4\sqrt{2}$

c $2\sqrt{3}-4\sqrt{2}+\sqrt{3}$

C $4\sqrt{2}+2\sqrt{3}$

d $4-\sqrt{2}-\left(3\sqrt{2}-2\right)$

D $6-4\sqrt{2}$

e $4\left(\sqrt{2}+\sqrt{3}\right)-\left(\sqrt{3}+\sqrt{2}\right)$

E $8-4\sqrt{2}$

5 Copy and complete the number wall below. The number in each box is found by adding the two numbers below it.

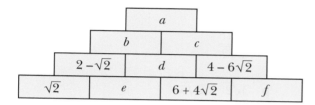

3.4 Multiplication, division and simplification of surds

WORKED EXAMPLE 4

Expand and simplify $\left(2+3\sqrt{5}\right)^{2}$.

Answer

$\left(2+3\sqrt{5}\right)^{2}=\left(2+3\sqrt{5}\right)\left(2+3\sqrt{5}\right)$

$=2\times2+2\times3\sqrt{5}+2\times3\sqrt{5}+3\sqrt{5}\times3\sqrt{5}$

$=4+6\sqrt{5}+6\sqrt{5}+45$

$=49+12\sqrt{5}$

REMEMBER

$\sqrt{a}\times\sqrt{b}=\sqrt{ab}$

$\sqrt{\dfrac{a}{b}}=\dfrac{\sqrt{a}}{\sqrt{b}}$

Exercise 3.4

1 Simplify.

a $\sqrt{5}\times\sqrt{5}$

b $\left(\sqrt{3}\right)^{2}$

c $\left(\sqrt{2}\right)^{3}$

d $\sqrt{5}\times\sqrt{7}$

e $2\sqrt{3}\times\sqrt{3}$

f $3\sqrt{2}\times4\sqrt{3}$

g $\left(2\sqrt{3}\right)^{2}$

h $4\sqrt{5}\times2\sqrt{5}$

i $\left(2\sqrt{5}\right)^{3}$

j $\left(3\sqrt{3}\right)^{3}$

2 Simplify.

a $\dfrac{\sqrt{60}}{\sqrt{10}}$

b $\dfrac{\sqrt{40}}{\sqrt{10}}$

c $\dfrac{\sqrt{28}}{\sqrt{4}}$

d $\dfrac{\sqrt{120}}{\sqrt{60}}$

e $\dfrac{\sqrt{20}}{\sqrt{4}}$

f $\dfrac{\sqrt{63}}{\sqrt{7}}$

g $\dfrac{\sqrt{10}}{\sqrt{40}}$

h $\dfrac{\sqrt{48}}{\sqrt{3}}$

i $\left(\dfrac{4}{\sqrt{7}}\right)^2$

j $\dfrac{\sqrt{14}}{\sqrt{126}}$

k $\dfrac{3\sqrt{12}}{\sqrt{4}}$

l $\dfrac{3\sqrt{12}}{\sqrt{3}}$

m $\dfrac{6\sqrt{40}}{2\sqrt{10}}$

n $\dfrac{3\sqrt{50}}{\sqrt{10}}$

o $\dfrac{15\sqrt{140}}{3\sqrt{10}}$

3 Simplify.

a $\sqrt{24}$

b $\sqrt{40}$

c $\sqrt{48}$

d $\sqrt{45}$

e $\sqrt{72}$

f $\sqrt{27}$

g $\sqrt{80}$

h $\sqrt{68}$

i $\sqrt{500}$

j $\sqrt{162}$

k $\dfrac{\sqrt{50}}{5}$

l $\dfrac{3\sqrt{18}}{2\sqrt{2}}$

m $\dfrac{\sqrt{54}}{\sqrt{3}}$

n $\dfrac{\sqrt{72}}{2}$

o $\left(\dfrac{2\sqrt{6}}{3}\right)^2$

p $3\sqrt{2}\times 2\sqrt{6}$

q $\sqrt{8}\times\sqrt{20}$

r $\sqrt{2}\times\sqrt{22}$

s $\left(\dfrac{4\sqrt{5}}{2\sqrt{10}}\right)^2$

4 Simplify.

a $\sqrt{8}+\sqrt{18}$

b $\sqrt{75}-\sqrt{27}$

c $\sqrt{20}+2\sqrt{45}$

d $\sqrt{18}+\sqrt{27}$

e $\sqrt{28}-\sqrt{12}$

f $\sqrt{48}-2\sqrt{3}$

g $5\sqrt{12}+\sqrt{27}$

h $\sqrt{3}+\sqrt{27}-\sqrt{12}$

i $12\sqrt{3}-\sqrt{27}$

j $6\sqrt{5}+2\sqrt{180}$

k $\sqrt{60}-\sqrt{15}$

l $\sqrt{80}-\sqrt{125}$

m $3\sqrt{20}-3\sqrt{80}-2\sqrt{45}$

n $2\sqrt{50}-\left(\sqrt{8}\right)^3$

o $2\sqrt{5}\sqrt{75}-3\sqrt{15}$

5 Expand and simplify.

a $\sqrt{2}\left(\sqrt{2}-3\right)$

b $\sqrt{3}\,(2\sqrt{3}-\sqrt{5})$

c $2\sqrt{2}\left(3\sqrt{2}-\sqrt{12}\right)$

d $3\sqrt{2}\left(4\sqrt{2}+\sqrt{18}\right)$

e $\sqrt{6}\left(\sqrt{2}+4\sqrt{2}\right)$

f $\sqrt{15}\left(\sqrt{5}+\sqrt{2}\right)$

g $(\sqrt{3}-1)(\sqrt{3}-1)$

h $\left(\sqrt{3}-1\right)\left(\sqrt{3}+1\right)$

i $\left(2-\sqrt{3}\right)\left(2+\sqrt{3}\right)$

j $\left(\sqrt{5}-2\sqrt{7}\right)\left(\sqrt{5}-\sqrt{7}\right)$

k $\left(2\sqrt{3}-1\right)\left(1+3\sqrt{3}\right)$

l $(\sqrt{15}-\sqrt{5})\left(\sqrt{15}-\sqrt{5}\right)$

m $(4\sqrt{2}-\sqrt{3})\left(\sqrt{3}-\sqrt{2}\right)$

n $\left(4+2\sqrt{2}\right)\left(5+2\sqrt{2}\right)$

o $(2\sqrt{5}-3\sqrt{2})\left(\sqrt{5}+3\sqrt{2}\right)$

6 Expand and simplify.

a $\left(3-\sqrt{5}\right)^2$

b $\left(3+2\sqrt{5}\right)^2$

c $4\sqrt{3}-\left(2-2\sqrt{3}\right)^2$

7 A right angled triangle ABC has $AB = \left(5 - 2\sqrt{2}\right)$ cm and $BC = (5 + 2\sqrt{2})$ cm.

    a Find the area of the triangle.

    b Find the length of AC.

8 A triangle PQR has angle $PQR = 60°$, $PQ = 3\sqrt{3}$ cm and $QR = 4\sqrt{3}$ cm. Find the length of PR in an exact form.

3.5 Rationalising the denominator of a fraction

REMINDER

This means to turn an irrational denominator to a rational number.

Using the following rules:

- For fractions of the form $\dfrac{1}{\sqrt{a}}$, multiply numerator and denominator by $\sqrt{a}$.

- For fractions of the form $\dfrac{1}{a + b\sqrt{c}}$, multiply numerator and denominator by $a - b\sqrt{c}$.

- For fractions of the form $\dfrac{1}{a - b\sqrt{c}}$, multiply numerator and denominator by $a + b\sqrt{c}$.

REMEMBER

$\sqrt{y} \times \sqrt{y} = \sqrt{y^2} = y$

REMEMBER

$\left(x - \sqrt{y}\right)\left(x + \sqrt{y}\right) = x^2 - y$

WORKED EXAMPLE 5

Rationalise the denominator and simplify $\dfrac{3}{3 - 2\sqrt{2}}$.

Answer

$$\frac{3}{3 - 2\sqrt{2}} = \frac{3}{3 - 2\sqrt{2}} \times \frac{3 + 2\sqrt{2}}{3 + 2\sqrt{2}}$$

$$= \frac{9 + 6\sqrt{2}}{9 - 6\sqrt{2} + 6\sqrt{2} - 8} \qquad 2\sqrt{2} \times 2\sqrt{2} = 8$$

$$= \frac{9 + 6\sqrt{2}}{1}$$

$$= 9 + 6\sqrt{2}$$

Exercise 3.5

1 Rationalise the denominators and simplify where possible.

  a $\dfrac{2}{\sqrt{3}}$ **b** $\dfrac{5}{\sqrt{2}}$ **c** $\dfrac{3}{\sqrt{12}}$ **d** $\dfrac{12}{\sqrt{8}}$

  e $\dfrac{\sqrt{3}}{\sqrt{18}}$ **f** $\left(\dfrac{\sqrt{3}}{2\sqrt{6}}\right)^2$ **g** $\dfrac{12}{2\sqrt{3}}$ **h** $\dfrac{1 + \sqrt{3}}{\sqrt{3}}$

  i $\dfrac{\sqrt{2} - 5}{\sqrt{2}}$ **j** $\dfrac{5 + \sqrt{2}}{\sqrt{2}}$ **k** $\dfrac{21}{\sqrt{3}} - \sqrt{27}$ **l** $\left(\dfrac{4}{\sqrt{6}}\right)^2$

  m $\dfrac{1 + \sqrt{2}}{1 - \sqrt{2}}$ **n** $\dfrac{2 + \sqrt{2}}{1 + 2\sqrt{2}}$ **o** $\dfrac{7 - \sqrt{3}}{2 + \sqrt{3}}$ **p** $\dfrac{7 + 2\sqrt{7}}{10 - 2\sqrt{7}}$

2 Find the value of k if $\sqrt{32} + \dfrac{2}{\sqrt{50}} = k\sqrt{2}$.

3 The sides of a right-angled triangle with an angle of 60° are $\sqrt{3}$ units, 3 units and $2\sqrt{3}$ units. Find the sine, cosine and tangent of 30° and 60° giving your answers with rational denominators.

4 Write as a single fraction $\dfrac{4+\sqrt{5}}{1+\sqrt{5}} + \dfrac{4-\sqrt{5}}{1-\sqrt{5}}$.

5 The area of a right-angled triangle is $18\,\text{cm}^2$. If its height is $\left(7-\sqrt{13}\right)$ cm, find the length of its base.

6 Express $\dfrac{-8+4\sqrt{3}}{4+2\sqrt{3}}$ in the form $a+b\,\sqrt{3}$ where a and b are integers.

7 Copy and complete each of the following.

   a $\left(\sqrt{3}-1\right)(\ldots\ldots\ldots) = 2$

   b $\left(2\sqrt{3}+4\sqrt{5}\right)(\ldots\ldots\ldots) = 68$

8 This diagram represents a 90° triangle with sides $\sqrt{2}$ units and $\sqrt{3}$ units.

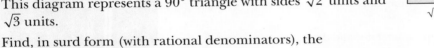

   Find, in surd form (with rational denominators), the

   a sine

   b cosine of angle x

9 Express $\left(1-\sqrt{5}\right)^2 - \dfrac{8}{2-\sqrt{5}}$ in the form $p+q\sqrt{5}$, where p and are q integers.

3.6 Solving equations involving surds

> **WORKED EXAMPLE 6**
>
> Solve the equation $2\sqrt{x} = 8 - x$.
>
> **Answer**
>
> $2y = 8 - y^2$ write $y = \sqrt{x}$
>
> $y^2 + 2y - 8 = 0$ rearrange
>
> $\left(y-2\right)\left(y+4\right) = 0$ factorise
>
> $\left(y-2\right) = 0$ gives $y = 2$ and $\left(y+4\right) = 0$ gives $y = -4$
>
> $\sqrt{x} = 2$ gives $x = 4$ but $\sqrt{x} = -4$ has no solution.

> **TIP**
> Squaring is not a reversible step. Notice that $x = 16$ does **not** satisfy the original equation.

Exercise 3.6

Solve these equations giving your answers as exact roots with simplified surds.

1 **a** $\left(4-\sqrt{2}\right)y = 1 + 3\sqrt{2}$ (Hint: divide both sides by $\left(4-\sqrt{2}\right)$.)

   b $x^2 - 8\sqrt{2}x - 4 = 0$

   c $\sqrt{x} + 11 = x$ (Hint: isolate $\sqrt{x}$ first, then square both sides of equation.)

   d $\sqrt{4x-4} - 3\sqrt{3-x} = 0$

   e $\sqrt{2x+3} = 5$

   f $\sqrt{5x-6} - \sqrt{2} = 2$

   g $\left(2+3\sqrt{2}\right)x - 5\sqrt{2} + 1 = \left(1+\sqrt{2}\right)x$

> **TIP**
> Use the quadratic formula
> $$x = \frac{-b \pm \sqrt{b^2 - 4ac}}{2a}.$$

> **TIP**
> For these type of equations, isolate the x terms on one side of the equation, then factorise.

2 Solve the equation $2 + 3\sqrt{y} = 6\sqrt{3} + 5$ giving your answer in the form $a + b\sqrt{3}$ where a and b are integers.

3 Given that $\left(2 - x\sqrt{3}\right)\left(5 + 4\sqrt{3}\right) = -2 + y\sqrt{3}$ find the values of x and y.

4 Find the exact solutions to the simultaneous equations
$\sqrt{3}x + \sqrt{2}y = 10$ and $\sqrt{2}x - \sqrt{3}y = 0$

5 Solve the following equation, giving your answers as simply as possible in exact form.
$2x^2 - 2x - 1 = 0$

Summary

Rules of indices

RULE 1: $a^m \times a^n = a^{m+n}$

RULE 2: $a^m \div a^n = a^{(m-n)}$ or $\dfrac{a^m}{a^n} = a^{m-n}$

RULE 3: $\left(a^m\right)^n = a^{mn}$

RULE 4: $a^n \times b^n = (ab)^n$

RULE 5: $\dfrac{a^n}{b^n} = \left(\dfrac{a}{b}\right)^n$

RULE 6: $a^0 = 1$

RULE 7: $a^{-n} = \dfrac{1}{a^n}$

RULE 8: $a^{\frac{1}{n}} = \sqrt[n]{a}$

RULE 9: $a^{\frac{m}{n}} = \left(\sqrt[n]{a}\right)^m = \sqrt[n]{a^m}$

Rules of surds

RULE 1: $\sqrt{ab} = \sqrt{a} \times \sqrt{b}$

RULE 2: $\sqrt{\dfrac{a}{b}} = \dfrac{\sqrt{a}}{\sqrt{b}}$

RULE 3: $\sqrt{a} \times \sqrt{a} = a$

The product of conjugate surds $a + b\sqrt{c}$ and $a - b\sqrt{c}$ is a rational number.

Exercise 3.7 (In this exercise, you may assume all bases are positive real numbers).

1 Simplify each of the following.

   a $\left(64x^6\right)^{\frac{3}{2}}$ **b** $\dfrac{30a^4\sqrt{25b^2}}{6a^2}$ **c** $a^{-1}\left(ab^{-2}\right) + b^{-2}$

2 Given that $\dfrac{72x^{\frac{2}{3}}}{\left(6x^{-3}\right)^3} = 3^a x^b$, find the value of a and the value of b.

3 Solve each of the following equations.

   a $\dfrac{8^x}{16^{2x+2}} = 128$ **b** $4^{2x} \times 64^x = \left(\dfrac{1}{2}\right)^{-1}$ **c** $4x^{\frac{2}{3}} - 5 = 2^3 + 3$

4 Solve the following pair of simultaneous equations.
$5^{x+1} \div 5^y = 1$ $8^x \times 2^y = 32$

5   **a** Solve the equation $\dfrac{1}{2}y^2 = 2 + \dfrac{3}{2}y$.

    b Use your answer to part **a** to solve $\sqrt[3]{x^2} - 3\sqrt[3]{x} = 4$.

6

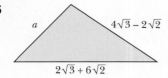

a $4\sqrt{3} - 2\sqrt{2}$

$2\sqrt{3} + 6\sqrt{2}$

Diagram not to scale.

The perimeter of this triangle is $10\sqrt{3} + 10\sqrt{2}$.

Find the exact length of side a.

7 The coordinates of two points are $A = (6 + 3\sqrt{2},\ 4)$ and $B = \left(2 - 2\sqrt{2}, -2\right)$. Find the coordinates of the midpoint of the line AB.

8 Expand and simplify $\left(5 + 2\sqrt{3}\right)\left(5 - 2\sqrt{3}\right) - \left(1 - \sqrt{3}\right)\left(1 + \sqrt{3}\right)$.

9 Rationalise the denominators and simplify.

a $\dfrac{6}{\sqrt{2}} + 4\sqrt{2}$ **b** $\dfrac{8}{3 + \sqrt{2}}$

10 Find the value of k if $\sqrt{27} + 3\sqrt{48} - \dfrac{3}{\sqrt{12}} = k\sqrt{3}$.

11 Find the distance between the points $\left(\sqrt{5}, 2\sqrt{3}\right)$ and $\left(2\sqrt{5}, -\sqrt{3}\right)$ giving your answer as a surd.

12 Solve $x - 5\sqrt{x} - 14 = 0$.

Chapter 4:
Factors and polynomials

This section will show you how to:

- use the remainder and factor theorems
- find factors of polynomials
- solve cubic equations.

REMINDER

A **polynomial** is an expression of the form:

$$a_n x^n + a_{n-1} x^{n-1} + a_{n-2} x^{n-2} + \ldots + a_2 x^2 + a_1 x^1 + a_0$$

where:

- x is a variable
- n is a non-negative integer
- the coefficients $a_n, a_{n-1}, a_{n-2}, \ldots, a_2, a_1, a_0$ are constants
- a_n is called the leading coefficient and $a_n \neq 0$
- a_0 is called the constant term.

TIP

$5x^4 + 4x^3 - 3x + 12$ is a quartic polynomial with 4 terms, a variable 'x' and the constant term 12.

4.1 Adding, subtracting and multiplying polynomials

WORKED EXAMPLE 1

If $P(x) = 3x^3 + 2x^2 - 1$ and $Q(x) = x^3 + 5x + 3$, find an expression for

a $P(x) + Q(x)$ **b** $P(x) - 2Q(x)$ **c** $P(x)Q(x)$.

Answers

a $P(x) + Q(x) = (3x^3 + 2x^2 - 1) + (x^3 + 5x + 3)$ collect like terms

$$= 4x^3 + 2x^2 + 5x + 2$$

b $P(x) - 2Q(x) = (3x^3 + 2x^2 - 1) - 2(x^3 + 5x + 3)$ remove brackets

$$= 3x^3 + 2x^2 - 1 - 2x^3 - 10x - 6$$ collect like terms

$$= x^3 + 2x^2 - 10x - 7$$

c $P(x)Q(x) = (3x^3 + 2x^2 - 1)(x^3 + 5x + 3)$

$$= 3x^3(x^3 + 5x + 3) + 2x^2(x^3 + 5x + 3) - 1(x^3 + 5x + 3)$$

$$= 3x^6 + 15x^4 + 9x^3 + 2x^5 + 10x^3 + 6x^2 - x^3 - 5x - 3$$

$$= 3x^6 + 2x^5 + 15x^4 + 18x^3 + 6x^2 - 5x - 3$$

Exercise 4.1

1 Expand and simplify each of the following.

   a $\left(x^2 + 2x + 1\right)(x - 1)$ **b** $(x - 3)(x - 2)(x - 1)$ **c** $(x + 2)(x + 3)^2$

   d $\left(2x^2 + 2x - 1\right)^2$ **e** $\left(3x^2 + 2x - 1\right)(x - 2)^2$ **f** $(2x - 3)^3$

2 If $P(x) = 3x^3 - 2x^2 + 1$ and $Q(x) = x^3 + 3x - 7$ find expressions for

   a $P(x) + Q(x)$ **b** $2P(x) - Q(x)$ **c** $P(x)Q(x)$

3 Simplify each of the following.

   a $(3x - 2)(x + 1) + (x + 2)(x + 3)$

   b $(2x + 1)\left(3x^2 + 2x - 1\right) - (x - 2)^2$

   c $\left(2x^2 - 3x^3 - 2x + 1\right)\left(2x^2 + x - 3\right) - (x + 2)\left(x^3 - 2x^2 + 3x + 2\right)$

4.2 Division of polynomials

WORKED EXAMPLE 2

Divide $x^3 - x^2 - 5x - 3$ by $x - 3$.

Answer

$$
\begin{array}{r}
x^2 + 2x + 1 \\
x - 3 \overline{\smash{)}\; x^3 - x^2 - 5x - 3} \\
\underline{x^3 - 3x^2} \\
2x^2 - 5x - 3 \\
\underline{2x^2 - 6x} \\
x - 3 \\
\underline{x - 3} \\
0
\end{array}
$$

divide the first term of the polynomial by x, $x^3 \div x = x^2$

divide $2x^2$ by x, $2x^2 \div x = 2x$

divide x by x, $x \div x = 1$

So $\left(x^3 - x^2 - 5x - 3\right) \div (x - 3) = x^2 + 2x + 1$.

Exercise 4.2

1 Simplify each of the following.

   a $\left(x^3 + x + 2\right) \div (x + 1)$ **b** $(x^3 - 2x^2 - 5x + 6) \div (x - 3)$

   c $(x^3 + 7x^2 + 8x + 2) \div (x + 1)$ **d** $\left(6x^3 + 7x^2 - 15x + 2\right) \div (x - 1)$

   e $\left(4x^3 - 4x^2 - 21x - 9\right) \div (x - 3)$ **f** $\left(2x^3 + 3x^2 + 3x + 1\right) \div (2x + 1)$

   g $\left(12x^3 + 4x^2 - 3x - 1\right) \div (2x - 1)$ **h** $\left(8x^3 - 12x^2 + 6x - 1\right) \div (2x - 1)$

   i $\left(9x^3 + 27x^2 - x - 3\right) \div (3x - 1)$ **j** $(6x^3 + 7x^2 - x - 2) \div (3x + 2)$

2 Simplify each of the following.

   a $\dfrac{x^4 - x^3 + 2x^2 - 7x - 2}{x - 2}$ **b** $\dfrac{2x^3 + x^2 - 3x - 14}{x - 2}$ **c** $\dfrac{x^4 + 2x^3 - 7x^2 - 8x + 12}{x + 3}$

3 **a** Divide $x^3 + 8$ by $x + 2$.   **b** Divide $4x^3 - 13x - 6$ by $x - 2$.

4.3 The factor theorem

 REMINDER

- If for a polynomial $P(x), P(c) = 0$ then $x - c$ is a factor of $P(x)$.
- If for a polynomial $P(x)$, $P\left(\dfrac{b}{a}\right) = 0$ then $ax - b$ is a factor of $P(x)$.

WORKED EXAMPLE 3

Use the factor theorem to show that $2x + 1$ is a factor of $2x^3 - x^2 - 5x - 2$.

Answer

Let $2x^3 - x^2 - 5x - 2$.   If $f\left(-\dfrac{1}{2}\right) = 0$, then $2x + 1$ is a factor.

$$f\left(-\frac{1}{2}\right) = 2\left(-\frac{1}{2}\right)^3 - \left(-\frac{1}{2}\right)^2 - 5\left(-\frac{1}{2}\right) - 2$$

$$= -\frac{1}{4} - \frac{1}{4} + \frac{5}{2} - 2$$

$$= 0$$

So $2x + 1$ is a factor of $2x^3 - x^2 - 5x - 2$.

Exercise 4.3

1 Use the factor theorem to show

  a $x + 3$ is a factor of $x^3 - x^2 - 9x + 9$

  b $x + 1$ is a factor of $x^3 + 6x^2 + 11x + 6$

  c $x - 7$ is a factor of $x^3 - 4x^2 - 21x$

  d $2x - 1$ is a factor of $2x^3 - x^2 - 2x + 1$

2 Find the value of a in each of the following.

  a $x - 1$ is a factor of $8x^3 - 3x^2 + ax + 15$.

  b $x + 4$ is a factor of $x^3 - x^2 - 16x + a$.

  c $3x + 2$ is a factor of $3x^3 + ax^2 + 15x - 2$.

3 $x - 5$ is a factor of $x^3 + ax^2 + bx - 25$.

  Express b in terms of a.

4 Find the value of a and the value of b in each of the following.

  a $x^2 + 3x - 10$ is a factor of $ax^3 + 10x^2 + bx - 10$.

  b $2x^2 - 9x - 18$ is a factor of $4x^3 + ax^2 - 27x + b$.

5 $x - 3$ and $x + 3$ are factors of $x^3 + ax^2 + bx + ab$.

  Find the value of a and the value of b.

6 $x - 3$ is a common factor of $3x^3 + (p + q)x - 30$ and $3x^3 + (p - q)x - 12$.

  Find the value of p and the value of q.

4.4 Cubic expressions and equations

WORKED EXAMPLE 4

Solve $2x^3 - x^2 - 41x - 20 = 0$.

Answers

Let $f(x) = 2x^3 - x^2 - 41x - 20$.

The positive and negative factors of 20 are $\pm 1, \pm 2, \pm 4, \pm 5, \pm 10$.

$$f(5) = 2(5)^3 - (5)^2 - 41 \times (5) - 20 = 0$$

So $x - 5$ is a factor of $f(x)$.

$$2x^3 - x^2 - 41x - 20 = (x - 5)\left(ax^2 + bx + c\right)$$

coefficient of x^3 is 1, so $a = 2$ since $1 \times 2 = 2$	constant term is -20, so $c = 4$ since $-5 \times 4 = -20$

$$2x^3 - x^2 - 41x - 20 = (x - 5)\left(2x^2 + bx + 4\right) \qquad \text{expand and collect like terms}$$
$$2x^3 - x^2 - 41x - 20 = 2x^3 + (b - 10)x^2 + (4 - 5b)x - 20$$

Equating coefficients of x^2: $b - 10 = -1$

$$b = 9$$

$$f(x) = (x - 5)\left(2x^2 + 9x + 4\right)$$
$$= (x - 5)(2x + 1)(x + 4)$$

Hence $(x - 5)(2x + 1)(x + 4) = 0$.

So $x = -4$ or $x = -\dfrac{1}{2}$ or $x = 5$.

Exercise 4.4

1 Factorise these cubic expressions completely.

   a $x^3 + 3x^2 - 13x - 15$ **b** $2x^3 + 7x^2 + 2x - 3$

   c $3x^3 - x^2 + 3x - 1$ **d** $5x^3 + 14x^2 + 7x - 2$

   e $3x^3 + 2x^2 - 7x + 2$

> **TIP**
> Write down the positive and negative factors of the constant term first. Then use the factor theorem to find the first factor.

2 Solve the following equations.

   a $x^3 + x^2 - 10x + 8 = 0$ **b** $x^3 - 6x^2 + 12x - 8 = 0$

   c $x^3 - 7x - 6 = 0$ **d** $x^3 - 3x = 2$

   e $5x^3 + 23x = 34x^2 - 6$

3 Solve the following equations. Express roots in the form $a \pm b\sqrt{c}$, where necessary.

   a $x^3 + 8x^2 + 11x - 2 = 0$ **b** $x^3 + 30x = 10x^2 + 27$

   c $x^3 + 5 = 8x - 2x^2$

4 Factorise $x^3 + 3x^2 + 3x + 2$ fully.

5 Factorise $x^3 + x^2 - x - 1$.

6 Given that $2x^4 + 2x^3 + 5x^2 + 3x + 3 = \left(x^2 + x + 1\right)\left(ax^2 + bx + c\right)$ find the values of the constants a, b and c.

7 Solve the equation $\dfrac{2}{x} = x^2 - 3$.

4.5 The remainder theorem

REMINDER

- If a polynomial $P(x)$ is divided by $x - c$, the remainder is $P(c)$

which can be extended to:

- If a polynomial $P(x)$ is divided by $ax - b$, the remainder is $P\left(\dfrac{b}{a}\right)$.

WORKED EXAMPLE 5

$f(x) = 2x^3 + ax^2 + bx + 15$

When $f(x)$ is divided by $x - 1$, the remainder is 5.

When $f(x)$ is divided by $x - 4$, the remainder is 11.

Find the value of a and of b.

Answers

$f(x) = 2x^3 + ax^2 + bx + 15$

When $f(x)$ is divided by $x - 1$, the remainder is 5 means that: $f(1) = 5$

$2(1)^3 + a(1)^2 + b(1) + 15 = 1$

$\qquad 2 + a + b + 15 = 5$

$\qquad\qquad a + b = -12$ ------------(1)

When $f(x)$ is divided by $x - 4$, the remainder is 11 means that: $f(4) = 11$

$2(4)^3 + a(4)^2 + b(4) + 15 = 11$

$\qquad 128 + 16a + 4b + 15 = 11$

$\qquad\qquad 16a + 4b = -132$

$\qquad\qquad\quad 4a + b = -33$ ---------(2)

(2) − (1) gives $3a = -21$

$\qquad\qquad\quad a = -7$

Substituting $a = -7$ in equation (1) gives $b = -5$.

$a = -7$ and $b = -5$

Exercise 4.5

1 Find the remainders when the polynomial $x^3 + 5x^2 - 17x - 21$ is divided by

  a $x + 1$ **b** $x - 4$ **c** $2x + 1$

2 Find the remainders when

  a $2x^3 + 4x^2 - 6x + 5$ is divided by $x - 1$

  b $6x^3 - 2x^2 + 5x - 4$ is divided by x

  c $8x^3 + 4x + 3$ is divided by $2x - 1$

TIP

If you are only asked for the remainder when one polynomial is divided by another then use the remainder theorem and not long division.

3 The expression $2x^3 - 3x^2 + ax - 5$ gives a remainder of 7 when divided by $x - 2$. Find the value of the constant a.

4 The cubic polynomial $3x^3 + bx^2 - 7x + 5$ gives a remainder of 17 when divided by $x + 3$. Find the value of the constant b.

5 When $x^3 + 2x^2 + ax - 3$ is divided by $x + 1$ the remainder is the same as when it is divided by $x - 2$. Find the value of a.

6 The polynomial $x^3 - x^2 + ax + b$ has a factor of $x + 3$ and leaves a remainder of 6 when divided by $x - 3$.

   a Find the values of the constants a and b.

   b Factorise the expression fully.

Summary

The **factor theorem**:

If for a polynomial $P(x)$, $P(c) = 0$ then $x - c$ is a factor of $P(x)$.

If for a polynomial $P(x)$, $P\left(\dfrac{b}{a}\right) = 0$ then $ax - b$ is a factor of $P(x)$.

The **remainder theorem**:

If a polynomial $P(x)$ is divided by $x - c$, the remainder is $P(c)$.

If a polynomial $P(x)$ is divided by $ax - b$, the remainder is $P\left(\dfrac{b}{a}\right)$.

Exercise 4.6

1 Given that $x^2 - 4$ is a factor of the cubic polynomial $x^3 + ax^2 + bx - 12$,

   a find the values of the constants a and b

   b using these values of a and b, solve the equation $x^3 + ax^2 + bx - 12 = 0$.

2 $f(x) = x^3 - 9x^2 + 24x - 16$

   a Evaluate $f(1)$.

   b Show that $f(x)$ can be written in the form $f(x) = (x + a)(x + b)^2$ where a and b are integers to be found.

3 The polynomial $g(x) = 2x^3 + x^2 + ax + b$ gives a remainder of 20 when divided by $x + 2$.

   a Find an expression for b in terms of a.

   Given that $2x - 1$ is also a factor of $g(x)$,

   b find the values of a and b

   c fully factorise $g(x)$.

4 The polynomial $f(x)$ is given as $f(x) = x^3 + kx^2 - 7x - 15$.

   When it is divided by $x + 1$ the remainder is r.

   When it is divided by $x - 3$, the remainder is $3r$.

   a Find the values of k and r.

   b With these values of k and r, fully factorise $f(x) = x^3 + kx^2 - 7x - 15$.

5 A polynomial $g(x) = x^3 + 7x^2 + ax - 6$ gives the solution $x = -3$ when $g(x) = 0$.

  a Find the value of a.

  b Using this value of a, find the remainder when $g(x)$ is divided by $x - 2$.

  c Find all the solutions to the equation $g(x) = 0$ giving your answers in a simplified surd form if necessary.

6 Given the polynomial function $f(x) = x^3 - 3x^2 + x + 1$.

  a Find f(1) and f(–2) and hence write down a factor of f(x).

  b Express f(x) in the form $(x + a)(x^2 + bx + c)$ where a, b and c are constants to be found.

  c Solve the equation $x^3 - 3x^2 + x + 1 = 0$.

    (Write your answers to 2 decimal places where necessary.)

7 Find the quotient and the remainder when $8x^3 - 24x^2 + 32x - 16$ is divided by $x + 1$.

8 Find the quotient and the remainder when $20x^3 - x^2 - 4x - 7$ is divided by $4x + 3$.

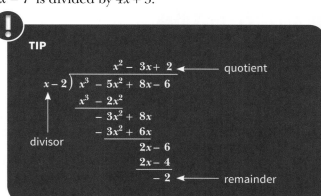

TIP

$$\begin{array}{r} x^2 - 3x + 2 \quad \longleftarrow \text{quotient} \\ x-2\,\overline{)\,x^3 - 5x^2 + 8x - 6} \\ \underline{x^3 - 2x^2} \\ -3x^2 + 8x \\ \underline{-3x^2 + 6x} \\ 2x - 6 \\ \underline{2x - 4} \\ -2 \quad \longleftarrow \text{remainder} \end{array}$$

divisor

9 a Find the value of a for which $x - 2$ is a factor of $3x^3 + ax^2 + x - 2$.

  b Using this value of a, show that the cubic equation $3x^3 + ax^2 + x - 2 = 0$ has only one real root.

41

10 a Find the values of the constants a, b and c for which:

    $(x + 5)(x - 4)(x - a) = x^3 + bx^2 - 23x + c$

  b Using these values for b and c, solve the inequality $x^3 + bx^2 - 23x + c < 0$.

Chapter 5:
Equations, inequalities and graphs

This section will show you how to:

- solve graphically or algebraically equations of the type $|ax + b| = |cx + d|$
- solve graphically or algebraically inequalities of the type $|ax + b| > c$ $(c \geqslant 0)$, $|ax + b| \leqslant c$ $(c > 0)$ and $|ax + b| \leqslant |cx + d|$
- solve cubic inequalities in the form $k(x - a)(x - b)(x - c) \leqslant d$ graphically
- sketch the graphs of cubic polynomials and their moduli, when given in factorised form
- use substitution to form and solve quadratic equations.

5.1 Solving equations of the type $|ax + b| = |cx + d|$

> **WORKED EXAMPLE 1**
>
> Solve the equation $|2x - 5| = |4 - x|$ using an algebraic method.
>
> **Answers**
>
> **Method 1**
>
> $$|2x - 5| = |4 - x|$$
>
> $2x - 5 = 4 - x$ or $2x - 5 = -(4 - x)$
>
> $x = 3$ or $x = 1$
>
> CHECK: $|6 - 5| = |4 - 3|$ CHECK: $|2 - 5| = |4 - 1|$
>
> Solutions are: $x = 3$, $x = 1$
>
> **Method 2**
>
> $$|2x - 5| = |4 - x|$$ use $|a| = |b| \Leftrightarrow a^2 = b^2$
>
> $$(2x - 5)^2 = (4 - x)^2$$ expand
>
> $$4x^2 - 20x + 25 = 16 - 8x + x^2$$ simplify
>
> $$3x^2 - 12x + 9 = 0$$
>
> $$x^2 - 4x + 3 = 0$$
>
> $$(x - 3)(x - 1) = 0$$
>
> $$x = 3, x = 1$$

The equation $|2x - 5| = |4 - x|$ could also have been solved graphically:

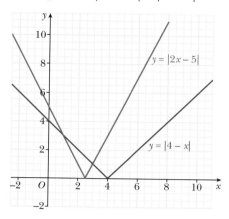

The solutions are the x-coordinates where the two graphs intersect.

WORKED EXAMPLE 2

Solve the equation $|x - 2| + |3x - 4| = 8$ using an algebraic method.

Answers

$|x - 2| + |3x - 4| = 8$ subtract $|3x - 4|$ from both sides

$\qquad |x - 2| = 8 - |3x - 4|$ split the equation into two parts

$\qquad\quad x - 2 = 8 - |3x - 4| \text{———(1)}$

$\qquad\quad x - 2 = |3x - 4| - 8 \text{———(2)}$

Using equation (1):

$\quad |3x - 4| = 10 - x$ split this equation into two parts

$3x - 4 = 10 - x \quad$ or $\quad 3x - 4 = -(10 - x)$

$\quad 4x = 14 \qquad\quad$ or $\qquad 2x = -6$

$\quad\; x = 3.5 \qquad\qquad\qquad\; x = -3$

Using equation (2):

$\quad |3x - 4| = x + 6$ split this equation into two parts

$3x - 4 = x + 6 \quad$ or $\quad 3x - 4 = -(x + 6)$

$\quad 2x = 10 \qquad\quad$ or $\qquad 4x = -2$

$\quad\; x = 5 \qquad\qquad\qquad\;\; x = -0.5$

CHECK: $|3.5 - 2| + |10.5 - 4| = 8 \qquad$ CHECK: $|-3 - 2| + |-9 - 4| = 18$

CHECK: $|5 - 2| + |15 - 4| = 14 \qquad$ CHECK: $|-0.5 - 2| + |-1.5 - 4| = 8$

Solutions are: $x = 3.5, \; x = -0.5$

Exercise 5.1

1 Solve.

   a $|x + 1| = |2x - 3|$ **b** $|2x + 1| = |3x + 9|$ **c** $|5x + 1| = |11 - 2x|$

   d $|x - 3| = |1 + 3x|$ **e** $|2x - 1| = |x - 2|$ **f** $\left|2 - \dfrac{x}{3}\right| = |3x + 2|$

   g $|2x - 1| = \left|\dfrac{x}{2} + 5\right|$ **h** $|2 + 3x| = 3|2 - x|$ **i** $3|2 - x| = 4\left|x - \dfrac{1}{2}\right|$

43

2 Solve the simultaneous equations $y = |4x - 5|$ and $y = |3 - 2x|$.

3 Solve the equation $3|2x + 1|^2 + 2|2x + 1| - 1 = 0$.

4 **a** On the same set of axes sketch the graphs of $y = 2 - |x - 1|$ and $y = |x + 2| - 3$.

    b By solving the simultaneous equations algebraically, indicate the points of intersection of the two graphs.

5 Solve the equation $|x^2 - 2x - 4| = |1 - 2x|$, leaving your answers in surd form.

6 Solve the equation $|x - 2| + |1 - x| = 2$.

7 **a** Solve the equation $|x - 6| = 2$.

    b Hence solve the equation $|y^3 - 6| = 2$, leaving your answers in exact form where appropriate.

8 Find the three roots of the equation $|x^2 - 2x + 1| = |x^2 - 3x - 4|$.

5.2 Solving modulus inequalities

WORKED EXAMPLE 3

Solve $|2x + 4| < 8$.

Answers

Method 1 (using algebra)

$|2x + 4| < 8$

$\quad -8 < 2x + 4 < 8$

$\quad -12 < 2x < 4$

$\quad -6 < x < 2$

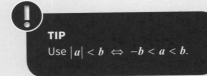

TIP

Use $|a| < b \iff -b < a < b$.

Method 2 (using a graph)

The graphs of $y = |2x + 4|$ and $y = 8$ intersect at the points A and B.

$$|2x + 4| = \begin{cases} 2x + 4 & \text{if } x \geqslant -2 \\ -(2x + 4) & \text{if } x < -2 \end{cases}$$

At A, the line $y = -(2x + 4)$ intersects the line $y = 8$.

$\quad -(2x + 4) = 8$

$\quad\quad -2x - 4 = 8$

$\quad\quad\quad -2x = 12$

$\quad\quad\quad\quad x = -6$

At B, the line $y = 2x + 4$ intersects the line $y = 8$.

$\quad 2x + 4 = 8$

$\quad\quad 2x = 4$

$\quad\quad\ x = 2$

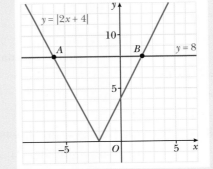

To solve the inequality $|2x + 4| < 8$ you must find where the graph of the function $y = |2x + 4|$ is below the graph of $y = 8$.

Hence, the solution is $-6 < x < 2$.

WORKED EXAMPLE 4

Solve $|2x - 1| \leqslant |3 - x|$.

Answers

Method 1 (using algebra)

$|2x - 1| \leqslant |3 - x|$ $\qquad$ use $|a| \geqslant |b| \Leftrightarrow a^2 \geqslant b^2$

$(2x - 1)^2 \leqslant (3 - x)^2$

$4x^2 - 4x + 1 \leqslant 9 - 6x + x^2$

$3x^2 + 2x - 8 \leqslant 0$ $\qquad$ factorise

$(3x - 4)(x + 2) \leqslant 0$

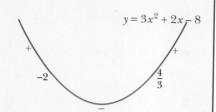

$y = 3x^2 + 2x - 8$

Critical values are $\dfrac{4}{3}$ and -2.

Hence, $-2 \leqslant x \leqslant \dfrac{4}{3}$

Method 2 (using a graph)

The graphs of $y = |2x - 1|$ and $y = |3 - x|$ intersect
at the points A and B.

$|2x - 1| = \begin{cases} 2x - 1 & \text{if } x \geqslant \dfrac{1}{2} \\ -(2x - 1) & \text{if } x < \dfrac{1}{2} \end{cases}$

$|3 - x| = |x - 3| = \begin{cases} x - 3 & \text{if } x \geqslant 3 \\ -(x - 3) & \text{if } x < 3 \end{cases}$

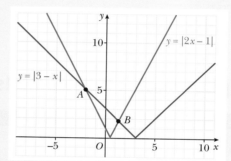

At A, the line $y = -(2x - 1)$ intersects the line $y = -(x - 3)$.

$2x - 1 = x - 3$

$x = -2$

At B, the line $y = 2x - 1$ intersects the line $y = -(x - 3)$.

$2x - 1 = -(x - 3)$

$3x = 4$

$x = \dfrac{4}{3}$

To solve the inequality $|2x - 1| \leqslant |3 - x|$ you must find where the graph of the function
$y = |2x - 1|$ is below the graph of $y = |3 - x|$.

Hence, $-2 \leqslant x \leqslant \dfrac{4}{3}$

Exercise 5.2

1 The graphs of $y = |3x - 1|$ and $y = |2 - x|$ are shown on the grid.
Write down the set of values of x that satisfy the inequality $|3x - 1| < |2 - x|$.

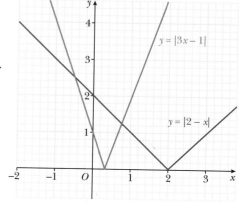

2 **a** On the same axes sketch the graphs of $y = |3 - 2x|$ and $y = |x - 3|$.
   b Solve the inequality $|3 - 2x| \geqslant |x - 3|$.

3 Solve.

   a $|3x - 2| > 4$ $\qquad$ **b** $|4 - 2x| \leqslant 6$ $\qquad$ **c** $|10 - 2x| < 3$

   d $|2x + 4| > 6$ $\qquad$ **e** $|5x + 1| > 12$ $\qquad$ **f** $|4 - 2x| \leqslant 2$

4 Solve.

a $|2x - 5| \le x + 1$

b $|5 - x| > 3 - 2x$

c $|x + 2| - 3x \le 1$

5 Solve.

a $|3x - 1| \le |2x|$

b $|2x + 4| > |2x|$

c $|4x| > |3 - 2x|$

d $|x + 2| > |2x + 3|$

e $|2 - x| \ge |3 - 2x|$

f $|1 - 2x| < |x + 3|$

6 Solve.

a $|x + 3| > |2x - 4|$

b $|x + 2| \ge |2x + 5|$

c $|x - 1| \le |3x + 7|$

d $|2x + 1| \le |3 - 2x|$

e $|x + 3| < \left|\dfrac{1}{3}x + 5\right|$

f $\left|\dfrac{1}{2}x - 2\right| \ge \left|\dfrac{1}{3}x + 4\right|$

7 Solve.

a $|x + 6| > 3|x|$

b $|x - 7| < 2|x + 3|$

c $\left|\dfrac{1}{2}x - 5\right| \le \dfrac{1}{3}|2x + 1|$

8 Find the value for a if $|2x + a| < 3|x|$, where a is positive and $x < -2$.

9 Solve the inequality $\left|\sqrt{2x + 1}\right| < \left|\sqrt{x - 5}\right|$.

10 Solve $|2x - 2| + |3x - 2| \le 4$.

5.3 Sketching graphs of cubic polynomials and their moduli

REMINDER

When sketching graphs of the form

$$y = k(x - a)(x - b)(x - c)$$

you should show the general shape of the curve and all of the axis intercepts.

The shape of the graph is

 if k is positive   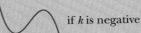 if k is negative

To help find the general shape of the curve you need to consider what happens to

- y as x tends to positive infinity (i.e. as $x \to +\infty$)
- y as x tends to negative infinity (i.e. as $x \to -\infty$)

WORKED EXAMPLE 5

a Sketch the graph of the function $y = (x - 1)(2x + 1)(x + 3)$.

b Hence, sketch the graph of $y = |(x - 1)(2x + 1)(x + 3)|$.

Answers

a When $x = 0$, $y = -1 \times 1 \times 3 = -3$.

∴ The curve intercepts the y-axis at $(0, -3)$.

When $y = 0$, $(x - 1)(2x + 1)(x + 3) = 0$

$x - 1 = 0$ $2x + 1 = 0$ $x + 3 = 0$

    $x = 1$ $x = -\dfrac{1}{2}$ $x = -3$

∴ The curve intercepts the x-axis at $(1, 0)$, $\left(-\dfrac{1}{2}, 0\right)$ and $(-3, 0)$.

As $x \to +\infty$, $y \to \infty$

As $x \to -\infty$, $y \to -\infty$

The graph of the function $y = (x - 1)(2x + 1)(x + 3)$ is:

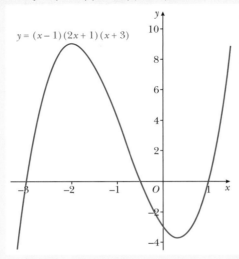

b To sketch the curve $y = \left|(x - 1)(2x + 1)(x + 3)\right|$ you reflect in the x-axis the parts of the curve $y = (x - 1)(2x + 1)(x + 3)$ that are below the x-axis.

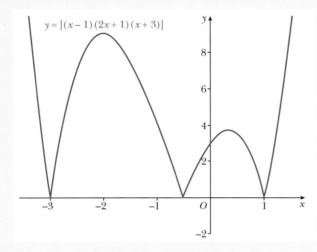

WORKED EXAMPLE 6

The sketch graphs below are examples of cubic functions of the form $y = k(x - a)(x - b)(x - c)$

Using the sketches, find the equation of each graph.

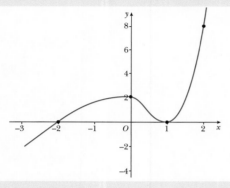

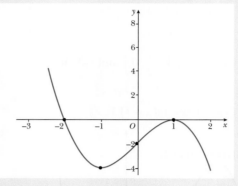

Figure 1   Figure 2

Answers

Figure 1 is a cubic graph of the form $y = k(x - a)(x - b)(x - c)$ where k is **positive**.

$y = k(x - a)(x - b)(x - c)$ when $y = 0$,

   $k(x - a)(x - b)(x - c) = 0$ the x axis intercepts are $x = 1$, $x = -2$

                                there is a repeated root at $x = 1$

$y = k(x - 1)(x - 1)(x + 2)$ to find k, substitute $x = 2$, $y = 8$

$8 = k(2 - 1)(2 - 1)(2 + 2)$

$k = 1$

$\therefore y = (x - 1)(x - 1)(x + 2)$

$y = (x - 1)^2(x + 2)$

Figure 2 is a cubic graph of the form $y = k(x - a)(x - b)(x - c)$ where k is **negative**.

$y = k(x - a)(x - b)(x - c)$ when $y = 0$,

   $k(x - a)(x - b)(x - c) = 0$ the x axis intercepts are $x = 1$, $x = -2$

                                  there is a repeated root at $x = 1$

$y = k(x - 1)(x - 1)(x + 2)$ to find k, substitute $x = -1$, $y = -4$

$-4 = k(-1 - 1)(-1 - 1)(-1 + 2)$

$k = -1$

$\therefore y = -(x - 1)(x - 1)(x + 2)$

$y = -(x - 1)^2(x + 2)$

WORKED EXAMPLE 7

a Sketch the graph of the function $y = x(x-2)^2$.

b Hence sketch the graph of $y = \left| x(x-2)^2 \right|$.

Answers

a When $x = 0$, $y = 0 \times (-2)^2 = 0$

∴ The curve intercepts the y-axis at $(0, 0)$.

When $y = 0$, $x(x-2)^2 = 0$

$x = 0$ $(x-2)^2 = 0$

$x = 0$ $x = 2$ (repeated root)

∴ The curve intercepts the x-axis at $(0, 0)$ and $(2, 0)$.

As $x \to +\infty$, $y \to +\infty$

As $x \to -\infty$, $y \to -\infty$

The graph of the function $y = x(x-2)^2$ is:

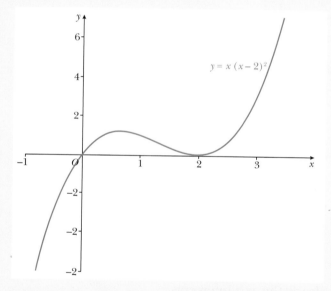

b To sketch the curve $y = \left| x(x-2)^2 \right|$ you reflect in the x-axis the part of

the curve $y = x(x-2)^2$ that is below the x-axis.

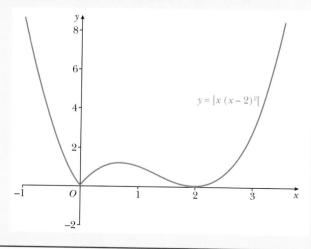

Exercise 5.3

1 Find the coordinates of the points A, B and C where the curve intercepts the x-axis and the point D where the curve intercepts the positive y-axis.

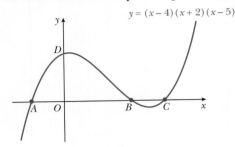

$$y = (x-4)(x+2)(x-5)$$

2 Sketch each of these curves and indicate clearly the axis intercepts.

a $y = (x-1)(x-4)(x+2)$

b $y = (x+3)(x+2)(4-x)$

c $y = (2x-3)(x+3)(x-3)$

d $y = (1-2x)(x-2)(x+2)$

3 Find the coordinates of the point A and the point B, where A is the point where the curve intercepts the positive x-axis and B is the point where the curve intercepts the positive y-axis.

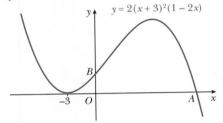

$$y = 2(x+3)^2(1-2x)$$

4 Sketch each of these curves and indicate clearly the axis intercepts.

a $y = x(x-2)^2$

b $y = x^2\left(1 - \dfrac{1}{2}x\right)$

c $y = (x+3)^2(x+1)$

d $y = (x-1)^2(1-x)$

5 Sketch each of these curves and indicate clearly the axis intercepts.

a $y = \left|(x-1)(x+2)(x-2)\right|$

b $y = \left|3(1-2x)(x+2)(1-x)\right|$

c $y = \left|x(4-x^2)\right|$

d $y = \left|3x^2(x+1)\right|$

6 Factorise each of these functions and then sketch the graph of each function indicating clearly the axis intercepts.

a $y = 4x - x^3$

b $y = -x^3 + x^2 + 4x - 4$

c $y = 2x^3 - x^2 - 5x - 2$

d $y = 3x^3 - 12x^2 + 12x$

7 a On the same axes sketch the graphs of $y = x - x^3$ and $y = x^2 - 1$, showing clearly the points at which the curves meet the coordinate axes.

b Use algebra to find the coordinates of all the points where the graphs intersect.

8 a On the same axes sketch the graphs of $y = \left|(x-2)(x+1)^2\right|$ and $y = \left|(x-2)(x+1)\right|$, showing clearly the points at which the curves meet the coordinate axes.

b Use algebra to find the coordinates of all the points where the graphs intersect.

9 The diagram shows the graph of $y = k(x + a)^2 (x - b)$.

Find the values of a, b and k.

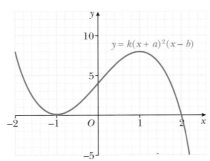

10 a On the same axes sketch the graphs of $y = \left| -(x + 2)(x - 1)^2 \right|$ and $y = \left| (-x - 2) \right|$, showing clearly the points at which the curves meet the coordinate axes.

b Use algebra to find the coordinates of all the points where the graphs intersect.

5.4 Solving cubic inequalities graphically

WORKED EXAMPLE 8

The diagram shows part of the graph of $y = \dfrac{1}{2}(x + 3)(x - 1)(x + 1)$.

Use the graph to solve the inequality $(x + 3)(x - 1)(x + 1) \geqslant 2$.

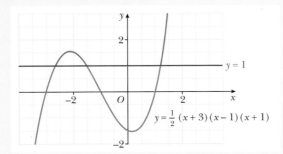

Answers

$(x + 3)(x - 1)(x + 1) \geqslant 2$ divide both sides by 2

$\dfrac{1}{2}(x + 3)(x - 1)(x + 1) \geqslant 1$

You need to find where the curve $y = \dfrac{1}{2}(x + 3)(x - 1)(x + 1)$ is above the line $y = 1$.

The red sections of the graph represent where the curve $y = \dfrac{1}{2}(x + 3)(x - 1)(x + 1)$ is above the line $y = 1$.

The solution is $-2.7 \leqslant x \leqslant -1.5$ or $x \geqslant 1.2$ to 1 d.p.

Exercise 5.4

1

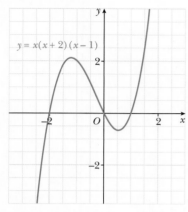

The diagram shows part of the graph of $y = x(x+2)(x-1)$.

Use the graph to solve each of the following inequalities.

a $x(x+2)(x-1) \leq 0$, **b** $x(x+2)(x-1) \geq 1$, **c** $x(x+2)(x-1) \leq -2$.

2

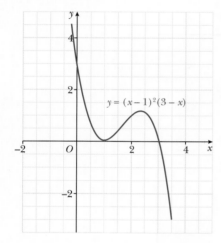

The diagram shows part of the graph of $y = (x-1)^2(3-x)$.

Use the graph to solve each of the following inequalities.

a $(x-1)^2(3-x) \geq 0$ **b** $(x-1)^2(3-x) \leq 0.5$ **c** $(x-1)^2(3-x) \leq -1$

3

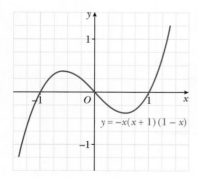

The diagram shows part of the graph of $y = -x(x+1)(1-x)$.

Use the graph to solve each of the following inequalities.

a $-x(x+1)(1-x) < 0$ **b** $-x(x+1)(1-x) \leq 0.2$

c $-x(x+1)(1-x) > -1$

5.5 Solving more complex quadratic equations

You may be asked to solve an equation that is quadratic in some function of x.

WORKED EXAMPLE 9

Solve the equation $x^4 - 3x^2 - 4 = 0$.

Answers

Method 1 (substitution method)

$$x^4 - 3x^2 - 4 = 0 \qquad \text{use the substitution } y = x^2$$

$$y^2 - 3y - 4 = 0 \qquad \text{factorise}$$

$$(y+1)(y-4) = 0 \qquad \text{solve}$$

$$y + 1 = 0 \quad \text{or} \quad y - 4 = 0$$

$$y = -1 \quad \text{or} \quad y = 4 \qquad \text{substitute } x^2 \text{ for } y$$

$$x^2 = -1 \quad \text{or} \quad x^2 = 4 \qquad x^2 = -1 \text{ has no real solutions}$$

$$x = \pm 2$$

Method 2 (factorise directly)

$$x^4 - 3x^2 - 4 = 0$$

$$(x^2 + 1)(x^2 - 4) = 0$$

$$x^2 + 1 = 0 \quad \text{or} \quad x^2 - 4 = 0$$

$$x^2 = -1 \quad \text{or} \quad x^2 = 4$$

$$x = \pm 2$$

WORKED EXAMPLE 10

Use the substitution $y = x^{\frac{1}{3}}$ to solve the equation $x^{\frac{2}{3}} - x^{\frac{1}{3}} - 6 = 0$.

Answers

$$x^{\frac{2}{3}} - x^{\frac{1}{3}} - 6 = 0 \qquad \text{let } y = x^{\frac{1}{3}}$$

$$y^2 - y - 6 = 0 \qquad \text{factorise}$$

$$(y - 3)(y + 2) = 0 \qquad \text{solve}$$

$$y - 3 = 0 \quad \text{or} \quad y + 2 = 0$$

$$y = 3 \quad \text{or} \quad y = -2 \qquad \text{substitute } x^{\frac{1}{3}} \text{ for } y$$

$$x^{\frac{1}{3}} = 3 \quad \text{or} \quad x^{\frac{1}{3}} = -2 \qquad \text{cube both sides}$$

$$x = 3^3 \quad \text{or} \quad x = (-2)^3$$

$$x = 27 \quad \text{or} \quad x = -8$$

WORKED EXAMPLE 11

Solve the equation $x + \sqrt{x} - 20 = 0$.

Answers

$x + \sqrt{x} - 20 = 0$ use the substitution $y = \sqrt{x}$

$y^2 + y - 20 = 0$

$(y - 4)(y + 5) = 0$

$y - 4 = 0$ or $y + 5 = 0$

     $y = 4$ or $y = -5$ substitute $\sqrt{x}$ for y

    $\sqrt{x} = 4$ or $\sqrt{x} = -5$ $\sqrt{x} = -5$ has no real solutions

$\therefore x = 16$

WORKED EXAMPLE 12

Solve the equation $9^x - 10(3^x) + 9 = 0$.

Answers

$9^x - 10(3^x) + 9 = 0$ 9^x can be written as $(3^2)^x = (3^x)^2$

$(3^x)^2 - 10(3^x) + 9 = 0$ let $y = 3^x$

     $y^2 - 10y + 9 = 0$

    $(y - 1)(y - 9) = 0$

    $y = 1$ or $y = 9$ substitute 3^x for y

    $3^x = 1$ or $3^x = 9$ $1 = 3^0$ and $9 = 3^2$

    $x = 0$ or $x = 2$

Exercise 5.5

1 Find the real values of x satisfying the following equations.

   a $x^4 - 11x^2 + 30 = 0$ **b** $x^4 - 6x^2 + 8 = 0$ **c** $4x^4 - 25x^2 + 36 = 0$

   d $12x^4 + 10x^2 - 2 = 0$ **e** $6x^4 - x^2 - 2 = 0$ **f** $6x^4 - 11x^2 + 3 = 0$

   g $x^4 + 36 = 13x^2$ **h** $x^{\frac{2}{3}} - x^{\frac{1}{3}} - 6 = 0$ **i** $\dfrac{21}{x^2} + \dfrac{18}{x^4} = 9$

2 Use the quadratic formula to find the real values of x satisfying the following equations.

Write your answers correct to 3 significant figures.

   a $x^4 - 6x^2 + 8 = 0$ **b** $x^4 + x^2 - 12 = 0$ **c** $65x^4 - 4x^8 - 16 = 0$

   d $x^6 - 9x^3 + 8 = 0$ **e** $x^6 - 2x^3 - 8 = 0$ **f** $x^8 - 17x^4 + 16 = 0$

3 Solve $(x+2)^2 - 3(x+2) - 4 = 0$

4 Solve.

    a $2x + \sqrt{x} - 1 = 0$ **b** $x - 5\sqrt{x} + 6 = 0$ **c** $x - 6\sqrt{x} + 5 = 0$

    d $\sqrt{x}\left(8 - \sqrt{x}\right) = 15$ **e** $x - 12\sqrt{x} + 35 = 0$ **f** $\sqrt{x}\left(\sqrt{x} - 6\right) + 9 = 0$

    g $x = 4\sqrt{x} - 3$ **h** $\dfrac{12}{\sqrt{x}} - \sqrt{x} + 4 = 0$ **i** $\dfrac{9}{\sqrt{x}} - \dfrac{10}{x} = 2$

5 Solve the equation $x^{\frac{1}{2}} - x^{\frac{1}{4}} - 6 = 0$.

6 The curves $y = 7 - \sqrt{x}$ and $y = \dfrac{10}{\sqrt{x}}$ intersect at the points P and Q.

    a   Write down an equation satisfied by the x-coordinates of P and Q.

    b   Solve your equation in **part a** and hence find the coordinates of P and Q.

7 Solve.

    a $2^{2x} - 3(2^{x+2}) + 32 = 0$ **b** $4^x - 2^{x+2} = 0$ **c** $2^{2x} - 10(2^x) + 16 = 0$

    d $4^{x+1} + (4^{1-x}) - 10 = 0$ **e** $3^{2x+2} - 10(3^x) + 1 = 0$ **f** $4^x - 9(2^{x-1}) + 2 = 0$

8 $f(x) = 2x$ and $g(x) = 4x^2 - 9x + 2$. Solve $gf(x) = 0$.

9 The diagonal of a rectangle is $10\,\text{cm}$ and its area is $45\,\text{cm}^2$.

    a   If its width is x cm, show that its area can be expressed as $x\sqrt{100 - x^2} = 45$

    b   By solving this equation, find the dimensions of the rectangle to 3 significant figures.

10 Challenge question

    Solve $\left(x^2 + 2x\right)^2 - 11\left(x^2 + 2x\right) + 24 = 0$

Summary

Solving modulus equations

To solve modulus equations you can use the property:

$$|a| = |b| \Leftrightarrow a^2 = b^2$$

Solving modulus inequalities

To solve modulus inequalities you can use the properties:

$$|a| \leqslant b \Leftrightarrow -b \leqslant a \leqslant b$$
$$|a| \geqslant b \Leftrightarrow a \leqslant -b \ \text{ or } \ a \geqslant b$$
$$|a| > |b| \Leftrightarrow a^2 > b^2$$
$$|a| < |b| \Leftrightarrow a^2 < b^2, b \neq 0$$

The graph of $y = k(x - a)(x - b)(x - c)$

The x-axis intercepts are $(a, 0)$, $(b, 0)$ and $(c, 0)$.

The shape of the graph is

if k is positive   if k is negative

The graph of $y = |k(x - a)(x - b)(x - c)|$

To sketch the curve $y = |k(x - a)(x - b)(x - c)|$ you reflect in the x-axis the parts of the curve $y = k(x - a)(x - b)(x - c)$ that are below the x-axis.

Exercise 5.6

1 Solve the equation $|x - 3| = |4x - 1|$.

2 Solve the inequality $|3x - 1| < 8$.

3 Solve the inequality $|5 - 2x| < 1$.

4 Solve the inequality $|2x| > |1 - 3x|$.

5 Solve the inequality $|2x - 1| \leqslant 3|x + 1|$.

6 Solve the inequality $\left|\dfrac{1}{3}x + 3\right| < \left|\dfrac{1}{2}x - 1\right|$.

7 The diagram below shows the graph of $y = f(x)$.

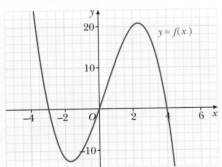

On separate axes

a sketch the graph of $y = |f(x)|$

b sketch the graph of $y = -|f(x)|$.

In each case, mark the points where the curves meet the coordinate axes.

8 Solve the inequality $|x + 3k| > |2x - k|$ where k is a positive constant.

9 Sketch the graph of $y = -x(3-x)^2$, showing clearly the points at which the curve meets the coordinate axes.

10 a Sketch the graph of $y = (x-1)(x+3)(x+2)$, showing clearly the points at which the curve meets the coordinate axes.

  b Hence sketch the curve $y = |(x-1)(x+3)(x+2)|$.

11 a Factorise completely $x^3 - x^2 - 2x$.

  b On the same axes sketch the graphs of $y = x^3 - x^2 - 2x$ and $y = (x+1)(2-x)$, showing clearly the points at which the curves meet the coordinate axes.

12 a On the same axes sketch the graphs of $y = (x-1)(x+2)^2$ and $y = \dfrac{1}{x}$, showing clearly the points at which the curves meet the coordinate axes.

  b Hence, state the number of real roots of the equation $(x-1)(x+2)^2 = \dfrac{1}{x}$.

Chapter 6:
Logarithmic and exponential functions

This section will show you how to:

- use simple properties of the logarithmic and exponential functions including $\ln x$ and e^x
- use graphs of the logarithmic and exponential functions including $\ln x$ and e^x and graphs of $ke^{nx} + a$ and $k\ln(ax + b)$ where n, k, a and b are integers
- use the laws of logarithms, including change of base of logarithms
- solve equations of the form $a^x = b$.

6.1 Logarithms to base 10

« REMINDER

The rule for base 10 is: If $y = 10^x$ then $x = \log_{10} y$.

$$\log_{10} 10 = 1$$

$$\log_{10} 1 = 0$$

$$\log_{10} 10 = 1 \text{ for } x \in \mathbb{R}$$

$$x = 10^{\log_{10} x} \text{ for } x > 0$$

! TIP

$\log_{10} x$ can also be written as $\lg x$.

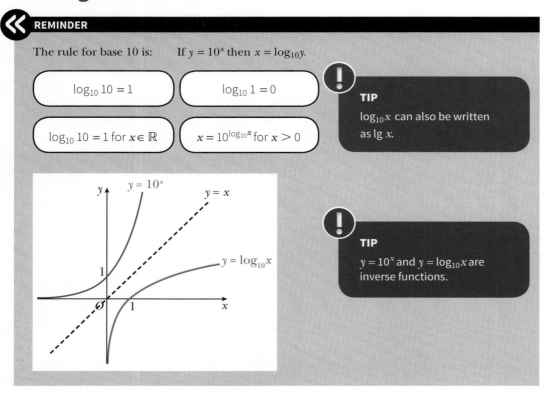

! TIP

$y = 10^x$ and $y = \log_{10} x$ are inverse functions.

WORKED EXAMPLE 1

a Convert $10^x = 150$ to logarithmic form.

b Convert $\log_{10} x = 6.4$ to exponential form.

Answers

a $10^x = 150$

   $\log_{10} 10^x = \log_{10} 150$

   $x = \log_{10} 150.$

b $\log_{10} x = 6.4$

   $x = 10^{6.4}$

Exercise 6.1

1 Convert from exponential form to logarithmic form.

    a $10^4 = 10000$ **b** $10^x = 80$ **c** $10^x = 0.002$

2 Solve each of these equations, giving your answers correct to 3 sf.

    a $10^x = 22$ **b** $10^x = 220$ **c** $10^x = 0.22$

3 Convert from logarithmic form to exponential form.

    a $\lg 1000 = 3$ **b** $\lg\left(\dfrac{1}{100}\right) = -2$ **c** $\lg x = 6$

    d $\lg x = -0.5$

4 Solve these equations, giving your answers correct to 3 sf.

    a $\lg x = 3.1$ **b** $\lg x = -0.1$ **c** $\lg x = \dfrac{1}{8}$

5 Without using a calculator, find the value of

    a $\lg 0.1$ **b** $\lg \sqrt[5]{10}$ **c** $\lg\left(1000\sqrt{10}\right)$

    d $\lg 10\sqrt[4]{10}$ **e** $\lg 10^{2.5}$ **f** $\lg (10^{-1.2})$

6.2 Logarithms to base a

REMINDER

The rule for base a is: If $y = a^x$ then $x = \log_a y$.

$\log_{10} a = 1$

$\log_a 1 = 0$

$\log_a a^x = x$

$x = a^{\log_a x}$

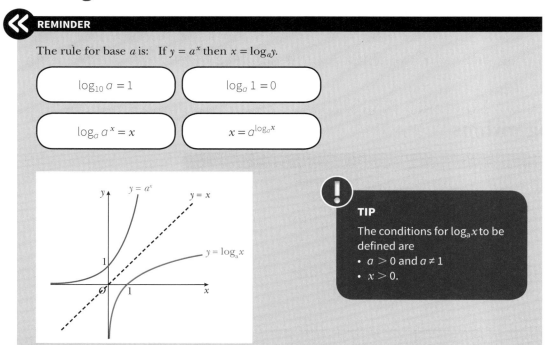

TIP

The conditions for $\log_a x$ to be defined are
- $a > 0$ and $a \neq 1$
- $x > 0$.

WORKED EXAMPLE 2

Find the value of

a $\log_5 125$ **b** $\log_3 \dfrac{1}{243}$.

Answers

a $\log_5 125 = \log_5 5^3$ write 125 as a power of 5, $125 = 5^3$

   $\qquad\qquad = 3$

b $\log_3 \dfrac{1}{243} = \log_3 3^{-5}$ write $\dfrac{1}{243}$ as a power of 3, $\dfrac{1}{243} = 3^{-5}$

   $\qquad\qquad = -5$

Exercise 6.2

1 Convert from exponential form to logarithmic form.

   a $4^2 = 16$ **b** $4^{-2} = \dfrac{1}{16}$ **c** $a^3 = b$ **d** $y^x = 6$

2 Convert from logarithmic form to exponential form.

   a $\log_3 27 = 3$ **b** $\log_4 64 = 3$ **c** $\log_{25} 5 = 0.5$ **d** $\log_{16} 2 = \dfrac{1}{4}$

> **TIP**
>
> $a^{\log_a x} = x$ and $\log_a a^x = x$

3 Solve.

   a $\log_2 x = 6$ **b** $\log_5 x = 2$ **c** $\log_5 x = \dfrac{1}{2}$ **d** $\log_x 125 = 3$

   e $\log_2 (2x + 1) = 5$ **f** $\log_4 (2 - 4x) = 2$

4 Find the value of

   a $\log_9 3$ **b** $\log_6 \sqrt{6}$ **c** $\log_2 0.125$ **d** $\log_2 16\sqrt{2}$

   e $\log_3 \sqrt[3]{3}$ **f** $\log_5 \dfrac{5}{\sqrt{5}}$

6.3 The laws of logarithms

« REMINDER

If x and y are both positive and $a > 0$ and $a \neq 1$, then the following laws apply.

$$\log_a (xy) = \log_a x + \log_a y$$

$$\log_a \left(\dfrac{x}{y}\right) = \log_a x - \log_a y$$

$$\log_a (x)^m = m \log_a x$$

$$\log_a \left(\dfrac{1}{x}\right) = -\log_a x$$

WORKED EXAMPLE 3

Use the laws of logarithms to simplify these expressions.

a $\lg 7 + \lg 3$ **b** $\log_3 18 \div \log_3 3$ **c** $3 \log_7 2 + 4 \log_7 3$

Answers

a $\lg 7 + \lg 3$ **b** $\log_3 18 \div \log_4 3$ **c** $3 \log_7 2 + 4 \log_7 3$

   $= \lg (7 \times 3)$ $\quad = \log_3 \left(\dfrac{18}{3}\right)$ $\quad = \log_7 2^3 + \log_7 3^4$

   $= \lg 21$ $\qquad = \log_3 6$ $\qquad\quad = \log_7 (8 \times 81)$

   $\qquad\qquad\qquad\qquad\qquad\qquad\qquad\qquad\quad = \log_3 648$

Exercise 6.3

1 Write as a single logarithm, simplifying your answer if necessary.

a $\lg 3 + \lg 5$ **b** $\lg 3 + \lg 15$ **c** $\log_4 15 - \log_4 5$

d $\log 4 + \log 25$ **e** $2\log_7 2 + \log_7 5$ **f** $\frac{1}{2}\log_4 16 - 2\log_4 4$

g $\frac{1}{3}\log_4 64 + 2\log_4 2$ **h** $3\log_5 5 - 1$ **i** $3\lg 2 + \lg 4 - \lg 8$

j $2\log_4\left(\frac{1}{2}\right) - \log_4 2$ **k** $-\log_2\left(\frac{1}{2}\right)$ **l** $2\log_3 15 - \log_3 9 - \log_3 5$

2 Simplify.

a $\dfrac{\lg 8}{\lg 2}$

b $\dfrac{\lg 81}{\lg 9}$

> **TIP Q2a**
>
> Be careful, a common error is to write lg4 next.
> You need to rewrite $\dfrac{\lg 8}{\lg 2}$ as $\dfrac{\lg 2^3}{\lg 2}$ which is $\dfrac{3\lg 2}{\lg 2}$.
> Answer is 3.

c $\dfrac{\log_2 49}{\log_2 343}$

d $\dfrac{\log 125 - 2\log 5}{-\log 5}$

e $\dfrac{\log 0.1}{2\log 100}$

3 Express as a single logarithm.

a $2\log_a 5 + \log_a 4 - \log_a 10$ **b** $2\log_a 3 - \log_a 15 + \log_a 5$

c $\log_a 12 - \left(\frac{1}{2}\log_a 9 + \frac{1}{3}\log_a 8\right)$

4 Given that $\log 2 = 0.3$ and $\log 5 = 0.7$ (both correct to 1 sf), use these values to find the values of the following to 1 sf.

a $\log 2.5$ **b** $\log 4$ **c** $\log 25$ **d** $\log 32$

e $\log 0.5$

5 Express $\log pq^2\sqrt{r}$ in terms of $\log p$, $\log q$ and $\log r$.

6 Simplify $3\log p + n\log q - 4\log r$.

7 Express each of the following in terms of $\log p$, $\log q$ and $\log r$.

a $\log p^2 q$ **b** $\log \dfrac{p}{qr}$ **c** $\log \sqrt{\dfrac{q}{r}}$

d $\log \dfrac{1}{100p^2}$ **e** $\log p^n q^m$

6.4 Solving logarithmic equations

WORKED EXAMPLE 4

Solve $\log_x 32 - \log_x 2 = 2\log_x x$.

Answer

$\log_x 32 - \log_x 2 = 2\log_x x$

$$\log_x\left(\frac{32}{2}\right) = \log_x x^2$$

$$\log_x(16) = \log_x x^2$$

$$16 = x^2$$

$$x = 4 \qquad\qquad x = 4, \ (x = -4 \text{ not a solution})$$

Exercise 6.4

1 Solve each of the following equations.

a $\log_2 5x = \log_2(2x + 9)$

b $\log_2(-2x + 9) = \log_2(7 - 4x)$

c $-2\log_5 7x = 2$

d $\log_4 x + \log_4 4 - \log_4 5 = \log_4 12$

e $\log_4 x - \log_4 7 = \dfrac{3}{2}$

f $\log_9(x + 6) - \log_9 x = \log_9 2$

g $\log_5 2x + \log_5 6 = \log_5(2x + 3)$

h $\log 2 + \log p = 1$

i $\log_2 x + \log_2(x - 3) = 2$

j $\log_2(x + 5) - \log_2(x - 2) = 3$

k $\log 2x = 3$

l $\log_2(x + 4) = 1 + \log_2(x - 5)$

2 Solve the following simultaneous equations.

a $x^2 - 11 = y^2$
   $\log x - \log y = 1$

b $\log x + \log y = 5$
   $\log x - \log y = 1$

c $\log x - \log 2 = 2\log y$
   $x - 5y + 2 = 0$

d $\log x + \log 2 = 2\log y$
   $2^y = 4^x$

6.5 Solving exponential equations

WORKED EXAMPLE 5

Solve $25^x - 3 \times 5^x = 0$.

Answer

$25^x - 3 \times 5^x = 0$

$5^{2x} - 3 \times 5^x = 0 \qquad 25^x = \left(5^2\right)^x$

$5^x\left(5^x - 3\right) = 0$

$5^x = 0 \qquad \text{or} \qquad 5^x - 3 = 0$

No solutions $\qquad\qquad 5^x = 3 \qquad$ take logs of both sides

$\qquad\qquad\qquad \lg 5^x = \lg 3 \qquad$ use the power rule

$\qquad\qquad\qquad x\lg 5 = \lg 3 \qquad$ divide both sides by lg5

$$x = \frac{\lg 3}{\lg 5}$$

$$x \approx 0.683$$

Exercise 6.5

1 Solve, giving your answers correct to 3 sf.

a $5^{2x} = 8$ **b** $4^{2x} = 9$

c $6^{x-2} = 4$ **d** $3^{2x-1} = 5^x$

e $2^{-3x} = 5$ **f** $5^{4x-1} = 7^{x+2}$

> **TIP**
>
> Parts **a–f**:
>
> Use $y = a^x$ then $x = \log_a y$.
>
> Take the $\log_{10}$ of both sides of the equation first, then use your calculator.

2 Solve, giving your answers correct to 3 sf.

a $5 \times 2^x = 3 \times 7^x$

b $3 \times 2^x = 7$

c $9 \div 4^x = 20$

d $5 \div 2^x = 6 \times 5^x$

e $5 \times 2^x = 21 \times 3^x$

f $5(2^{3x+1}) = 62$

3 Solve, giving your answers correct to 3 sf.

a $2^{2x} - 2^x = 6$

b $2^{2x} - 5 \times 2^x + 4 = 0$

c $3^{2x} - 30 \times 3^x + 81 = 0$

d $4^{2x} - 5 \times 4^x + 6 = 0$

e $2 \times 2^{2x} - 11 \times 2^x + 5 = 0$

f $8^x - 5 \times 4^x = 0$

> **TIP**
>
> Use $\log_{10}(xy) = \log_{10} x + \log_{10} y$ and $\log_{10}(x)^m = m \log_{10} x$

6.6 Change of base of logarithms

REMINDER

- $\log_b a = \dfrac{\log_c a}{\log_c b}$

- If $c = a$ in the change of base rule, then the rule gives:

  $\log_b a = \dfrac{1}{\log_a b}$

WORKED EXAMPLE 6

Solve $\log_5 x^2 = \log_{25} 8x$.

Answer

$\log_5 x^2 = \log_{25} 8x$ change $\log_{25} 8x$ to base 5

$\log_5 x^2 = \dfrac{\log_5 8x}{\log_5 25}$ $\log_5 25 = \log_5 5^2 = 2$

$\log_5 x^2 = \dfrac{\log_5 8x}{2}$ multiply both sides by 2

$2\log_5 x^2 = \log_5 8x$ use the power rule

$\log_5 x^4 = \log_5 8x$ use equality of logs

$x^4 = 8x$

$x^4 - 8x = 0$

$x(x^3 - 8) = 0$

$x = 0$ or $x^3 = 8$

$\therefore x = 2$

Exercise 6.6

1 Use the change of base rule to evaluate the following to 3 sf.

    a $\log_3 3.3$ **b** $\log_4 5$ **c** $\log_5 10$

2 Show that $\log_8 1000 = \log_2 10$.

3 Solve $\log_3 x = 4\log_x 3$.

4 Solve, giving your answers correct to 3 sf.

    a $\log_4 x^3 + \log_2 \sqrt{x} = 8$ **b** $\log_{16} x^5 = \log_{64} 125 - \log_4 \sqrt{x}$

5 Solve the following simultaneous equations.

$$\log_{10} y + 2\log_{10} x = 3$$
$$\log_2 y - \log_2 x = 3$$

6.7 Natural logarithms

REMINDER

If $y = e^x$ then $x = \ln y$.

$y = \ln x$ is the reflection of $y = e^x$ in the line $y = x$.

$y = \ln x$ and $y = e^x$ are inverse functions.

All the rules of logarithms that you have learnt so far, also apply for natural logarithms.

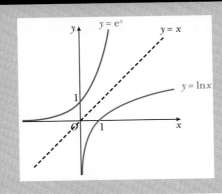

Exercise 6.7

1 Use a calculator to evaluate correct to 3 sf.

   a e^3 **b** $e^{2.5}$ **c** $e^{0.3}$ **d** e^{-4}

2 Use a calculator to evaluate correct to 3 sf.

   a $\ln 5$ **b** $\ln 3.1$ **c** $\ln 0.75$ **d** $\ln 1.39$

3 Without using a calculator, find the value of.

   a $e^{\ln 2}$ **b** $e^{\frac{1}{2}\ln 9}$ **c** $2e^{-\ln 5}$

   d $\ln e^5$ **e** $\ln \dfrac{1}{e}$

> **TIP**
>
> Remember $e^{\ln x} = x$ and $\ln e^x = x$.

4 Solve.

   a $e^{\ln x} = 5$ **b** $\ln e^x = 12$ **c** $e^{3\ln x} = 8$ **d** $e^{-\ln x} = 4$

5 Solve, giving your answers correct to 3 sf.

   a $e^x = 34$ **b** $e^{2x} = 40$ **c** $e^{x+1} = 21$ **d** $e^{2x-1} = 7$

6 Solve, giving your answers in terms of natural logarithms.

   a $e^x = 5$ **b** $2e^x - 6 = 10$ **c** $\dfrac{1}{2}e^{2x-3} = 12$

7 Solve, giving your answers correct to 3 sf.

   a $\ln x = 4$ **b** $\ln x = -6$ **c** $\ln(x+1) = 8$ **d** $\ln(2x-5) = 2$

8 Solve, giving your answers correct to 3 sf.

   a $4e^{0.5x+3} = 13$ **b** $\ln x + \ln x^2 = 16$

   c $e^{3x} = 4e^{2x+1}$ **d** $\ln(3x-2) - \ln x = 0.5$

9 Solve, giving your answers in exact form.

   a $\ln(2x-1) = 4$ **b** $5 - e^{1-2x} = 0$ **c** $2e^{2x} + 12 = 11e^x$

10 Solve the following giving your answers to 3 sf.

   a $2e^{2x} + e^x - 5 = 0$ **b** $e^x + 5e^{-x} - 70 = 0$

11 Solve the following simultaneous equations giving your answers to 3 sf if necessary.

   a $e^{5x} - y = 0$ **b** $\ln(x-y) - 0$

      $\ln y^4 + x = 7$ $2\ln x = \ln(y+4)$

6.8 Practical applications of exponential equations

WORKED EXAMPLE 7

The volume of water in a container, $V \text{cm}^3$, at time t minutes, is given by the formula

$V = 1000\,e^{-kt}$.

When $V = 740$, $t = 12$.

a   Find the value of k.

b   Find the value of V when $t = 25$.

Answers

a $740 = 1000\,e^{-12k}$

$0.74 = e^{-12k}$ Divide both sides by 1000.

$\ln 0.74 = -12k$

$k = \dfrac{\ln 0.74}{-12} = 0.025$

b $V = 1000\,e^{-0.025t}$

$V = 1000\,e^{-0.025 \times 25}$

$V = 535\,\text{cm}^3$ (3 sf)

Exercise 6.8

1   The population of rabbits are decreasing in a city park. Initially there were 250 rabbits recorded. After t years the number of rabbits R was modelled by $R = 250e^{-0.2t}$. How many rabbits are there after 3 years?

2   A 20 g sample of radioactive iodine decays so that the mass remaining after t days is given by the equation $A = 20e^{-0.087t}$, where A is measured in grams. After how many days (to the nearest whole day) is there only 5 grams remaining?

3   A type of moss grows according to the formula $N = 4(2.5)^{kt}$, where N is the quantity of moss in grams after t days.

   a   What is the initial amount of moss?

   After 6 days there are 5.5 grams of moss.

   b   Calculate the value of the constant k to 3 sf.

   c   After what period of time does the quantity of moss reach 10 grams? (Give your answer as a whole number.)

4   The value of a car depreciates so that when it is t years old its value $\$V$ is given by the formula, $V = 15000e^{-0.6t}$.

   a   What is the initial price of the car?

   b   What is the value of the car after 4 years? Give your answer to 3 sf.

   c   If the owner of the car decides to sell it when its value is halved, find, to the nearest month, the age of the car when it is sold.

6.9 The graphs of simple logarithmic and exponential functions

 REMINDER

You should know the properties of the graph $y = e^x$ and its relationship with the graphs $y = ke^{nx} + a$ and $y = k \ln (ax + b)$ where n, k, a and b are all integers.

To sketch the curve of an **exponential** function, consider the following:

Is the equation of the form $y = ke^{nx} + a$ where $n < 0$?

Is the equation of the form $y = ke^{nx} + a$ where $n < 0$?

If so the graph will look like:

If so the graph will look like:

Next investigate:

- When $x = 0$ (this will give you the y intercept).
- When $y = 0$ (this will give you the x intercept).
- Finally, consider what happens to the value of y when $x \to +\infty$ and $x \to -\infty$. This will give you the y asymptote.

  $y = ke^{nx} + a$ has a y asymptote at $y = a$.

To sketch the curve of a **logarithmic function**, consider the following:

Remember $\ln x$ only exists for **positive** values of x.

Graphs of $y = k \ln (ax + b)$ look like:

If $k > 0$.

Graphs of $y = k \ln (ax + b)$ look like:

If $k < 0$.

- When $x = 0$ (this will give you the y intercept).
- When $y = 0$ (this will give you the x intercept).
- Consider what happens to the value of y when $x \to +\infty$.
- 'Solving' $ax + b = 0$ gives $x = \dfrac{-b}{a}$. The asymptote is at $x = \dfrac{-b}{a}$.

Exercise 6.9

1 Match the following graphs with the correct equation from the list below.

a $y = 2\ln x$

b $y = e^x + 2$

c $y = 2e^x$

d $y = \ln x + 2$

e $y = \ln (2x)$

f $y = e^{2x}$

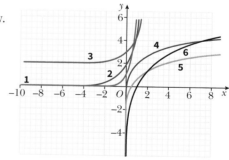

6.10 The graphs of $y = ke^{nx} + a$ and $y = k \ln(ax + b)$ where n, k, a and b are integers

Exercise 6.10

1 Sketch the graphs of each of the following exponential functions.

(Remember to show the axis crossing points and the asymptotes.)

a $y = 2e^x - 3$ **b** $y = -2e^x + 3$ **c** $y = 2e^{-x} - 3$

d $y = -2e^{-x} + 3$ **e** $y = 2e^x + 3$ **f** $y = -2e^x - 3$

g $y = 2e^{-x} + 3$ **h** $y = -2e^{-x} - 3$

2 Sketch the graphs of each of the following logarithmic functions.

(Remember to show the axis crossing points and the asymptotes.)

a $y = \ln(2x + 4)$ **b** $y = -\ln(2x + 4)$ **c** $y = 2\ln(2x + 4)$

d $y = -2\ln(2x + 4)$

6.11 The inverse of logarithmic and exponential functions

 REMINDER

To find the inverse of a function f, use the following steps:

- confirm that f is one-to-one

- replace $f(x)$ with y

- interchange x and y

- solve for y

- replace y with $f^{-1}(x)$

- the domain of f^{-1} is equal to the range of f; and the range of f^{-1} is equal to the domain of f

---

WORKED EXAMPLE 8

Find the inverse of each function and state its domain.

a $f(x) = 3e^{-2x} + 5$ for $x \in \mathbb{R}$ **b** $f(x) = 4\ln(3x - 9)$ for $x > 3$

Answers

a $f(x) = 3e^{-2x} + 5$ for $x \in \mathbb{R}$

Step 1: Write the function as $y =$ $\longrightarrow$ $y = 3e^{-2x} + 5$

Step 2: Interchange the x and y variables. $\longrightarrow$ $x = 3e^{-2y} + 5$

Step 3: Rearrange to make y the subject. $x - 5 = 3e^{-2y}$

$$\frac{x - 5}{3} = e^{-2y}$$

$$\ln\left(\frac{x - 5}{3}\right) = -2y$$

$$y = -\frac{1}{2}\ln\left(\frac{x - 5}{3}\right)$$

$f^{-1}(x) = -\dfrac{1}{2}\ln\left(\dfrac{x - 5}{3}\right)$ for $x > 5$

b $f(x) = 4\ln(3x - 9)$ for $x > 3$

Step 1: Write the function as $y =$ ⟶ $y = 4\ln(3x - 9)$

Step 2: Interchange the x and y variables. ⟶ $x = 4\ln(3y - 9)$

Step 3: Rearrange to make y the subject. ⟶ $\dfrac{x}{4} = \ln(3y - 9)$

Step 4: ⟶ $e^{\frac{x}{4}} = 3y - 9$

Step 5: ⟶ $e^{\frac{x}{4}} + 9 = 3y$

Step 6: ⟶ $y = \dfrac{1}{3}\left(e^{\frac{x}{4}} + 9\right)$

$f^{-1}(x) = \dfrac{1}{3}\left(e^{\frac{x}{4}} + 9\right)$

Exercise 6.11

1 The following functions are each defined for $x \in \mathbb{R}$.
Find $f^{-1}(x)$ for each function and state its domain.

a $f(x) = e^x + 3$ **b** $f(x) = 3e^x - 1$ **c** $f(x) = 4e^{2x} + 1$

d $f(x) = 5e^{-2x} + 4$ **e** $f(x) = 2 - 3e^{-x}$ **f** $f(x) = 6 - 3e^{-2x}$

2 Find $f^{-1}(x)$ for each function.

a $f(x) = \ln(x + 2)$, $x > -2$ **b** $f(x) = 2\ln(x + 3)$, $x > -3$

c $f(x) = 2\ln(2x + 3)$, $x > -1\dfrac{1}{2}$ **d** $f(x) = -4\ln(3x - 1)$, $x > \dfrac{1}{3}$

3 $f(x) = e^{3x} + 1$ for $x \in \mathbb{R}$

a State the range of $f(x)$.   **b** Find $f^{-1}(x)$.

c State the domain of $f^{-1}(x)$.   **d** Find $f^{-1}f(x)$.

e Sketch the functions f and f^{-1}. What is the relationship between f and f^{-1}?

4 $f(x) = e^{3x}$ for $x \in \mathbb{R}$, $g(x) = 2\ln x$ for $x > 0$

a Find **i** $fg(x)$ **ii** $fg(3)$.

b Find the value of x for which $fg(x) = 20$.

> **TIP**
>
> Remember $ff^{-1} = f^{-1}f = x$ for one-to-one functions.

Summary

The rules of logarithms

If $y = a^x$ then $x = \log_a y$.

$\log_a a = 1$ $\log_a 1 = 0$ $\log_a a^x = x$ $x = a^{\log_a x}$

Product rule: $\log_a(xy) = \log_a x + \log_a y$

Division rule: $\log_a\left(\dfrac{x}{y}\right) = \log_a x - \log_a y$

Power rule: $\log_a(x)^m = m\log_a x$

Change of base: $\log_b a = \dfrac{\log_c a}{\log_c b}$

$\left[\text{special case: } \log_a\left(\dfrac{1}{x}\right) = -\log_a x\right]$

$\left[\text{special case: } \log_b a = \dfrac{1}{\log_a b}\right]$

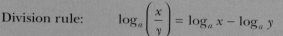
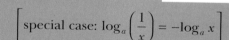
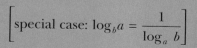

Natural logarithms

Logarithms to the base of e are called natural logarithms.

$\ln x$ is used to represent $\log_e x$.

If $y = e^x$ then $x = \ln y$.

All the rules of logarithms apply for natural logarithms.

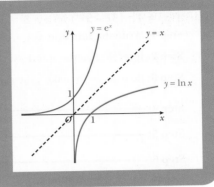

Exercise 6.12

1 Solve each of the following equations.

   a $\log_x x^2 - \log_x 2 = \log_x 8$
                b $\left(\log_5 x\right)^2 - 4\log_5(x) = -3$

2 Solve the following simultaneous equations.

   a $\log_2(x - 3y + 2) = 0$
                b $\log_y x = 2$

     $\log_2(x + 1) - 1 = 2\log_2 y$
                 $5y = x + 12\log_x y$

3 Solve $8 \times 9^x - 3^x = 0$, giving your answers correct to 3 sf.

4 a Factorise $x^3 - 13x^2 + 39x - 27$.

   b Hence solve the equation $3^{3x} - 13 \times 3^{2x} + 39 \times 3^x - 27 = 0$.

5 a Factorise $4x^3 - 29x^2 + 47x - 10$.

   b Hence solve the equation, $4 \times 4^{3x} - 29 \times 4^{2x} + 47 \times 4^x - 10 = 0$ giving your answer to 3 sf.

6 a Show that $x = 1$ is a solution of the equation $2^{3x} - 4 \times 2^{2x} + 2^x + 6 = 0$.

   b By using the substitution $y = 2^x$, show that the equation can be written as

     $y^3 - 4y^2 + y + 6 = 0$

   c Hence find the other solution to equation $2^{3x} - 4 \times 2^{2x} + 2^x + 6 = 0$ giving your answer correct to 3 sf.

7 Solve the following equation giving your answers to 3 sf.

   $\log_3 x^2 - \log_9 x = 4$

8 The variables x and y are connected by the equation $y = ax^n$ where a and n are constants. Given that $y = 6360$ when $x = 10$, find the values of a and n to 3 sf.

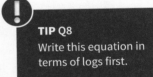

TIP Q8

Write this equation in terms of logs first.

9 A pan of water is heated and then allowed to cool. Its temperature, $T°C$, t minutes after cooling begun is given by the formula

   $T = 60e^{-0.2t}$

   a What is the temperature of the water as it starts to cool?

   b What is its temperature after 4 minutes? Give your answer to 3 sf.

   c Find to the nearest minute the time taken for the water to reach a temperature of 10°C.

10 $f(x) = e^{2x}$ for $x \in \mathbb{R}$ $g(x) = \ln 4x$ for $x > 0$

   a Find **i** $fg(x)$ **ii** $gf(x)$.

   b Solve $g(x) = 3f^{-1}(x)$.

Chapter 7:
Straight line graphs

This section will show you how to:

- solve questions involving midpoint and length of a line
- know and use the condition for two lines to be parallel or perpendicular, including finding the equation of perpendicular bisectors
- interpret the equation of a straight line graph in the form $y = mx + c$
- transform given relationships, including $y = ax^n$ and $y = Ab^x$, to straight line form and hence determine unknown constants by calculating the gradient or intercept of the transformed graph.

7.1 Problems involving length of a line and midpoint

REMINDER

If P is the point (x_1, y_1), Q is the point (x_2, y_2) and M is the midpoint of the line PQ.

- The length of the line $PQ = \sqrt{(x_2 - x_1)^2 + (y_2 - y_1)^2}$.

- The gradient of the line $PQ = \dfrac{y_2 - y_1}{x_2 - x_1}$.

- The coordinates of M are $\left(\dfrac{x_1 + x_2}{2}, \dfrac{y_1 + y_2}{2} \right)$.

WORKED EXAMPLE 1

Find the length of the line segment joining $(2, -3)$ and $(7, 7)$.

Answer

The length of the line $= \sqrt{(7 - 2)^2 + (7 - -3)^2}$

$= \sqrt{5^2 + 10^2}$

$= \sqrt{25 + 100}$

$= \sqrt{125}$

$= 5\sqrt{5}$

Exercise 7.1

1 Find the length of the line segment joining

  a (2, 1) and (5, 5)   **b** (3, 6) and (8, 18)   **c** (−3, 2) and (5, 8)

  d (0, −2) and (8, 13)   **e** (−3, −4) and (−15, 12)   **f** (2, 5) and (6, 1)

  g (−7, 3) and (−2, 5)   **h** (6, 0) and (−4, 0)

2 The three points P, Q and R have coordinates (−1, 3), (6, 4) and (1, −1). Show that the distance PQ is equal to the distance QR.

3 Prove that the points $A(1, 2)$, $B(13, 7)$ and $C(6, 14)$ form a right-angled triangle ABC.

4 Calculate the area of the right-angled triangle *ABC* whose vertices are *A*(2, 5), *B*(5, 4) and *C*(8, 13).

5 The points *P*, *Q* and *R* have coordinates (3, 1), (2, 6) and (*a*, 5) respectively. Given that the length *PQ* is equal to the length *QR*, calculate the possible values of *a*.

6 Given that the distance from *P*(13, 10) to *Q*(1, *y*) is three times the distance from *Q* to *R* (−3, −2), calculate the possible values of *y*.

7 *B* is the midpoint of the straight line joining the point *C*(−5, 3) to the point *D*. Given that *B* has coordinates (2, 1), find the coordinates of *D*.

8 Find the coordinates of the midpoints of the line segments joining these pairs of points:

$(p + 2q, 2p + 13q)$ and $(5p - 2q, -2p - 7q)$

7.2 Parallel and perpendicular lines

REMINDER

- If two lines are parallel then their gradients are equal.
- If a line has a gradient of m, a line perpendicular to it has a gradient of $-\dfrac{1}{m}$.
- If the gradients of the two perpendicular lines are m_1 and m_2, then $m_1 \times m_2 = -1$.

WORKED EXAMPLE 2

$A(8, -5)$ and $B(2, 4)$. Find the gradient of the line perpendicular to AB.

Answer

Gradient of AB $\dfrac{4 - -5}{2 - 8} = \dfrac{9}{-6} = -\dfrac{3}{2}$.

Gradient of perpendicular line $= -\dfrac{1}{-\dfrac{3}{2}} = \dfrac{2}{3}$

Exercise 7.2

1 Find the gradient of the line *AB* for each of the following pairs of points.

  a *A*(2, 3)   *B*(4, 7)   **b** *A*(−1, 2)   *B*(1, 8)

  c *A*(5, 4)   *B*(3, 3)   **d** *A*(7, 4)   *B*(−1, −2)

  e *A*(3, 2)   *B*(−5, 4)   **f** *A*(−2, −1)   *B*(5, 3)

2 Find the gradient of the line joining $(p + q - 1, q + p - 3)$ and $(p - q + 1, q - p + 3)$.

3 Write down the gradient of lines perpendicular to a line with gradient

  a 4   **b** $-\dfrac{2}{3}$ **c** $\dfrac{2}{7}$ **d** $2\dfrac{3}{4}$ **e** $-3\dfrac{1}{2}$

4 Given the points *P*(2, 3), *Q*(5, 5), *R*(7, 2) and *S*(4, 0). Prove that *PR* is perpendicular to *QS*.

5 A triangle has vertices D (3, –2), B(2, –14) and C(–2, –4). Find the gradients of the straight lines AB, BC and CA. Hence prove the triangle is right-angled.

6 The origin O and the points A(–2, 3), B(4, 7) and C(6, 4) form a quadrilateral.
   a Show that OC is parallel to AB.   b Show that OA is parallel to CB.
   c Show that $OB = AC$.   d What shape is $OABC$?

7 Show that the points (–1, 3), (4, 7) and (–11, –5) are collinear.

8 Three of the following four points A(–1, 7), B(5, –5), C(–7, 5), D(7, –1) lie on a circle whose centre is at the origin.
   a Which are they?   b What is the radius of the circle?

9 A and B are the points (–1, –6) and (5, –8) respectively. Which of the following points lie on the perpendicular bisector of AB?
   P(3, –4), Q(4, 0), R(5, 2), S(6, 5)

7.3 Equations of straight lines

 REMINDER

- The equation of a straight line is $y = mx + c$ where m = the gradient and c = the y-intercept.

- Alternatively, the equation of a straight line, with gradient m, which passes through the point (x_1, y_1) is:
  $y - y_1 = m(x - x_1)$

WORKED EXAMPLE 3

Find the equation of the line with gradient $-\dfrac{2}{3}$ and passing through the point (–4, 2).

Answer

$y - 2 = -\dfrac{2}{3}(x - -4)$
$3y - 6 = -2x - 8$
$3y = -2x - 2$

Exercise 7.3

1 Find the equation of the line with
   a gradient 2 and passing through the point (5, 3),
   b gradient –2 and passing through the point (6, –3),

2 Find the equation of the line passing through
   a (–2, –4) and (–3, –8)   b (3, 7) and (4, –5)   c (3, 9) and (–5, 9).

3 Find the equation of the line
   a parallel to the line $y = 3x + 5$, passing through the point (4, 3)
   b parallel to the line $2x + y = 3$, passing through the point (4, –1)
   c perpendicular to the line $3x + 4y = 8$, passing through the point (–6, 3).

73

4 A straight line L, has a positive gradient, passes through the point $(2, 5)$ and makes an angle of $45°$ with the horizontal. Find the equation of L.

5 Find the equation of the perpendicular bisector of the line segment joining the points

   a $(2, 3)$ and $(6, 5)$ **b** $(2, -5)$ and $(4, -1)$ **c** $(3, 2)$ and $(-4, 1)$.

6 **a** Write down the gradient of the straight line joining (a, b) with (p, q).

   b Write down the two conditions that that these points should lie on the line $y = 7x - 3$.

   c Hence, find the gradient of the line.

7 Find the coordinates of the foot of the perpendicular from $P(-2, -4)$ to the line joining the points $Q(0, 2)$ and $R(-1, 4)$.

8 $A(1, 6)$, $B(-5, 2)$ and $C(3, 4)$ are the three vertices of a triangle.

   a Find the equations of the perpendicular bisectors of AB and BC.

   b Hence find the coordinates of the circumcentre of triangle ABC.

   (Hint: the circumcentre of a triangle is the point where the perpendicular bisectors of the sides intersect.)

7.4 Areas of rectilinear figures

The formula below is often referred to as the 'shoestring' or 'shoelace' method. You do not have to know this method for the examination but you may find it useful to know.

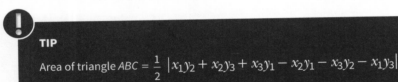

TIP

Area of triangle $ABC = \dfrac{1}{2} \left| x_1y_2 + x_2y_3 + x_3y_1 - x_2y_1 - x_3y_2 - x_1y_3 \right|$

WORKED EXAMPLE 4

A triangle PQR has coordinates $(0, a)$, $(-2, -6)$ and $(5, -4)$ respectively (in a clockwise direction).

Find the value of a if the triangle's area is 33 units^2.

Answers

$x_1 = 0$, $y_1 = a$ $x_2 = -2$, $y_2 = -6$ $x_3 = 5$, $y_3 = -4$

$33 = \dfrac{1}{2} \left| (0 \times -6) + (-2 \times -4) + (5 \times a) - (-2 \times a) - (5 \times -6) - (0 \times -4) \right|$

$33 = \dfrac{1}{2} \left| 0 + 8 + 5a + 2a + 30 + 0 \right|$

$33 = \dfrac{1}{2} \left| 38 + 7a \right|$

$66 = \left| 38 + 7a \right|$

$66 = 38 + 7a$ or $-66 = 38 + 7a$

$28 = 7a$ or $-104 = 7a$

$a = 4$ or $a = \dfrac{-104}{7}$

Exercise 7.4

1 Find the area of these triangles.

  a $A(2, -3), B(-2, -1), C(4, 3)$

  b $P(-8, -4), Q(-3, 10), R(5, 6)$

2 Find the area of these quadrilaterals.

  a $A(3, 4), B(-4, 2), C(6, -1), D(20, 3)$

  b $P(3, 5), Q(11, 4), R(7, 0), S(9, 8)$

3 A triangle PQR has coordinates $(1, 3), (5, 1)$ and $(3, k)$ respectively (in an anticlockwise direction).

Find the value of k if the triangle's area is 6 units².

4 $PQRS$ is a parallelogram in which the coordinates of P, Q and R are $(1, 2), (7, -1), (-1, -2)$ respectively.

  a Find the equations of PS and RS.

  b Find the coordinates of S.

  c Prove that angle QPR is 90°.

  d Calculate the area of the parallelogram.

  e Find the length of the perpendicular from P to QR leaving your answer in surd form.

5 Calculate the area of the triangle that has sides given by the equations $2y - x = 1$, $y + 2x = 8$, and $4y + 3x = 7$

6 A straight line L has a gradient 3 and passes through the point $P(-6, 4)$.

  a Find the equation of the line L.

  b Another straight line, M, has the equation $7y = x + 14$.
     M crosses the y-axis at the point Q and intersects L at the point R.

     i Find the coordinates of Q and R.

     ii Show that angle QPR is 90°.

     iii Find the area of triangle PQR.

7 A straight line L has the equation $y = 14 - 2x$ and crosses the x axis at point P.

  a Find the coordinates of P.

  b Another straight line, M, is parallel to L and passes through the point $Q(-6, 6)$.
     Find the equation of M.

  c The line M crosses the x-axis at point R.
     Find the coordinates of point R.

  d The point S lies on L and is such that RS is perpendicular to L.
     Show that S has coordinates $(5, 4)$.

  e Find the area of triangle PRS.

7.5 Converting from a non-linear equation to linear form

 REMINDER

To convert a non-linear equation involving x and y into a linear equation, express the equation in the form $Y = mX + c$, where X and Y are expressions in x and/or y.

WORKED EXAMPLE 5

Convert $y = \dfrac{x^a}{b}$ into the form $Y = mX + c$, where a and b are constants.

Answer

Multiplying both sides of the equation by b gives:

$$by = x^a$$

Taking natural logarithms of both sides gives:

$$\ln(by) = \ln(x^a)$$
$$\ln(by) = a\ln(x)$$
$$\ln(b) + \ln(y) = a\ln(x)$$
$$\ln(y) = a\ln(x) - \ln(b)$$

Now compare $\ln(y) = a\ln(x) - \ln(b)$ with $Y = mX + c$:

$$\underset{\underset{Y}{\uparrow}}{\ln(y)} = \underset{\underset{m}{\uparrow}}{a} \underset{\underset{X}{\uparrow}}{\ln(x)} - \underset{\underset{c}{\uparrow}}{\ln(b)}$$

The non-linear equation $y = \dfrac{x^a}{b}$ becomes the linear equation:

$Y = mX + c$, where $Y = \ln y$, $X = \ln(x)$, $m = a$ and $c = -\ln b$

Exercise 7.5

1 Convert each of these non-linear equations into the form $Y = mX + c$, where a and b are constants. State clearly what the variables X and Y and the constants m and c represent.

(Note: there may be more than one method to do this this.)

a $y = ax^3 + b$　　　　**b** $y = ax + \dfrac{b}{x^2}$　　　　**c** $y = a + b\sqrt{x}$

d $y = \dfrac{a}{x} + b$　　　　**e** $x = ay + by^2$　　　　**f** $y = \dfrac{1}{(x-a)(x-b)}$

g $y^2 = ax - b$　　　　**h** $xy = ax + by$

2 Convert each of these non-linear equations into the form $Y = mX + c$, where a and b are constants. State clearly what the variables X and Y and the constants m and c represent.

(Note: there may be more than one way to do this.)

a $y = \dfrac{x^a}{b}$　　　　**b** $y^a = e^{x+k}$　　　　**c** $y = ax^{n+2}$

d $x^2 - bx = ae^y$　　　　**e** $x^b e^a = y$　　　　**f** $e^y = ab^x$

 TIP

It is best to use ln for questions with terms involving powers of e. For other questions with powers, you can use ln or lg, e.g. in parts a and b.

7.6 Converting from linear form to a non-linear equation

WORKED EXAMPLE 6

Find y in terms of x.

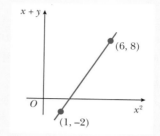

Answer

The linear equation is $Y = mX + c$, where $Y = x + y$ and $X = x^2$.

Gradient $= m = \dfrac{8 - -2}{6 - 1} = \dfrac{10}{5} = 2.$

Using $Y = mX + c$, $m = 2$, $X = 6$ and $Y = 8$:

$8 = 2 \times 6 + c$

$8 = 12 + c$

$c = -4$

The non-linear equation is: $x + y = 2x^2 - 4$

$\qquad\qquad\qquad\qquad\qquad\quad y = 2x^2 - x - 4$

Exercise 7.6

1 The graphs show part of a straight line obtained by plotting y against some function of x.

For each graph, express y in terms of x.

a
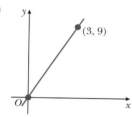

b
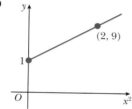

c
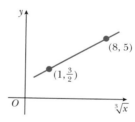

d
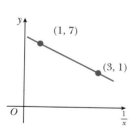

e
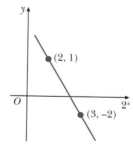

f
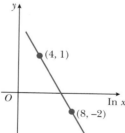

2 For each of the following relations,

i express y in terms of x **ii** find the value of y when $x = 4$.

a
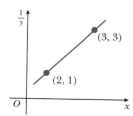

b
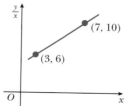

c
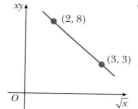

d
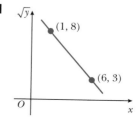

77

3 Variables x and y are related so that, when $\dfrac{y}{x^2}$ is plotted on the vertical axis and $\sqrt{x}$ is plotted on the horizontal axis, a straight-line graph passing through (2, 16) and (6, 4) is obtained.

Express y in terms of x.

4 Variables x and y are related so that, when y^2 is plotted on the vertical axis and 3^x is plotted on the horizontal axis, a straight-line graph which passes through the point $\left(-\dfrac{1}{2}, 16\right)$ with gradient -2 is obtained.

  a Express y in terms of 3^x.

  b Find the value of x when $y = 3$.

5 Variables x and y are related so that, when e^y is plotted on the vertical axis and $\sqrt{x}$ is plotted on the horizontal axis, a straight-line graph passing through the points (3, 2) and (5, 6) is obtained.

  a Express e^y in terms of x.   **b** Express y in terms of x.

6 Variables x and y are related so that, when $\lg y$ is plotted on the vertical axis and x is plotted on the horizontal axis, a straight-line graph passing through the points (6, 4) and (8, 10) is obtained.

  a Express $\lg y$ in terms of x.

  b Express y in terms of x, giving your answer in the form $y = a \times 10^{bx}$.

7 Variables x and y are related so that, when $\lg y$ is plotted on the vertical axis and $\lg x$ is plotted on the horizontal axis, a straight-line graph passing through the points (3, 6) and (5, 9) is obtained.

  a Express y in terms of x, giving your answer in the form $y = a \times x^{b}$.

  b Find the value of x when $y = 12$.

8 Variables x and y are related so that, when $\ln y$ is plotted on the vertical axis and $\ln x$ is plotted on the horizontal axis, a straight-line graph passing through the points (3, 7) and (5, 13) is obtained.

  a Express $\ln y$ in terms of x.   **b** Express y in terms of x.

7.7 Finding relationships from data

 REMINDER

When experimental data is collected for two variables, it is useful to be able to establish the mathematical relationship between the variables in the form of an equation. If the raw data is plotted on a graph, it is unusual for the points to form a perfectly straight line. It is more usual for a curve to be seen which indicates that the variables are connected by a non-linear equation.

Exercise 7.7

1

x	1	2	3	4	5
y	12.5	14.0	16.5	20.0	24.5

The table shows experimental values of the variables x and y which are thought to be related by an equation of the form $y = ax^2 + b$.

a Copy and complete the following table.

x	1	2	3	4	5
x^2					

b Draw the graph of x^2 against x.

c Express y in terms of x.

d Using your equation find the value of x when $y = 15$.

2

x	1	2	3	4	5
y	74	126	162	172	175

The table shows experimental values of the variables x and y which are thought to be connected by the equation $y = px^2 + qx$.

a Copy and complete the following table.

x	1	2	3	4	5
$\dfrac{y}{x}$					

b Draw the graph of $\dfrac{y}{x}$ against x and use it to estimate the values of p and q to the nearest whole number.

c Express y in terms of x.

d Find the value of x when $y = 103.5$.

3

x	1.5	2.5	3	4	10
y	−6.0	10.0	6.0	4.0	2.5

The table shows experimental values of the variables x and y.

a Draw the graph of $\dfrac{1}{y}$ against $\dfrac{1}{x}$.

b Use your graph to express y in terms of x.

c Find the value of y when $x = 5$.

4 It is thought that the variables s and t satisfy a relation of the form $\left(\dfrac{s}{t}\right)^{p} = qe^{-t}$ where the constants p and q are positive integers.

By drawing a linear graph, find the values of p and q.

t	0.2	0.4	0.6	0.8	1.0
s	1.09	1.96	2.67	3.22	3.64

5 Two variables x and y satisfy a law of the form $y = ab^{x}$ where a and b are constants.

By drawing a suitable straight line graph show that this is approximately correct. Hence calculate estimates for a and b.

x	2.0	2.4	2.8	3.2	3.6
y	69	88	101	131	138

6 Two variables d and p are thought to be connected by the equation $p = kd^{m}$.

d	1	2	3	5	10
p	0.02	0.32	1.62	12.53	199.8

a Draw a graph of $\lg d$ against $\lg p$.

b Use your graph to find the relationship $p = kd^{m}$.

7

x	2	4	6	8	10
y	81	70	61	52	45

The table shows experimental values of the variables x and y.

The variables are known to be related by the equation $y = ka^{x}$ where k and a are constants.

a Draw the graph of $\lg y$ against x.

b Use your graph to estimate the value of k and the value of a.

Summary

Length of a line segment, gradient and midpoint

Length of $PQ = \sqrt{\left(x_2 - x_1\right)^2 + \left(y_2 - y_1\right)^2}$.

Gradient of $PQ = \dfrac{y_2 - y_1}{x_2 - x_1}$.

Midpoint of $PQ = \left(\dfrac{x_1 + x_2}{2}, \dfrac{y_1 + y_2}{2}\right)$.

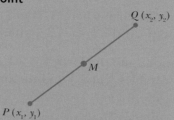

Parallel and perpendicular lines

If two lines are parallel then their gradients are equal.

If a line has a gradient of m, a line perpendicular to it has a gradient of $-\dfrac{1}{m}$.

If the gradients of the two perpendicular lines are m_1 and m_2, then $m_1 \times m_2 = -1$.

The equation of a straight line

$y = mx + c$ where $m = $ the gradient and $c = $ the y-intercept.

$y - y_1 = m(x - x_1)$ where $m = $ the gradient and (x_1, y_1) is a known point on the line.

Non-linear equations

To convert a non-linear equation involving x and y into a linear equation, express the equation in the form $Y = mX + c$, where X and Y are expressions in x and/or y.

81

Exercise 7.8

1 Show that the vertices $A(-2, 0)$, $B\left(0, 2\sqrt{3}\right)$ and $C(2, 0)$ are the vertices of an equilateral triangle.

2 The point A has coordinates $(3, a)$ and the point B has coordinates $(15, 6)$. AB has length 13 units. Find all the possible values of a.

3 The straight line joining the point $A(5, 6)$ to the point $B(a, 2)$ is perpendicular to the straight line joining the point B to the point $C(9, -1)$. Calculate the possible values of a.

4 Find the equation of the line perpendicular to the line $3y + 10x = 8$, passing through the point $\left(-\dfrac{1}{3}, -\dfrac{2}{5}\right)$.

5 The perpendicular bisector of the straight line joining the points $(3, 2)$ and $(5, 6)$ meets the x-axis at P and the y-axis at Q. Prove that the distance PQ is $6\sqrt{5}$.

6 a Find the equation of the line through the point $(1, 1)$ which is perpendicular to the line
$3y - 2x + 12 = 0$

   b Find the coordinates of the point of intersection of the two lines.

7 a Given that the points $(4, 2)$, $(1, 6)$ and $(5, k)$ lie on a straight line, calculate the value of k.

b The line meets the x and y axes at P and Q respectively. If O is the origin, calculate the lengths of OP and OQ.

c Find the area of triangle POQ.

8 Given that $A = (2, a)$, $B = (3 + a, 2)$ and $C = (3, 4)$ where A, B and C are in an anticlockwise direction. Find the values of a if the area is 2.5 units^2.

9 Convert each of these non-linear equations into the form $Y = mX + c$, where a and b are constants. State clearly what the variables X and Y and the constants m and c represent.

(Note: there may be more than one method to do this.)

a $\dfrac{1}{x} + \dfrac{1}{y} = \dfrac{1}{a}$

b $y^a = e^{x+k}$

10 For the following relation,

a express y in terms of x

b find the value of y when $x = 4$.

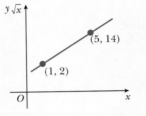

11 Variables x and y are related so that, when $\dfrac{y}{x}$ is plotted on the vertical axis and $\dfrac{1}{x^2}$ is plotted on the horizontal axis, a straight-line graph passing through the points $(2, 3)$ and $(4, 11)$ is obtained.

a Express y in terms of x.

b Find the value of x and the value of y such that $\dfrac{y}{x} = 4$.

12 Variables x and y are such that, when $\ln y$ is plotted on the vertical axis and e^x is plotted on the horizontal axis, a straight-line graph passing through the points $(2, 2)$ and $(4, 6)$ is obtained.

a Express $\ln y$ in terms of x.

b Find the value of $\ln y$ when $x = \ln 4$.

c Find the value of x when $\ln y = 8$.

13 The table below shows the experimental data obtained between two variables p and t.

t	5	10	15	20	25
p	212	49.1	10.6	2.31	0.532

a By drawing a suitable graph, show that these values satisfy a relationship $p = ae^{kt}$ where a and k are constants.

b Use your graph to estimate the values of a and k to 2 sf.

14 The table below shows values of the variables x and y which are thought to be connected by the equation $bx^2 + y^2 = c$, where b and c are constants.

x	1	2	3	4	4.5
y	2.96	2.83	2.60	2.24	1.98

a By drawing a suitable graph, find the values of b and c.

b Calculate the value of y when $x = 3.5$.

This section will show you how to:

- use radian measure
- solve problems involving the arc length and sector area of a circle.

8.1 Circular measure

REMINDER

An arc equal in length to the radius of a circle subtends an angle of 1 radian at the centre.

π radians = 180°

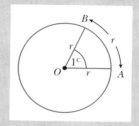

WORKED EXAMPLE 1

a Change 45° to radians, giving your answer in terms of π.

b Change $\dfrac{11\pi}{6}$ radians to degrees.

Answers

a $45° = \left(45 \times \dfrac{\pi}{180}\right)$ radians

$\qquad$ **b** $\dfrac{11\pi}{6}$ radians $= \left(\dfrac{11\pi}{6} \times \dfrac{180}{\pi}\right)°$

$45° = \dfrac{\pi}{4}$ radians

$\qquad\qquad \dfrac{11\pi}{6}$ radians $= 330°$

Exercise 8.1

1 Change these angles to radians, in terms of π.

a 30° $\qquad$ **b** 60° $\qquad$ **c** 140° $\qquad$ **d** 250°

e 315° $\qquad$ **f** 540° $\qquad$ **g** 900° $\qquad$ **h** 750°

i 5° $\qquad$ **j** 350°

TIP

To change from degrees to radians, multiply by $\dfrac{\pi}{180}$.

2 Change these angles to degrees.

a $\dfrac{3\pi}{2}$ $\qquad$ **b** $\dfrac{5\pi}{6}$ $\qquad$ **c** $\dfrac{7\pi}{12}$ $\qquad$ **d** $\dfrac{2\pi}{9}$

e $\dfrac{5\pi}{3}$ $\qquad$ **f** $\dfrac{3\pi}{5}$ $\qquad$ **g** $\dfrac{9\pi}{10}$ $\qquad$ **h** $\dfrac{7\pi}{15}$

i $\dfrac{9\pi}{20}$ $\qquad$ **j** $\dfrac{6\pi}{5}$

TIP

To change from radians to degrees, multiply by $\dfrac{180}{\pi}$.

3 Write each of these angles in radians correct to 3 sf.

   a 27°   **b** 48°   **c** 88°   **d** 113°

   e 265°

> **TIP**
> Your calculator can be in radian or degree mode.

4 Write each of these angles in degrees correct to 1 decimal place.

   a 1.5 rad   **b** 2.2 rad   **c** 1.06 rad   **d** 1.93 rad

   e 0.68 rad

5 Use your calculator to find

   a $\sin 1.2$ rad   **b** $\cos 0.8$ rad   **c** $\tan 1.2$ rad,   **d** $\sin \dfrac{\pi}{3}$

   e $\cos \dfrac{\pi}{5}$ **f** $\tan \dfrac{3\pi}{4}$.

> **TIP**
> You do not need to change the angle into degrees first. Make sure that your calculator is in radian mode.

8.2 Length of an arc

« REMINDER

Arc length $= r\theta$.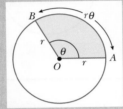

WORKED EXAMPLE 2

A sector has radius of 2.5 cm and perimeter of 6.5 cm.

Find the angle of the sector.

Answer

$6.5 = 5 + 2.5 \times \theta$ Perimeter $= 2r + r\theta$.

$1.5 = 2.5 \times \theta$

$\theta = 0.6$ radians

Exercise 8.2

1 Find, in terms of π, the arc length of a sector of

   a radius 8 cm and angle $\dfrac{\pi}{2}$ **b** radius 5 cm and angle $\dfrac{2\pi}{9}$

   c radius 10 cm and angle $\dfrac{3\pi}{4}$ **d** radius 18 cm and angle $\dfrac{5\pi}{12}$

2 Find the arc length of a sector of

   a radius 8 cm and angle 1.5 radians   **b** radius 2.5 cm and angle 0.6 radians

3 Find, in radians, the angle of a sector of

   a radius 5 cm and arc length 8 cm   **b** radius 12 cm and arc length 16 cm

4 Find the perimeter of each of these sectors.

a

1.5 rad

3 cm

b

1.6 rad

8 cm

c

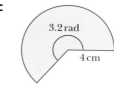

3.2 rad

4 cm

5 A sector has angle 2.5 radians and perimeter of 18 cm.
Find the radius of the sector.

6 $ABCD$ is a rectangle with $AB = 5$ cm and $BC = 12$ cm.

O is the midpoint of BC.

$OAED$ is a sector of a circle, centre O. Find

   a AO

   b angle AOD, in radians

   c the perimeter of the shaded region.

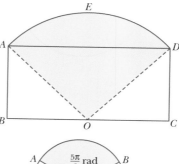

7 A sector AOB of angle $\dfrac{5\pi}{6}$ radians is cut
from a circle of radius 6 cm.
Calculate the perimeter of the sector remaining.

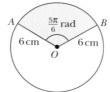

8.3 Area of a sector

 REMINDER

Area of sector $= \dfrac{1}{2}r^2\theta$.

(θ has to be in radians.)

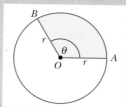

85

WORKED EXAMPLE 3

Calculate the area of the shaded segment of angle $\frac{\pi}{3}$ radians cut from a circle of radius 10 cm.

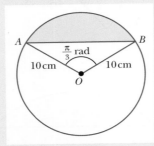

Answer

Area of triangle $AOB = \frac{1}{2} \times 10 \times 10 \times \sin\left(\frac{\pi}{3}\right)$ 　　　using area of triangle $= \frac{1}{2}\,ab\sin C$

$\qquad\qquad\qquad\quad = 43.3012\ldots$

Area of sector $AOB = \frac{1}{2} \times 10 \times 10 \times \frac{\pi}{3}$ 　　　using area of sector $= \frac{1}{2}\,r^2\,\theta$

$\qquad\qquad\qquad\quad = \dfrac{50\pi}{3}$

Area of segment = area of sector AOB – area of triangle AOB

$\qquad\qquad\qquad = \dfrac{50\pi}{3} - 43.3012\ldots$

$\qquad\qquad\qquad = 9.06\ \text{cm}^2$

Exercise 8.3

1　Find, in terms of π, the area of a sector of

　a　radius 6cm and angle $\dfrac{\pi}{4}$ 　　　　　　**b**　radius 15cm and angle $\dfrac{3\pi}{10}$

　c　radius 10cm and angle $\dfrac{7\pi}{6}$ 　　　　　**d**　radius 9cm and angle $\dfrac{5\pi}{3}$.

2　Find the area of a sector of

　a　radius 5cm and angle 1.3 radians 　　　**b**　radius 4.8cm and angle 0.8 radians.

3　Find, in radians, the angle of a sector of

　a　radius 3cm and area 7cm² 　　　　　　**b**　radius 5cm and area 25cm².

4　POQ is the sector of a circle, centre O, radius 12cm.

　The arc length PQ is 9cm. Find

　a　angle POQ, in radians 　　　　　　　**b**　the area of the sector POQ.

5　A sector of a circle, radius $r$cm, has a perimeter of 120cm.
　Find an expression, in terms of r, for the area of the sector.

6　The sector of a circle of radius r which subtends an angle of $\dfrac{\pi}{6}$ is shown below.

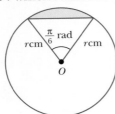

　　Show that the area of the shaded segment is given by: $\dfrac{r^2(\pi - 3)}{12}$

7   The diagram shows two intersecting circles with centres *X* and *Y* with radii 4 cm and 5 cm.

PQ is the common chord.

The distance from *X* to *Y* is 7 cm.

Find, giving your answers to 3 sf

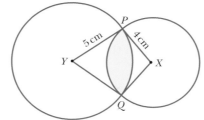

   a   angle *PYQ* in radians

   b   angle *PXQ* in radians

   c   the shaded area.

8   The diagram shows a triangle *ABC*.

$AB = 6$ cm

$AC = BC = 4$ cm

The arc *CP* is part of a circle centre *A* radius 4 cm.

The arc *CQ* is part of a circle centre *B* radius 4 cm.

Find, giving your answers to 3 sf

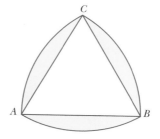

   a   angle *BAC* in radians

   b   the length of the perimeter of the shaded region *R* which is bounded by the arcs *CP*, *CQ* and *PQ*

   c   the area of the sector *ACP*

   d   the area of the region *R*.

9   The diagram shows a flag which is made up of an equilateral triangle of side 6 cm.

AB is a circular arc with centre *C*.

BC is a circular arc with centre *A*.

CA is a circular arc with centre *B*.

Calculate, giving your answers as exact values

   a   the area of triangle *ABC*

   b   the area of the sector *ABC*

   c   the area of the shaded region.

Summary

One radian $\left(1^{c}\right)$ is the size of the angle subtended at the centre of a circle, radius *r*, by an arc of length *r*.

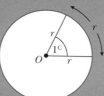

When θ is measured in radians:

- the length of arc $AB = r\theta$

- the area of sector $AOB = \dfrac{1}{2}r^{2}\theta$

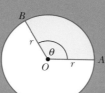

Exercise 8.4

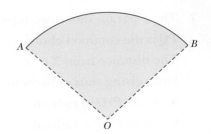

1 The diagram shows the sector *OAB* of a circle centre *O* in which angle *AOB* is 2.5 radians.

Given that the perimeter of the sector is 36cm, find the length of *OA*.

2 The minor arc *AB* of a circle, centre *O*, has length 46.2 cm.

Given that $\angle AOB = \dfrac{157\pi}{360}$ rad.

Find, giving your answers to 3 sf

  a the distance *OA*   **b** the perimeter of sector *OAB*.

3 The diagram shows a circle of radius 10 cm.

A and *B* are points on the circumference of the circle.

The centre of the circle is *O*.

Angle *AOB* is $\dfrac{2\pi}{3}$ radians.

Find the exact length of the major arc *AB*.

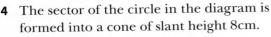

4 The sector of the circle in the diagram is formed into a cone of slant height 8cm.

The vertical height of the cone *h* is equal to the radius of its base *r*.

Find the size of its angle *θ* in radians.

5 The diagram represents the cross-section of a pipe which has the shape of a major segment of a circle whose centre is *O*.

The radius of the circle is 4cm and the size of angle *AOB* is 1.5 radians.

Calculate the perimeter of the cross-section to 3 sf.

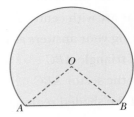

6 The diagram shows part of a circle centre *O* and radius 4cm.

Given that the length of the arc *XYZ* is 5cm, find

  a angle *XOZ* in radians

  b the area of the shaded region.

  (Give your answers to 3 sf.)

7 In the diagram, *BT* is a tangent to the circle at *T*.

The centre of the circle is *O* and its radius is 6cm.

OB = 12cm.

Find the shaded area to 3 sf.

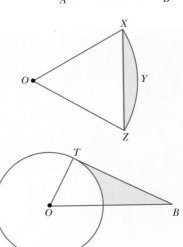

Chapter 9:
Trigonometry

This section will show you how to:

- find the trigonometric ratios of angles of any magnitude
- determine the amplitude and period of trigonometric functions
- describe the relationship between trigonometric graphs
- sketch graphs of $y = |f(x)|$, where f(x) is a trigonometric function
- draw and use the graphs of $y = a \sin bx + c$, $y = a \cos bx + c$, $y = a \tan bx + c$, where a is a positive integer, b is a simple fraction or integer and c is an integer
- use trigonometric relationships
- solve simple trigonometric equations
- prove simple trigonometric identities.

9.1 Angles between 0° and 90°

REMINDER

Angles between 0° and 90°

You should already know the following trigonometric ratios:

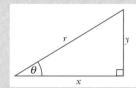

$$\sin\theta = \frac{\text{opposite}}{\text{hypotenuse}} \qquad \cos\theta = \frac{\text{adjacent}}{\text{hypotenuse}} \qquad \tan\theta = \frac{\text{opposite}}{\text{adjacent}}$$

$$\tan\theta = \frac{y}{x} \qquad \cos\theta = \frac{x}{r} \qquad \sin\theta = \frac{y}{r}$$

$$\sin 45° = \frac{1}{\sqrt{2}}\left(=\frac{\sqrt{2}}{2}\right) \qquad \sin\frac{\pi}{4} = \frac{1}{\sqrt{2}}\left(=\frac{\sqrt{2}}{2}\right)$$

$$\cos 45° = \frac{1}{\sqrt{2}}\left(=\frac{\sqrt{2}}{2}\right) \qquad \cos\frac{\pi}{4} = \frac{1}{\sqrt{2}}\left(=\frac{\sqrt{2}}{2}\right)$$

$$\tan 45° = 1 \qquad \tan\frac{\pi}{4} = 1$$

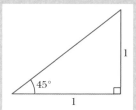

$$\sin 60° = \frac{\sqrt{3}}{2} \qquad \sin\frac{\pi}{3} = \frac{\sqrt{3}}{2}$$

$$\cos 60° = \frac{1}{2} \qquad \cos\frac{\pi}{3} = \frac{1}{2}$$

$$\tan 60° = \sqrt{3} \qquad \tan\frac{\pi}{3} = \sqrt{3}$$

$$\sin 30° = \frac{1}{2} \qquad \sin\frac{\pi}{6} = \frac{1}{2}$$

$$\cos 30° = \frac{\sqrt{3}}{2} \qquad \cos\frac{\pi}{6} = \frac{\sqrt{3}}{2}$$

$$\tan 30° = \frac{1}{\sqrt{3}}\left(=\frac{\sqrt{3}}{3}\right) \qquad \tan\frac{\pi}{6} = \frac{1}{\sqrt{3}}\left(=\frac{\sqrt{3}}{3}\right)$$

TIP

It may be useful to know the ratios of certain angles as exact values.

Exercise 9.1

1 Given that $\tan\theta = \dfrac{1}{3}$ and that θ is acute, find the exact values of

  a $\sin\theta$ **b** $\cos\theta$ **c** $\sin^2\theta$

  d $\sin^2\theta + \cos^2\theta$ **e** $\dfrac{2 + \sin\theta}{3 - \cos\theta}$.

2 Given that $\sin\theta = \dfrac{\sqrt{2}}{3}$ and that θ is acute, find the exact values of

  a $\cos\theta$ **b** $\tan\theta$ **c** $1 - \cos^2\theta$

  d $\sin\theta + \cos\theta$ **e** $\dfrac{\cos\theta - \sin\theta}{\tan\theta}$.

3 Given that $\cos\theta = \dfrac{1}{3}$ and that θ is acute, find the exact values of

  a $\sin\theta$ **b** $\tan\theta$ **c** $\tan\theta\cos\theta$

  d $\sin^2\theta + \cos^2\theta$ **e** $\dfrac{\cos\theta - \tan\theta}{1 - \cos^2\theta}$.

4 Find the exact value of each of the following.

  a $\tan 45°\sin 30°$ **b** $\tan^2 30°$ **c** $\dfrac{\tan 60°}{\cos 60°}$

  d $\sin 30° + \cos 30°$ **e** $\dfrac{\cos^2 60°}{\cos 30° + \cos 60°}$ **f** $\dfrac{\tan 30° - \sin 30°}{1 + \sin^2 30°}$.

5 Find the exact value of each of the following.

  a $\sin\dfrac{\pi}{3}\cos\dfrac{\pi}{4}$ **b** $\sin^2\dfrac{2\pi}{3}$ **c** $\dfrac{\tan\dfrac{\pi}{3}}{\cos\dfrac{\pi}{3}}$

  d $\dfrac{1 - \tan\dfrac{\pi}{4}}{\sin\dfrac{\pi}{6}}$ **e** $\dfrac{1}{\sin\dfrac{2\pi}{3}} - \dfrac{1}{\cos\dfrac{\pi}{3}}$ **f** $\dfrac{2\tan\dfrac{\pi}{4} - 2\sin\dfrac{\pi}{6}}{3\tan\dfrac{\pi}{6}\sin\dfrac{\pi}{3}}$.

9.2 The general definition of an angle

REMINDER

You need to be able to use the three basic trigonometric functions for any angle. To do this you need a general definition for an angle:

An angle is a measure of the rotation of a line *OP* about a fixed point *O*.

The angle is measured from the positive *x*-direction.

An anticlockwise rotation is taken as positive and a clockwise rotation is taken as negative.

The Cartesian plane is divided into four quadrants, and the angle θ, is said to be in the quadrant where *OP* lies. In the diagram shown, θ is in the first quadrant.

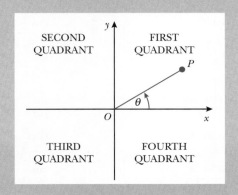

Exercise 9.2

1 Draw a diagram showing the quadrant in which the rotating line *OP* lies for each of the following angles. In each question indicate clearly the direction of rotation and find the acute angle that the line *OP* makes with the *x*-axis.

a $120°$
b $-45°$
c $240°$
d $-165°$

e $-280°$
f $\dfrac{3\pi}{8}$
g $\dfrac{7\pi}{5}$
h $-\dfrac{5\pi}{4}$

i $\dfrac{12\pi}{5}$
j $-\dfrac{3\pi}{5}$

2 State the quadrant that *OP* lies in when the angle that *OP* makes with the positive *x*-axis is:

a $170°$
b $320°$
c $-170°$
d $195°$

e $-400°$
f $\dfrac{2\pi}{3}$
g $\dfrac{12\pi}{5}$
h $-\dfrac{12\pi}{7}$

i $\dfrac{13\pi}{3}$
j $-\dfrac{10\pi}{3}$

9.3 Trigonometric ratios of general angles

REMINDER

- In general, trigonometric ratios of any angle θ in any quadrant are defined as:

  $\sin\theta = \dfrac{y}{r}$, $\cos\theta = \dfrac{x}{r}$, $\tan\theta = \dfrac{y}{x}$, $x \neq 0$

  where *x* and *y* are the coordinates of the point *P* and *r* is the length of *OP* and $r = \sqrt{x^2 + y^2}$.

- The diagram on the right, records which ratios are positive in each quadrant.

  You can memorise this diagram using a mnemonic such as:

  '**A**ll **S**tudents **T**rust **C**ambridge'.

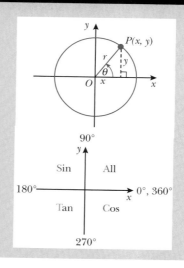

Exercise 9.3

1 Express the following as trigonometric ratios of acute angles.

a $\sin 320°$
b $\cos 200°$
c $\tan 190°$
d $\cos(-95°)$

e $\tan 500°$
f $\sin\dfrac{3\pi}{5}$
g $\tan\dfrac{-7\pi}{3}$
h $\cos\left(-\dfrac{5\pi}{6}\right)$

i $\tan\dfrac{3\pi}{5}$
j $\sin\dfrac{5\pi}{4}$

2 Given that $\sin\theta = \dfrac{3}{5}$ and that $180° \leqslant \theta \leqslant 270°$, find the value of

a $\tan\theta$
b $\cos\theta$.

3 Given that $\cos\theta = -\dfrac{\sqrt{3}}{2}$ and that $90° \leqslant \theta \leqslant 180°$, find the value of

a $\sin\theta$
b $\tan\theta$.

91

4 Given that $\sin\theta = \dfrac{12}{13}$ and that θ is obtuse, find the value of

a $\cos\theta$ **b** $\tan\theta$.

5 Given that $\tan\theta = \dfrac{3}{4}$ and that θ is reflex, find the value of

a $\sin\theta$ **b** $\cos\theta$.

6 Given that $\tan A = \dfrac{3}{4}$ and $\sin B = -\dfrac{\sqrt{3}}{2}$, where A and B are in the same quadrant, find the value of

a $\sin A$ **b** $\cos A$ **c** $\cos B$ **d** $\tan B$.

7 Given that $\sin A = -\dfrac{4}{5}$ and $\cos B = \dfrac{5}{13}$, where A and B are in the same quadrant, find the value of

a $\cos A$ **b** $\tan A$ **c** $\sin B$ **d** $\tan B$.

9.4 Graphs of trigonometric functions

REMINDER

The graph of $y = a\sin bx + c$

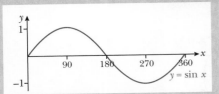

The sine function has a **period** of 360° (2π, if working in radians) and an **amplitude** 1.

$$y = a\sin bx + c$$

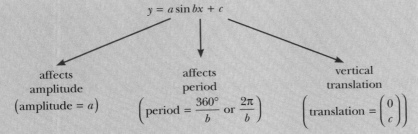

affects amplitude
$\left(\text{amplitude} = a\right)$

affects period
$\left(\text{period} = \dfrac{360°}{b} \text{ or } \dfrac{2\pi}{b}\right)$

vertical translation
$\left(\text{translation} = \begin{pmatrix} 0 \\ c \end{pmatrix}\right)$

The graph of $y = a\cos bx + c$

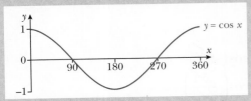

The cosine function has a **period** of 360° (2π, if working in radians) and an **amplitude** 1.

$$y = a\cos bx + c$$

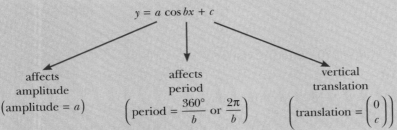

affects amplitude
$\left(\text{amplitude} = a\right)$

affects period
$\left(\text{period} = \dfrac{360°}{b} \text{ or } \dfrac{2\pi}{b}\right)$

vertical translation
$\left(\text{translation} = \begin{pmatrix} 0 \\ c \end{pmatrix}\right)$

92

The graph of $y = a \tan bx + c$

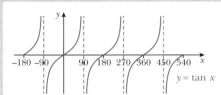

The tangent function has a **period** of 180°
(π, if working in radians).

$$y = a \tan bx + c$$

stretches the graph
Note: there is no
amplitude for a
tangent function

affects
period

$$\left(\text{period} = \frac{180°}{b} \text{ or } \frac{\pi}{b} \right)$$

vertical
translation

$$\left(\text{translation} = \begin{pmatrix} 0 \\ c \end{pmatrix} \right)$$

Exercise 9.4

1 a The following functions are defined for $0° \leqslant x \leqslant 360°$.

For each function, write down the amplitude, the period and the coordinates
of the maximum and minimum points.

i $f(x) = 3 \sin x$ **ii** $f(x) = 3 \cos 2x$ **iii** $f(x) = 2 \sin 3x$

iv $f(x) = 4 \cos \dfrac{1}{3} x$ **v** $f(x) = 4 \sin x + 2$ **vi** $f(x) = 5 \cos 2x - 2$

b Sketch the graph of each function in part **a** and use graphing software to check
your answers.

2 a The following functions are defined for $0 \leqslant x \leqslant 2\pi$.

For each function, write down the amplitude, the period and the coordinates
of the maximum and minimum points.

i $f(x) = 3 \cos x$ **ii** $f(x) = \sin 2x$ **iii** $f(x) = 3 \cos 2x$

iv $f(x) = 4 \sin \dfrac{1}{2} x$ **v** $f(x) = \cos 2x + 4$ **vi** $f(x) = 2 \sin 3x - 2$

b Sketch the graph of each function in part **a** and use graphing software to check
your answers.

3 The graph of $y = a + b \sin cx$, for $0 \leqslant x \leqslant 2\pi$, is shown.

Write down the value of a, the value of b and the value of c.

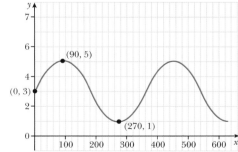

93

4   Part of the graph of $y = a \sin bx + c$ is shown.

Write down the value of a, the value of b and the value of c.

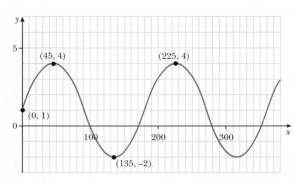

5   The graph of $y = a + b \cos cx$, for $0° \leqslant x \leqslant 360°$, is shown.

Write down the value of a, the value of b and the value of c.

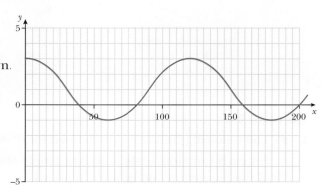

6   **a**   The following functions are defined for $0° \leqslant x \leqslant 360°$.

For each function, write down the period and the equations of the asymptotes.

   i $f(x) = \tan 3x$ **ii** $f(x) = 2 \tan \dfrac{1}{3} x$ **iii** $f(x) = 3 \tan 2x + 4$

   b   Sketch the graph of each function and use graphing software to check your answers.

7   **a**   The following functions are defined for $0 \leqslant x \leqslant 2\pi$.

For each function, write down the period and the equations of the asymptotes.

   i $f(x) = \tan \dfrac{1}{2} x - 1$ **ii** $f(x) = 4 \tan \dfrac{1}{3} x$ **iii** $f(x) = 4 \tan 2x - 1$

   b   Sketch the graph of each function and use graphing software to check your answers.

8   Part of the graph of $y = A \tan Bx + C$ is shown.

The graph passes through the point $P\left(\dfrac{\pi}{4}, \, 5\right)$.

Find the value of A, the value of B and the value of C.

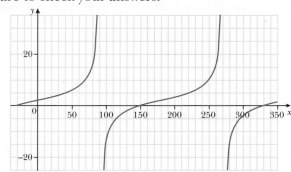

9   $f(x) = a + b \sin cx$

The maximum value of f is 7, the minimum value of f is -1 and the period is $180°$.

Find the value of a, the value of b and the value of c.

10 $f(x) = A + 2\cos Bx$ for $0° \leqslant x \leqslant 360°$.

The maximum value of f is 6 and the period is 120°.

a Write down the value of A and the value of B.

b Write down the amplitude of f.

11 $f(x) = A + B\sin Cx$ for $0° \leqslant x \leqslant 360°$.

The amplitude of f is 10, the period is 180° and the minimum value of f is -6.

Write down the value of A, the value of B and the value of C.

12 a On the same grid, sketch the graphs of $y = \sin x$ and $y = 2 + \sin 3x$ for
$0° \leqslant x \leqslant 360°$.

b State the number of roots of the equation $\sin 3x - \sin x + 2 = 0$ for
$0° \leqslant x \leqslant 360°$.

13 a On the same grid, sketch the graphs of $y = \sin x - 1$ and $y = 1 + \cos 2x$ for
$0° \leqslant x \leqslant 360°$.

b State the number of roots of the equation $\sin x - 1 = 1 + \cos 2x$ for
$0° \leqslant x \leqslant 360°$.

14 a On the same grid, sketch the graphs of $y = 2\sin 3x$ and $y = 1 + \cos x$ for
$0° \leqslant x \leqslant 360°$.

b State the number of roots of the equation $2\cos 3x = 1 + \cos x$ for $0° \leqslant x \leqslant 360°$.

9.5 Graphs of $y = |f(x)|$, where f(x) is a trigonometric function

---

WORKED EXAMPLE 1

a Sketch the graph of $f(x) = |\cos x|$ for $0 \leqslant x \leqslant 2\pi$.

b State the range of the function f.

Answers

a **Step 1** Sketch the graph of $y = \cos x$.

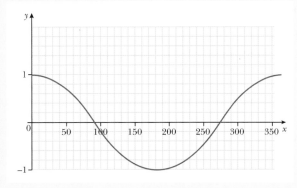

Step 2 Reflect in the x-axis the part of the curve $y = \cos x$ that is below the x-axis.

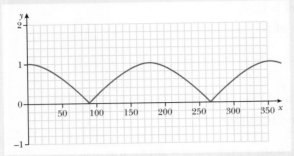

b The range of the function f is $0 \leqslant f(x) \leqslant 1$.

Exercise 9.5

Use graphing software to check your graphs in this exercise.

1 Sketch the graphs of each of the following functions, for $0° \leqslant x \leqslant 360°$, and state the range of each function.

   a $f(x) = |\tan 2x|$ **b** $f(x) = |\cos 3x|$ **c** $f(x) = |2 \sin x|$

   d $f(x) = \left|\sin \dfrac{1}{3}x\right|$ **e** $f(x) = \left|3 \cos \dfrac{1}{3}x\right|$ **f** $f(x) = |2 \sin 3x|$

   g $f(x) = |\sin 2x - 1|$ **h** $f(x) = |4 \sin 2x + 1|$ **i** $f(x) = |2 \cos 2x + 1|$

2 a Sketch the graph of $y = 3 \sin x - 2$ for $0° \leqslant x \leqslant 180°$.

   b Sketch the graph of $y = |3 \sin x - 2|$ for $0° \leqslant x \leqslant 180°$.

   c Write down the number of solutions of the equation $|3 \sin x - 2| = \dfrac{2}{3}$ for $0° \leqslant x \leqslant 180°$.

3 a Sketch the graph of $y = 1 + 2 \cos x$ for $0° \leqslant x \leqslant 180°$.

   b Sketch the graph of $y = |1 + 2 \cos x|$ for $0° \leqslant x \leqslant 180°$.

   c Write down the number of solutions of the equation $|1 + 2 \cos x| = 1$ for $0° \leqslant x \leqslant 180°$.

4 a Sketch the graph of $y = 1 + 2 \cos 2x$ for $0° \leqslant x \leqslant 180°$.

   b Sketch the graph of $y = |1 + 2 \cos 2x|$ for $0° \leqslant x \leqslant 180°$.

   c Write down the number of solutions of the equation $|1 + 2 \cos 2x| = 1$ for $0° \leqslant x \leqslant 180°$.

5 a On the same grid, sketch the graphs of $y = |\tan 2x|$ and $y = \sin x$ for $0° \leqslant x \leqslant 360°$.

   b State the number of roots of the equation $|\tan 2x| = \sin x$ for $0° \leqslant x \leqslant 360°$.

6 a On the same grid, sketch the graphs of $y = |\cos 2x|$ and $y = \tan 2x$ for $0 \leqslant x \leqslant 2\pi$.

   b State the number of roots of the equation $|\cos 2x| = \tan 2x$ for $0 \leqslant x \leqslant 2\pi$.

7 a On the same grid, sketch the graphs of $y = |0.5 + \sin 2x|$ and $y = 0.5 + \cos 2x$ for $0° \leqslant x \leqslant 360°$.

b State the number of roots of the equation $|0.5 + \sin 2x| = 0.5 + \cos 2x$ for $0° \leq x \leq 360°$.

8 a On the same grid, sketch the graphs of $y = |2 + 3\cos 2x|$ and $y = 1 + \sin x$ for $0° \leq x \leq 360°$.

b State the number of roots of the equation $|2 + 3\cos 2x| = 1 + \sin x$ for $0° \leq x \leq 360°$.

9 The equation $|2\cos 2x + 1| = k$, has 4 roots for the interval $0 \leq x \leq 2\pi$. Find the possible values of k.

10 The diagram shows the graph of $f(x) = |a + b\sin cx|$, where a, b and c are positive integers. Find the value of a, the value of b and the value of c.

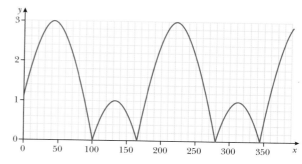

9.6 Trigonometric equations

WORKED EXAMPLE 2

Solve $\cos x = 0.6$ for $0° \leq x \leq 360°$.

$\cos x = 0.6$ use a calculator to find $\cos^{-1}(0.6)$ to 1 decimal place

$\quad x = 53.1°$

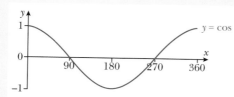

Answers

The graph shows there are two values of x, between $-360°$ and $360°$, for which $\cos x = 0.6$.

Using the symmetry of the curve, the second value is $(360° - 53.1°) = 306.9°$.

Hence the solution of $\cos x = 0.6$ for $0° \leq x \leq 360°$ is:

$\quad x = 53.1°$ or $306.9°$

Exercise 9.6

In this exercise give your answers correct to 3 sf

1 Solve each of these equations for $0° \leqslant x \leqslant 360°$.

    a $\sin x = 0.4$ **b** $\cos x = 0.3$ **c** $\tan x = 3$

    d $\sin x = -0.4$ **e** $\tan x = -3.4$ **f** $\sin x = -0.9$

    g $5\sin x - 3 = 0$ **h** $3\cos x + 1 = 0$

2 Solve each of the these equations for $0 \leqslant x \leqslant 2\pi$.

    a $\sin x = 0.5$ **b** $\tan x = 0.4$ **c** $\sin x = \dfrac{\sqrt{3}}{2}$

    d $\tan x = -\sqrt{3}$ **e** $\sin x = -1.5$ **f** $\cos x = -0.65$

    g $5\sin x = 1$ **h** $4\sin x + 3 = 0$

3 Solve each of these equations for $0° \leqslant x \leqslant 180°$.

    a $\sin 3x = 0.8$ **b** $\cos 2x = -0.9$ **c** $\tan 3x = 2$

    d $\sin 3x = -0.6$ **e** $4\cos 2x = 4$ **f** $5\sin 3x = -2$

    g $2 + 3\tan 2x = 0$ **h** $3 - 2\sin 2x = 0$

4 Solve each of these equations for the given domains.

    a $\sin(x - 60°) = 0.5$ for $0° \leqslant x \leqslant 2\pi$

    b $2\tan(x - 15°) = 3.7$ for $0° \leqslant x \leqslant 180°$

    c $\sin\left(x - \dfrac{\pi}{4}\right) - 0.5 = 0$ for $0° \leqslant x \leqslant 2\pi$

    d $\cos(2x + 70°) = 0.5$ for $0 < x < 180°$

    e $\sin\left(\dfrac{1}{2}x + 18°\right) = 0.572$ for $0 < x < 180°$

    f $\dfrac{1}{2}\tan\left(2x + \dfrac{\pi}{6}\right) = 1$ for $0 < x < 2\pi$ radians

5 Solve each of these equations for $0° \leqslant x \leqslant 360°$.

    a $4\sin x = 5\cos x$

    b $2\sin 2x + 5\cos 2x = 0$

    c $2\sin x = \dfrac{1}{\sin x}$

    d $2\sin x = \tan x$

6 Solve $2\sin(3x - 20°) - 5\cos(3x - 20°) = 0$ for $0° \leqslant x \leqslant 180°$.

7 Solve each of these equations for $0° \leqslant x \leqslant 360°$.

    a $\sin x \tan(x - 30°) = 0$ **b** $5\tan^2 x - 4\tan x = 0$

    c $3\cos^2 x = \cos x$ **d** $\sin^2 x + \sin x \cos x = 0$

    e $5\sin x \cos x = \cos x$ **f** $\sin x \tan x = \sin x$

8 Solve each of these equations for $0° \leqslant x \leqslant 360°$.

    a $4\cos^2 x = 1$ **b** $4\tan^2 x - 1 = 0$

9 Solve each of these equations for $0° \leqslant x \leqslant 360°$.

    a $\tan^2 x - 3\tan x + 2 = 0$ **b** $3\sin^2 x + \sin x = 1$

    c $6\cos^2 x - \cos x - 2 = 0$ **d** $\cos^2 x + 2\cos x - 1 = 0$

> **TIP**
>
> After rearranging to give '=0', remember to consider the positive and negative roots of the quadratic equation formed.

e $4\cos^2 x + 3\sin x = 4$

f $3 - 2\sin^2 x = 3$

g $10\sin^2 x - 5\cos^2 x + 2 = 4\sin x$

h $4\sin x \cos x = \sin x$

i $5\cos x = 6\tan x$

10 $f(x) = \cos x$ for $0 \leqslant x \leqslant 2\pi$ $g(x) = 3x + 1$ for $x \in \mathbb{R}$

Solve $gf(x) = 0.5$.

9.7 Trigonometric identities

 REMINDER

- When proving an identity, it is usual to start with the more complicated side of the identity and prove that it simplifies to the less complicated side.

WORKED EXAMPLE 3

Prove the identity $\dfrac{1}{\cos^2 x} - 1 = \tan^2 x$.

Answer

$\text{LHS} = \dfrac{1}{\cos^2 x} - 1$

$= \dfrac{1}{\cos^2 x} - \dfrac{\cos^2 x}{\cos^2 x}$

$= \dfrac{1 - \cos^2 x}{\cos^2 x}$

$= \dfrac{\sin^2 x}{\cos^2 x}$ use $1 - \cos^2 x = \sin^2 x$

$= \left(\dfrac{\sin x}{\cos x}\right)^2$

$= \tan^2 x$ use $\dfrac{\sin x}{\cos x} = \tan x$

$= \text{RHS}$

Exercise 9.7

1 Prove each of these identities.

a $\sin x \tan x + \cos x \equiv \dfrac{1}{\cos x}$

b $\dfrac{1}{\sin x} - \tan x \cos x \equiv \dfrac{\cos^2 x}{\sin x}$

c $\dfrac{\sin^2 x}{1 - \cos x} = 1 + \cos x$

d $\dfrac{1}{\cos x} + \tan x \equiv \dfrac{\cos x}{1 - \sin x}$

e $\dfrac{1}{\sin x} - \dfrac{1}{\tan x} \equiv \dfrac{1 - \cos x}{\sin x}$

f $\dfrac{\sin x \, \tan x}{1 - \cos x} \equiv 1 + \dfrac{1}{\cos x}$

2 Prove each of these identities.

a $(\sin x + \cos x)^2 \equiv 1 + 2\sin x \cos x$

b $(\cos x - \tan x)^2 + (\sin x + 1)^2 \equiv 2 + \tan^2 x$

c $\cos^4 x - \sin^4 x \equiv \cos^2 x - \sin^2 x$

d $(1 - \sin x + \cos x)^2 \equiv 2(1 - \sin x)(1 + \cos x)$

3 Prove each of these identities.

a $\sin x + \cos x \equiv \dfrac{1 - 2\cos^2 x}{\sin x - \cos x}$

b $\left(\sin x + \cos x\right)^2 - 1 \equiv 2\sin x \cos x$

c $\left(\sin x + \cos x\right)\left(1 - \sin x \cos x\right) \equiv \sin^3 x + \cos^3 x$

d $\dfrac{1 + \sin x + \cos x}{\cos x} \equiv \dfrac{1 - \sin x + \cos x}{1 - \sin x}$

9.8 Further trigonometric equations

REMINDER

- In addition to sine, cosine and tangent there are three further ratios, which you will have to learn and use.

- These are **cosecant** (cosec), **secant** (sec) and **cotangent** (cot) where:

$$\operatorname{cosec} \theta = \frac{1}{\sin \theta} \qquad \sec \theta = \frac{1}{\cos \theta} \qquad \cot \theta = \frac{1}{\tan \theta}\left(= \frac{\cos \theta}{\sin \theta}\right)$$

- There are also two further identities for you to learn and use:

$$1 + \tan^2 x = \sec^2 x \qquad 1 + \cot^2 x = \operatorname{cosec}^2 x$$

WORKED EXAMPLE 4

Solve $3\cot^2 x - 8\operatorname{cosec} x + 7 = 0$ for $0° \leqslant x \leqslant 360°$.

Answers

$3\cot^2 x - 8\operatorname{cosec} x + 7 = 0$	use $1 + \cot^2 x = \operatorname{cosec}^2 x$
$3\left(\operatorname{cosec}^2 x - 1\right) - 8\operatorname{cosec} x + 7 = 0$	expand brackets and collect terms
$3\operatorname{cosec}^2 x - 3 - 8\operatorname{cosec} x + 7 = 0$	
$3\operatorname{cosec}^2 x - 8\operatorname{cosec} x - 4 = 0$	factorise

$\left(3\operatorname{cosec} x - 2\right)\left(\operatorname{cosec} x - 2\right) = 0$

$3\operatorname{cosec} x - 2 = 0$ or $\operatorname{cosec} x - 2 = 0$

$\operatorname{cosec} x = \dfrac{2}{3} \qquad \operatorname{cosec} x = 2$

$\sin x = \dfrac{3}{2} \qquad \sin x = \dfrac{1}{2}$

no solutions $\qquad x = 30$ or $180 - 30$

$x = 30$ or 150

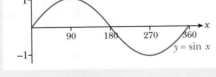

The solution of $3\cot^2 x - 8\operatorname{cosec} x + 7 = 0$ for $0° \leqslant x \leqslant 360°$ is

$x = 30°, 150°$

Exercise 9.8

In this exercise give your answers correct to 3 sf.

1 Solve each of these equations for $0° \leqslant x \leqslant 360°$.

a $\cot x = -0.2$ **b** $\sec x = -3$ **c** $\operatorname{cosec} x = 4$

d $2\sec x + 2 = 0$

2 Solve each of the these equations for $0 \leqslant x \leqslant 2\pi$.

   a $\operatorname{cosec} x = -3$ **b** $\cot x = 0.5$ **c** $\sec x = -6$

   d $2 \cot x + 1 = 4$

3 Solve each of these equations for $0° \leqslant x \leqslant 180°$.

   a $\cot 3x = 1$ **b** $\operatorname{cosec} x = \dfrac{2\sqrt{3}}{3}$ **c** $\cot(2x + 135°) = 1$

   d $5 \operatorname{cosec} 3x = -17$

4 Solve each of these equations for the given domains.

   a $\operatorname{cosec}(x + 30°) = 2$ for $0° \leqslant x \leqslant 360°$.

   b $\sqrt{3} \sec(x - 60°) = 2$ for $0° \leqslant x \leqslant 180°$.

   c $\cot\left(2x - \dfrac{\pi}{3}\right) = -1$ for $0 < x < \pi$.

   d $3 \sec(2x + 3) = 4$ for $0 < x < \pi$ radians.

5 Solve each of these equations for $0° \leqslant x \leqslant 360°$.

   a $\operatorname{cosec}^2 x = 4$ **b** $9 \cot^2 x = 16$ **c** $3 \sec^2 x = 4 \tan^2 x$

6 Solve each of these equations for $0° \leqslant x \leqslant 360°$.

   a $2 \operatorname{cosec}^2 x + 5 \operatorname{cosec} x = 12$ **b** $\sec^2 x - 2 \sec x - 3 = 0$

   c $2 \operatorname{cosec}^2 x - 9 \cot x + 2 = 0$ **d** $\cot^2 2x + \operatorname{cosec} 2x - 1 = 0$

   e $3 \operatorname{cosec}^2 x - 4 \sin^2 x - 1 = 0$ **f** $2 \cot^2 x + 3 \operatorname{cosec}^2 x - 3 = 4 \cot x$

   g $\sec x + 8 \sin^2 x = 8$ **h** $3 \tan^2 x - 3 \tan x + \sec^2 x = 2$

9.9 Further trigonometric identities

> **WORKED EXAMPLE 5**
>
> Prove the identity $\dfrac{1}{\tan x + \cot x} = \sin x \cos x$.
>
> **Answer**
>
> $\text{LHS} = \dfrac{1}{\tan x + \cot x}$ use $\cot x = \dfrac{1}{\tan x}$
>
> $= \dfrac{1}{\tan x + \dfrac{1}{\tan x}}$ multiply numerator and denominator by $\tan x$
>
> $= \dfrac{\tan x}{\tan^2 x + 1}$ use $1 + \tan^2 x = \sec^2 x$
>
> $= \dfrac{\tan x}{\sec^2 x}$
>
> $= \tan x \dfrac{1}{\sec^2 x}$ use $\sec x = \dfrac{1}{\cos x}$
>
> $= \tan x \cos^2 x$ use $\tan x = \dfrac{\sin 1}{\cos x}$
>
> $= \dfrac{\sin x}{\cos x} \cos^2 x$
>
> $= \sin x \cos x$
>
> $= \text{RHS}$

Exercise 9.9

1 Prove each of these identities.

    a $\sec x - \cos x \equiv \sin x \tan x$ **b** $\cot x - \cos x \equiv \cot x - \cot x \sin x$

    c $(1 - \cos x)(1 + \sec x) \equiv \sin x \tan x$ **d** $(\operatorname{cosec} x - \sin x)(\sec x - \cos x) \equiv \cos x \sin x$

2 Prove each of these identities.

    a $\operatorname{cosec}^2 x - 2\cot x \equiv (\cot x - 1)^2$ **b** $(1 + \cos x)(\operatorname{cosec} x - \cot x) \equiv \sin x$

    c $\operatorname{cosec}^2 x - \sec^2 x \equiv \cot^2 x - \tan^2 x$ **d** $(\operatorname{cosec}^2 x + \sec^2 x) \equiv \operatorname{cosec}^2 x \sec^2 x$

3 Prove each of these identities.

    a $\dfrac{\operatorname{cosec} x}{\operatorname{cosec} x - \sin x} \equiv \sec^2 x$ **b** $\dfrac{\tan^2 x + \cos^2 x}{\sin x + \sec x} = \sec x - \sin x$

    c $\dfrac{\cos x}{1 - \tan x} + \dfrac{\sin x}{1 - \cot x} \equiv \sin x + \cos x$ **d** $\dfrac{\sin x}{1 + \cos x} \equiv \dfrac{1 - \cos x}{\sin x}$

    e $\dfrac{\sin x}{1 + \cos x} + \dfrac{1 + \cos x}{\sin x} \equiv \dfrac{2}{\sin x}$ **f** $\dfrac{\cot x + \tan x}{\sec x} \equiv \operatorname{cosec} x$

4 Prove each of these identities.

    a $(\sin x + \tan x)(\cos x + \cot x) \equiv (1 + \sin x)((1 + \cos x)$

    b $(\sin x - \sec x)^2 \equiv \sin^2 x + (\tan x - 1)^2$

    c $(\cos x - 2\sec x)^2 \equiv \cos^2 x + 4\tan^2 x$

    d $(\sec^2 x + \tan^2 x)(\operatorname{cosec}^2 x + \cot^2 x) \equiv 1 + 2\sec^2 x \operatorname{cosec}^2 x$

Summary

Positive and negative angles

Angles measured anticlockwise from the positive x-direction are positive.

Angles measured clockwise from the positive x-direction are negative.

Diagram showing where sin, cos and tan are positive

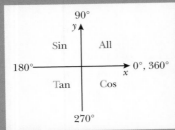

Useful mnemonic: 'All Students Trust Cambridge'.

Cosecant, secant and cotangent

$$\operatorname{cosec} \theta = \frac{1}{\sin \theta} \qquad \sec \theta = \frac{1}{\cos \theta} \qquad \cot \theta = \frac{1}{\tan \theta}$$

Trigonometric identities

$$\tan x = \frac{\sin x}{\cos x} \qquad 1 + \tan^2 x = \sec^2 x$$

$$\sin^2 x + \cos^2 x = 1 \qquad 1 + \cot^2 x = \operatorname{cosec}^2 x$$

Exercise 9.10

1 For the following graphs, find the cosine function representing them.

a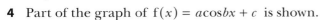

b

c

2 Solve the following, giving your answers in terms of π.

a $2\sin 3x + \sqrt{3} = 0$ for $0 \leqslant x \leqslant \pi$

b $\sqrt{2}\sin\left(x + \dfrac{\pi}{4}\right) = 1$ for $0 \leqslant x \leqslant 2\pi$

c $\cos\left(3x + \dfrac{2\pi}{3}\right) = 0.5$ for $0 \leqslant x \leqslant 2\pi$

d $\tan\left(2x - \dfrac{\pi}{6}\right) = \sqrt{3}$ for $0 \leqslant x \leqslant 2\pi$

3 a Given that $\tan x = \dfrac{1}{3}$, find the exact value of $\sec^2 x$.

b Given that $\operatorname{cosec} x = 1 + \sqrt{3}$, find the exact value of $\cot^2 x$.

c Given that $\sec x = \dfrac{3}{2}$, find the possible values of $\tan x$ giving your answers in the form $k\sqrt{5}$.

4 Part of the graph of $f(x) = a\cos bx + c$ is shown.

a Find the values of a, b and c.

b State the period and the amplitude of f.

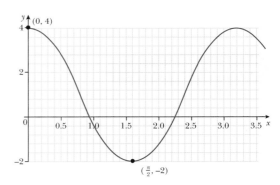

5 a Prove that $4 - \cos 2\theta + 5\sin\theta = 2\sin^2\theta + 5\sin\theta + 3$.

b Hence, solve the equation $4 - \cos 2\theta + 5\sin\theta = 0$ for $0 \leqslant x \leqslant 2\pi$.

6 On the axes shown, sketch for $0 \leqslant \theta \leqslant 360°$, the graph of

i $y = \sin 2x - 1$

ii $y = \cos 3x$

iii State the number of solutions to the equation $\cos 3x + 1 = \sin 2x$.

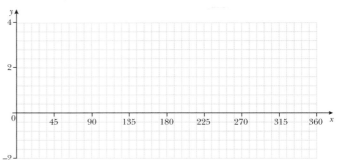

7 a Write $2\cos^2 x + \sin x$ in terms of $\sin x$ only.

b Solve the equation $2\cos^2 x + \sin x = 2$ for x in the interval $0 \leqslant x \leqslant \pi$, giving your answers exactly.

8 Given that $\sin A = \dfrac{3}{5}$, where A is acute, and $\cos B = -\dfrac{1}{2}$, where B is obtuse, find the exact values of

a $\sec A$ **b** $\cot A$ **c** $\cot B$ **d** $\operatorname{cosec} B$.

9 Prove the following identity: $\dfrac{1}{1 + \tan^2 x} + \dfrac{1}{1 + \cot^2 x} \equiv 1$

10 a Find all values of x in the interval $0 \leqslant x \leqslant 360°$ for which $\tan^2 x - \sec x = 1$.

b Find exact solutions of $\sqrt{2}\cos\left(\theta - \dfrac{3\pi}{4}\right) + 1 = 0$ for $0 \leqslant x \leqslant 2\pi$.

103

Chapter 10:
Permutations and combinations

This section will show you how to:

- calculate the number of arrangements of *n* distinct items
- calculate the number of permutations of *r* items from *n* distinct items
- calculate the number of combinations of *r* items from *n* distinct items
- solve problems using permutations and combinations.

10.1 Factorial notation

REMINDER

The **factorial** of a positive integer, *n*, written as *n*! is the product of all positive integers less than or equal to *n*.

$$5! = 5 \times 4 \times 3 \times 2 \times 1$$

WORKED EXAMPLE 1

a Find the value of $\dfrac{5!}{2!}$.

b Write $6 \times 5 \times 4$ using factorial notation.

Answers

a $\dfrac{5!}{2!} = \dfrac{5 \times 4 \times 3 \times \cancel{2} \times \cancel{1}}{\cancel{2} \times \cancel{1}} = 5 \times 4 \times 3 = 60$

b $6 \times 5 \times 4 = \dfrac{6 \times 5 \times 4 \times \cancel{3} \times \cancel{2} \times \cancel{1}}{\cancel{3} \times \cancel{2} \times \cancel{1}} = \dfrac{6!}{3!}$

Exercise 10.1

1 Without using a calculator, find the value of

a $6!$

b $\dfrac{12!}{10!}$

c $\dfrac{8!}{6!2!}$

d $\dfrac{(3!)^2}{2!4!}$

e $\dfrac{5!}{0!}$

TIP

Remember: $0! = 1$

2 Rewrite the following using factorial notation.

a $3 \times 2 \times 1$

b 11×10

c $\dfrac{8 \times 7 \times 6}{3 \times 2 \times 1}$

d $\dfrac{5 \times 4 \times 3}{3 \times 2 \times 1}$

e $\dfrac{39 \times 38}{2 \times 1}$

f $(n+2)(n+1)$

g $(n+1)\,n(n-1)$

h $\dfrac{n(n-1)(n-2)}{3 \times 2 \times 1}$

i $\dfrac{(n-1)(n-2)(n-3)(n-4)}{4 \times 3 \times 2 \times 1}$

TIP

Remember:
$n! = n \times (n-1)!$

104

10.2 Arrangements

 REMINDER

There are 3! = 6 possible **arrangements** of the three letters A, B and C:

- ABC, ACB, BCA, BAC, CAB and CBA
- The number of ways of arranging n distinct items in a line = $n!$

WORKED EXAMPLE 2

How many numbers less than 400 000 but greater than 200 000 can be formed using the digits 1, 2, 3, 4, 5, 6 only once?

Answer

Consider filling 6 spaces.

The first space can be filled in 2 ways with either 2 or 3.

There are 5! ways of filling the remaining five spaces.

The number of arrangements = $2 \times 5! = 240$.

Exercise 10.2

1 How many different 4-figure numbers can be made from the digits 1, 2, 3, 4, 5?

2 Find the number of different arrangements of letters in each of the following.
  a BRIDE **b** SAMPLE **c** SPECIAL

3 a Find the number of ways the letters in the word HEADS can be arranged.
  b Find the number of those arrangements which start and end in a vowel.

4 a Find how many different 4-digit numbers can be made using one of each of the digits 1, 2, 3 and 4.
  b If one of the numbers is selected at random, find the number of arrangements which will be less than 2000.

5 Five people A, B, C, D and E are asked to sit randomly in a line. How many arrangements are there if
  a they can sit in any order
  b A and B sit together
  c A and B do not sit together.

6 In how many different ways can the letters of the word OPTICAL be arranged so that the vowels are always together?

7 In how many different ways can the letters of the word RETAIL be arranged such that the vowels must occupy only the odd positions?

 TIP
Mark the positions as (1), 2, (3), 4, (5), 6 (the odd positions are bracketed).

8 How many arrangements of the letters in the word COMPUTING start with a vowel?

9 How many even numbers greater than 2000 can be made using the digits 1, 2, 4, 8 if I use each digit once?

10.3 Permutations

If you had three letters A, B and C and 3 spaces to fill, then the number of ways of filling the spaces was $3 \times 2 \times 1 = 3!$

If you have 8 letters A, B, C, D, E, F, G and H and 3 spaces to fill, then the number of different ways of arranging three letters chosen from eight letters $= 8 \times 7 \times 6 = 336$.

The different arrangements of the letters are called permutations.

The notation $_8P_3$ is used to represent the number of permutations of 3 items chosen from 8 items.

REMINDER

The general rule for finding the number of **permutations** of r items from n distinct items is:

$$^nP_r = \frac{n!}{(n-r)!}$$

In permutations, **order matters**.

WORKED EXAMPLE 3

How many odd numbers less than 3000 but greater than 2000 can be formed using the digits 2, 3, 4, 6 and 8 only once?

Answer

Consider filling 4 spaces.

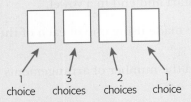

| 1 | 3 | 2 | 1 |
| choice | choices | choices | choice |

The first space has to be filled with a 2. The last space has to be a 3.

There are 3 choices for the second space and 2 choices for the third space.

The number of arrangements is 6 since $1 \times {_3P_2} \times 1 = 1 \times \frac{3!}{(3-2)!} \times 1 = 6$.

Exercise 10.3

1 Without using a calculator find the value of each of the following, and then use the $_nP_r$ key on your calculator to check your answers.

   a $^7P_5$ **b** $^6P_5$ **c** $^{10}P_8$ **d** $^5P_5$

TIP

Permutation questions can be phrased 'find the number of arrangements that can be made' or 'find the number of different ways in which something can be selected'.

2 Find the number of different ways that three books, chosen from 7 books can be arranged on a shelf.

3 How many permutations are there if I choose 6 items from 10 different items?

4 How many 4-digit numbers can be formed using 1, 2, 4, 6 and 8 if repetition of digits is not allowed?

5 There are 9 empty seats in a classroom. If 6 more pupils join the class, in how many different ways could they choose to take their seats?

6 Seven runners are competing in a race but the track only has 6 lanes. In how many ways can 6 of the 7 runners be assigned to the lanes?

7 Five books are chosen from 8 different books. In how many different ways can 5 books be arranged on a shelf?

8 How many 3-digit numbers can be formed from the digits 2, 3, 5, 6, 7 and 9 which are divisible by 5 and where none of the digits repeated?

9 Numbers are formed using the digits 2, 3, 4, 5, 6 and 7. No digit can be used more than once. Find how many different:

   a 4-digit numbers can be formed

   b numbers using 4 or more digits can be formed.

10 Find the number of ways of arranging 6 women and 3 men in a line so that all three men are standing together.

10.4 Combinations

There are $3! = 6$ possible **arrangements** of the three letters A, B and C:

- ABC, ACB, BCA, BAC, CAB and CBA

These are called **permutations** (the order is important).

There is only one **combination** of the letters A, B and C (the order is irrelevant).

Choosing the letters does not involve the order in which they are chosen. So ABC or CAB represents **two permutations** or **one combination**.

REMINDER

> The number of **combinations** of r items from n distinct items is:
>
> $$^nC_r = \binom{n}{r} = \frac{n!}{r!(n-r)!}$$
>
> In combinations, **order does not matter.**

WORKED EXAMPLE 4

In a group of 6 boys and 4 girls, four children are to be selected. In how many different ways can they be selected such that at least one boy is there?

Answer

1 boy, 3 girls:	$^6C_1 \times {}^4C_3 = 24$
2 boys, 2 girls:	$^6C_2 \times {}^4C_2 = 90$
3 boys, 1 girl:	$^6C_3 \times {}^4C_1 = 80$
4 boys:	$^6C_4 = 15$

Total arrangements $= 209$.

Exercise 10.4

1 Without using a calculator find the value of each of the following and then use the ^nC_r key on your calculator to check your answers.

a $^6C_1$ b $^5C_3$ c $^3C_3$ d $\begin{pmatrix} 7 \\ 4 \end{pmatrix}$

e $\begin{pmatrix} 4 \\ 4 \end{pmatrix}$ f $\begin{pmatrix} 8 \\ 2 \end{pmatrix}$

2 Show that $^7C_3 = {}^7C_4$.

3 How many different ways are there of selecting

a 5 photographs from 11 photographs

b 6 books from 10 books

c a team of 11 footballers from 18 footballers?

4 Find the number of ways of selecting a committee of 3 people from a group of 9 people.

5 There are 6 people in an office. A team of 3 people has to be formed. How many ways can the team be formed?

6 Find the number of ways of selecting a quiz team made up of 3 girls and 2 boys from a group containing 7 girls and 5 boys.

7 In a box there are 5 black pens, 3 white pens and 4 red pens. In how many ways can 2 black pens, 2 white pens and 2 red pens be chosen?

8 In how many ways can a group of 10 children be divided into two groups of 6 children and 4 children? Hint: each time 6 children are chosen, those **not** chosen must be a group of 4.

9 From a group of 7 men and 6 women, 5 people are to be selected. Find the number of different ways this could be done

a which include exactly 3 men

b if there are to be at least 3 men.

10 A committee of three is to be selected from 4 women and 5 men. There must be at least one man **and** one woman on the committee. How many different ways are there of doing this?

11 Nine people are going to travel in two taxis. The larger has 5 seats, and the smaller has 4. In how many ways can they travel?

12 A bag contains 2 white balls, 3 black balls and 4 red balls. In how many ways can 3 balls be picked from the bag if at least one black ball is to be included?

13 A question paper consists of 10 questions divided into 2 parts A and B. Each part contains 5 questions. A candidate is required to attempt 6 questions in total of which at least 2 should be from part A and at least 2 from part B. In how many ways could the candidate select the questions?

14 Find the number of ways which you could select a team of 5 from a group of 8 boys and 7 girls if there must not be less than two members of either sex in the team.

Summary

Arrangements in a line

The number of ways of arranging n distinct items in a line is:

$$n \times (n-1) \times (n-2) \times \ldots \times 3 \times 2 \times 1 = n!$$

Permutations

The number of **permutations** of r items from n distinct items is:

$$_n\mathrm{P}_r = \frac{n!}{(n-r)!}$$

In permutations, **order matters**.

Combinations

The number of **combinations** of r items from n distinct items is:

$$^n\mathrm{C}_r = \binom{n}{r} = \frac{n!}{r!(n-r)!}$$

In combinations, **order does not matter**.

Exercise 10.5

1 There are 5 books and 4 magazines. In how many ways can 4 books and 2 magazines be arranged on a shelf?

2 You are given the digits 1, 2, 3, 4 and 5 and the letters A, B, C and D. In how many ways can you arrange three of the digits and two of the letters? (Repeats are not allowed.)

TIP

Be careful! Some questions involve both permutations and combinations.

3 In how many ways can a committee of 4 men and 4 women be seated in a line if no one is sitting next to a person of the same sex?

4 There are 7 different books on a book shelf. Three of them are hardbacks and the rest are paperbacks.

  a In how many ways can the books be arranged if all the paperbacks are together and all the hardbacks are together?

  b In how many ways can the books be arranged if all the paperbacks are together?

5 Eight boys and two girls sit in a row. If the girls do not sit together, nor sit on the ends of the row, in how many ways can the 10 people be arranged?

6 A business has 4 vacancies for senior managers (each job has an identical description). 5 men and 3 women have applied for the positions.

  a How many ways are there of selecting 4 people to fill the positions?

  b If the 4 vacancies are filled at random, find the number of ways which contain at least 2 women.

  c Two of the people applying for the jobs are Mr and Mrs See. How many ways are there of filling the positions if these two must be chosen?

7 a How many odd three digit numbers can be formed from the digits 1, 2, 3, 4, 5, 6 and 8 (each digit can be used once)?

b How many of the arrangements from part **a** are over 500?

8 How many even numbers greater than 4000 can be made from the digits 2, 3, 6 and 8?

9 Ten people are arranged in line for a photograph. The 10 people come from three families.

Zara, Anya and Kyra come from the Patel family.

Mia, Jack and Tom come from the Smith family.

Irfan, Adam, Siti and Nor come from the Wan family.

a If the 10 people are arranged in a random order, how many arrangements are there?

b If members of the same family stand together, how many arrangements are there?

10 How many groups of 6 children can be chosen from a class of 20, if the class contains one set of twins who will not be separated?

11 Two sets of books contain six novels and 4 biographies. In how many ways can 4 novels and 2 biographies be arranged on a shelf?

12 How many arrangements can be formed using 3 consonants and 2 vowels chosen from 5 consonants and 4 vowels?

13 A board of directors of a company consists of 4 men and 4 women.

a Calculate the number of ways that the 8 directors could stand in a line for a photograph.

b Find the number of ways in which the 8 directors could stand in a line if the men and women stand alternately.

c Five members of the board are to be chosen to form a committee. Find the number of different possible committees which could be chosen if at least 2 women are on a committee.

14 A table tennis team consisting of 4 players is to be chosen from 7 boys and 5 girls.

a In how many different ways could the team be chosen?

b In how many of these ways will the team consist of 2 boys and 2 girls?

15 Each of 6 cards has a single different letter written on it. The letters on the cards are A, B, C, D, E and F. The cards are shuffled then placed in a row.

a How many different possible arrangements of the letters are there?

b In how many of these arrangements are the letters A and E next to each other?

16 A class consists of 7 students from Group A and 8 students from Group B.

a A team of 5 students is to be formed by choosing 2 students from Group A and 3 from Group B. How many different teams are possible?

b The chosen final team of 2 students from Group A and 3 from Group B are asked to sit in a line to watch a video. How many different arrangements can they sit in if no two students from Group B sit next to each other?

17 A test consists of 4 maths questions *A*, *B*, *C* and *D* and 4 English questions *G*, *H*, *I*, and *J*.

  a A teacher plans to arrange all 8 questions in a random order. How many different arrangements are possible?

    The teacher finally decides that the questions should be arranged in two sections, maths followed by English with the questions arranged in random order.

  b How many different arrangements are possible?

  c How many arrangements have questions *A* and *H* next to each other?

  d How many arrangements have questions *B* and *J* separated by more than 4 other questions?

18 How many odd numbers greater than 600 000 can be made from the digits 5, 6, 7, 8, 9 and 0 if each digit can only be used once in any number?

Chapter 11:
Series

- use the binomial theorem for expansion of $(a + b)^n$ for positive integral n

- use the general term $\binom{n}{r} a^{n-r} b^r$ for a binomial expansion

- recognise arithmetic and geometric progressions
- use the formula for the nth term and for the sum of the first n terms to solve problems involving arithmetic and geometric progressions
- use the condition for the convergence of a geometric progression, and the formula for the sum to infinity of a convergent geometric progression.

11.1 Pascal's triangle

REMINDER

Writing the expansions of $(a + b)^n$ out in order we get.......

$$(a + b)^1 = \qquad 1a + 1b$$
$$(a + b)^2 = \qquad 1a^2 + 2ab + 1b^2$$
$$(a + b)^3 = \qquad 1a^3 + 3a^2b + 3ab^2 + 1b^3$$
$$(a + b)^4 = \qquad 1a^4 + 4a^3b + 6a^2b^2 + 4ab^3 + 1b^4$$
$$(a + b)^5 = \qquad 1a^5 + 5a^4b + 10a^3b^2 + 10a^2b^3 + 5ab^4 + 1b^5$$

.....the coefficients of the terms define Pascal's Triangle:

$$1 \quad + \quad 1$$
$$1 \quad + \quad 2 \quad + \quad 1$$
$$1 \quad + \quad 3 \quad + \quad 3 \quad + \quad 1$$
$$1 \quad + \quad 4 \quad + \quad 6 \quad + \quad 4 \quad + \quad 1$$
$$1 \quad + \quad 5 \quad + \quad 10 \quad + \quad 10 \quad + \quad 5 \quad + \quad 1 \quad \text{and so on.}$$

WORKED EXAMPLE 1

a Expand $(3 - x)^4$.

b Find the coefficient of x^2 in the expansion of $(2 + 4x)(3 - x)^4$.

Answers

a $(3 - x)^4$ \qquad The index $= 4$ so use the 4th row in Pascal's triangle.

The 4th row of Pascal's triangle is 1, 4, 6, 4 and 1.

$$(3 - x)^4 = 1(3)^4 + 4(3)^3(-x) + 6(3)^2(-x)^2 + 4(3)^2(-x)^3 + 1(-x)^4$$
$$= 81 - 108x + 54x^2 - 12x^3 - x^4$$

b $(2 + 4x)(3 - x)^4 = (2 + 4x)(81 - 108x + 54x^2 - 12x^3 - x^4)$

The term in x^2 comes from the products:

$$(2 + 4x)(81 - 108x + 54x^2 - 12x^3 - x^5)$$

$$2 \times 54x^2 = 108x^2 \quad \text{and} \quad 4x \times (-108x) = -432x^2$$

So the coefficient of x^3 is $108 - 432 = -324$.

Exercise 11.1

1 Use Pascal's triangle to find the expansions of

a $(1 + x)^4$ **b** $(3 + x)^3$ **c** $(x + y)^4$ **d** $(1 - x)^5$

e $(x + y)^6$ **f** $(y + 3)^4$ **g** $(a - b)^4$ **h** $(3y + x)^4$

i $(x - 3y)^4$ **j** $(3x - 3)^4$ **k** $\left(x + \dfrac{3}{x}\right)^3$ **l** $\left(x^3 - \dfrac{1}{2x^2}\right)^3$

> **TIP**
> Remember to include the minus sign for $(-x), (-x)^2$ and so on.

2 Find the coefficient of x^3 in the expansions of

a $(2 + x)^4$ **b** $(3 + x)^4$ **c** $(2 - x)^4$ **d** $(3 - 2x)^3$

e $(x - 3)^4$ **f** $(1 - 2x)^4$ **g** $(3x - 3)^5$ **h** $\left(4 - \dfrac{1}{3}x\right)^4$

> **TIP**
> Remember the coefficient is just the number which comes with the x^3.

3 a Expand $(1 + x)^3$.

   b Hence expand $(1 + 2x)(1 + x)^3$.

4 a Expand $\left(1 + \sqrt{3}\right)^3$, leaving surds in your answer.

   b Expand $\left(1 - \sqrt{3}\right)^3$, leaving surds in your answer.

   c Use your answers from **a** and **b** to simplify $\left(1 + \sqrt{3}\right)^3 + \left(1 - \sqrt{3}\right)^3$.

5 Find the term independent of x in the expansion of $\left(x^2 + \dfrac{2}{x^2}\right)^4$.

6 Find the term independent of x in the expansion of $\left(2x + \dfrac{5}{x}\right)^6$.

7 a Expand $(1 + x)^5$ in ascending powers of x, simplifying your coefficients.

   b By replacing x with $y + y^2$, find the coefficient of y^4 in the expansion of $\left(1 + y + y^2\right)^5$.

8 Given that $a + b(1 + x)^3 + c(1 + 2x)^3 + d(1 + 3x)^3 = x^3$ for all values of x, find the values of the constants a, b, c and d.

9 Find the constant term in the expansion of $\left(2x^2 - \dfrac{1}{2x}\right)^6$.

10 Expand and simplify $(1 - x)(1 + 2x)^3$.

11.2 The binomial theorem for the expansion of $(a + b)^n$ where n is a positive integer

> **REMINDER**
>
> - $(a + b)^n = {}^nC_0\, a^n + {}^nC_1\, a^{n-1}b + {}^nC_2\, a^{n-2}b^2 + {}^nC_3\, a^{n-3}b^3 + \ldots + {}^nC_r\, a^{n-r}b^r + \ldots + {}^nC_n\, b^n$
>
> which can be written more simply as:
>
> - $(a + b)^n = a^n + {}^nC_1\, a^{n-1}b + {}^nC_2\, a^{n-2}b^2 + {}^nC_3\, a^{n-3}b^3 + \ldots + {}^nC_r\, a^{n-r}b^r + \ldots + b^n$
>
> or
>
> - $(a + b)^n = a^n + \dbinom{n}{1} a^{n-1}b + \dbinom{n}{2} a^{n-2}b^2 + \dbinom{n}{3} a^{n-3}b^3 + \ldots + \dbinom{n}{r} a^{n-r}b^r + \ldots + b^n$

WORKED EXAMPLE 2

Find the first four terms of the binomial expansion of:

a $(1-4x)^8$ **b** $(3+2y)^5$

Answers

a $(1-4x)^8 = 1 + 8(-4x) + \dfrac{8\times 7}{2!}(-4x)^2 + \dfrac{8\times 7\times 6}{3!}(-4x)^3 + \dots$

Replace x by $-4x$ and n by 8 in the formula.

$= 1 - 32x + 448x^2 - 3584x^3 + \dots$

b $(3+2y)^5 = \left[3\left(1+\dfrac{2y}{3}\right)\right]^5$

The formula is for $(1+x)^n$ so take out a factor of 3.

$= 3^5\left(1+\dfrac{2y}{3}\right)^5$

$= 3^5\left[1 + 5\left(\dfrac{2y}{3}\right) + \dfrac{5\times 4}{2!}\left(\dfrac{2y}{3}\right)^2 + \dfrac{5\times 4\times 3}{3!}\left(\dfrac{2y}{3}\right)^2 + \dots\right]$

Replace x by $\left(\dfrac{2y}{3}\right)$ and n by 5 in the formula.

$= 3^5\left[1 + \dfrac{10y}{3} + \dfrac{40}{9}y^2 + \dfrac{80}{27}y^3 + \dots\right]$

Multiply terms in brackets by 3^5.

$= 243 + 810y + 1080y^2 + 720y^3 + \dots$

Exercise 11.2

1 Write the following rows of Pascal's Triangle using combination notation.

a row 2 **b** row 6 **c** row 7

2 Use the binomial theorem to find the expansions of

a $(1+x)^3$ **b** $(1-x)^4$ **c** $(1-2x)^3$ **d** $(3+x)^4$

e $(1-2y)^4$ **f** $(2+x)^5$ **g** $(a-3b)^4$ **h** $(2x+5y)^4$

i $\left(\dfrac{1}{2}x-4\right)^4$ **j** $\left(2-\dfrac{x}{10}\right)^5$ **k** $\left(x-\dfrac{3}{x}\right)^4$ **l** $\left(x^2-\dfrac{1}{2x^2}\right)^5$

3 Find the term in x^3 for each of the following expansions.

a $(3+x)^5$ **b** $(6+x)^8$ **c** $(1+3x)^6$ **d** $(2+3x)^5$

e $(1+x)^6$ **f** $(3-x)^9$ **g** $(10-2x)^7$ **h** $(4-3x)^{10}$

TIP
Remember to include the x^3 in your answer.

4 Use the binomial theorem to find the first three terms in each of these expansions below, writing your answers in descending powers of x.

a $(2x+1)^{10}$ **b** $(1-2x)^8$ **c** $(1-4x)^7$ **d** $(3+3x)^6$

e $(3-x)^8$ **f** $\left(2+\dfrac{1}{4}x\right)^8$ **g** $(3-x^2)^8$ **h** $(2x-5y)^9$

5 a Find the the first 4 terms in the expansion of $(1+3x)^6$ in ascending powers of x.

b Find the coefficient of x^3 in the expansions of $\left(1-\dfrac{x}{3}\right)(1+3x)^6$.

6 a Find the the first 4 terms in the expansion of $\left(1+\dfrac{x}{4}\right)^{12}$ in ascending powers of x.

b Find the coefficient of x^3 in the expansions of $(1+2x)\left(1+\dfrac{x}{4}\right)^{12}$.

7 a Write down the first 4 terms in the expansion of $(1-5x)^8$ in ascending powers of x.

b Find the coefficient of x^3 in the expansions of $(1-4x)(1-5x)^8$.

8 a Find the first 3 terms of the expansion of $(3+2x)^6$ in ascending powers of x.

b Hence find the coefficient of x^2 in the expansion of $(3+2x)^6\left(1-2x+6x^2\right)$.

9 Find the coefficient of x in the binomial expansion of $\left(x-\dfrac{2}{x}\right)^7$.

10 Find the term independent of x in the binomial expansion of $\left(x^2+\dfrac{1}{3x^2}\right)^8$.

11.3 Arithmetic progressions

 REMINDER

A number sequence is also called a progression.

In an arithmetic progression, each term differs from the term before by a constant. This constant is called the **common difference**.

The notation used for arithmetic progressions is:

$a=$ first term $d=$ common difference $l=$ last term

nth term $= a+(n-1)d$

WORKED EXAMPLE 3

Find the number of terms in the arithmetic progression 1, 6, 11, 16...501, 506.

Answers

nth term $= a+(n-1)d$	use $a=1$, $d=5$ and nth term $=506$
$\quad506 = 1+5(n-1)$	solve
$5(n-1) = 505$	
$\quad\quad n = 102$	

WORKED EXAMPLE 4

The fifth term of an arithmetic progression is 23 and the twelfth term is 37. Find the first term and the common difference.

Answers

5th term $=23$ $\Rightarrow$ $a+4d=23$ ——(1)

12th term $=37$ $\Rightarrow$ $a+11d=37$ ——(2)

$(2)-(1)$, gives $7d=14$

$\quad\quad\quad\quad\quad d=2$

Substituting in (1) gives $a+8 = 23$

$\quad\quad\quad\quad\quad\quad\quad a = 15$

First term $=15$, common difference $=2$

WORKED EXAMPLE 5

The nth term of an arithmetic progression is $68 - 5n$. Find the first term and the common difference.

Answers

1st term $= 68 - 5(1) = 63$ substitute $n = 1$ into nth term $= 68 - 5n$

2nd term $= 68 - 5(2) = 58$ substitute $n = 2$ into nth term $= 68 - 5n$

Common difference $=$ 2nd term $-$ 1st term $= -5$

The sum of an arithmetic progression

 REMINDER

When the terms in a sequence are added together the resulting sum is called a **series**.

The sum of an arithmetic progression, S_n, can be written as:

$$S_n = \frac{n}{2}(a + l) \quad \text{or} \quad S_n = \frac{n}{2}\big[2a + (n-1)d\big]$$

nth term $= S_n - S_{n-1}$

WORKED EXAMPLE 6

In an arithmetic progression, the fifth term is 8, the ninth term is 14 and the last term is 32. Find the sum of all the terms in the progression.

Answers

nth term $= a + (n-1)d$

$\quad\quad 8 = a + 4d$ use nth term $= 8$ when $n = 5$

$\quad 14 = a + 8d$ use nth term $= 14$ when $n = 9$

$\quad 4d = 6$ solve

$\quad\quad d = 1.5$

$\quad\quad 8 = a + 4(1.5)$ substitute $d = 1.5$ into $8 = a + 4d$

$\quad\quad a = 2$

nth term $= a + (n-1)d$

$\quad 32 = 2 + 1.5(n-1)$

$\quad\quad n = 21$ solve

$\quad S_n = \frac{n}{2}(a + l)$ use $a = 2$, $l = 32$ and $n = 21$

$\quad S_{21} = \frac{21}{2}(2 + 32)$

$\quad\quad = 357$

WORKED EXAMPLE 7

The second term in an arithmetic progression is –12 and the sum of the first 12 terms is 18.
Find the first term of the progression and the common difference.

Answers

nth term $= a + (n-1)d$ use nth term $= -12$ when $n = 2$
$-12 = a + 1d$ —————— (1)

$S_n = \dfrac{n}{2}\left[2a + (n-1)d\right]$ use $n = 12$ and $S_{12} = 18$

$18 = \dfrac{12}{2}(2a + 11d)$ simplify

$18 = 12a + 66d$

$1.5 = a + 5.5d$ ——————— (2)

(1) – (2) gives $-4.5d = -13.5$

$d = 3$

Substituting $d = 3$ in equation (1) gives $a = -15$.

First term $= -15$, common difference $= 3$

WORKED EXAMPLE 8

The sum of the first n terms, S_n, of a particular arithmetic progression is given by $S_n = 17n - 3n^2$.

a Find the first term and the common difference.

b Find an expression for the nth term.

Answers

a $S_1 = 17(1) - 3(1)^2 = 14 \Rightarrow$ first term $= 14$
$S_2 = 17(2) - 3(2)^2 = 22 \Rightarrow$ first term + second term $= 22$
                    second term $= 22 - 14 = 8$

First term $= 14$, common difference $= -6$.

b **Method 1**

nth term $= a + (n-1)d$ use $a = 14$, $d = 6$
$\quad = 14 - 6(n-1)$
$\quad = 20 - 6n$

Method 2

nth term $= S_n - S_{n-1} = 17n - 3n^2 - \left[17(n-1) - 3(n-1)^2\right]$
$\quad = 17n - 3n^2 - (17n - 17 - 3n^2 - 6n + 3)$
$\quad = 20 - 6n$

Exercise 11.3

1 The first term in an arithmetic progression is a and the common difference is d.
Write down expressions, in terms of a and d, for the seventh term and the 12th term.

2 Find the sum of each of these arithmetic series.

a $2 + 6 + 10 + \dots$ (12 terms)   **b** $15 + 13 + 11 + \dots$ (16 terms)
c $7 + 3 - 1 - \dots$ (20 terms)   **d** $-9x - 7x - 5x - \dots$ (16 terms)

117

3 Find an expression for the nth term in the form $a + bn$ for each of these arithmetic series.

   a $7 + 9 + 11 + 13 + \ldots$ **b** $17 + 9 + 1 - 7 - \ldots$

4 Find the first term and the common difference for the arithmetic series

   $23 + 25 + 27 + 29$

5 The second and fifth terms of an arithmetic progression are 79 and 58.

   Find

   a   the first term and the common difference of the progression,

   b   the sum of the first 25 terms.

6 The sum of the first ten terms in an arithmetic progression is 120 and the sum of the first twenty terms is 840. Find the sum of the first thirty terms of this progression.

7 Three consecutive terms of an arithmetic progression are $3k + 1$, k and -3. Find the value of k.

8 The sum of the first ten terms of an arithmetic progression is 240. The fifth term is 23. Find

   a   the first term and the common difference of the progression,

   b   the sum of the first 60 terms of the series.

9 Find the sum of all the even numbers between 2 and 160 inclusive.

10 Find the sum of all positive integers less than 500 which are divisible by 3.

11 Five consecutive terms of an arithmetic progression have a sum of 40. The product of the first, third and fifth terms is 224. Find the terms of the sequence.

12 The first term of an arithmetic progression is -12 and the last term is 40. If the sum of the progression is 196, find the number of terms and the common difference.

13 In an arithmetic progression the sum of the first 10 terms is 50 and the fifth term is three times the second term. Find the first term and the sum of the first 20 terms.

14 In an arithmetic progression, the eighth term is twice the fourth term and the 20th term is 40. Find the common difference and the sum of the terms from the eighth to the 20th inclusive.

15 If the sum of the first n terms, S_n, of a particular arithmetic progression is given by $S_n = 2n^2 - n$. Find the sum of the terms from the third to the 12th inclusive.

16 The first, second and third terms of an arithmetic progression are $8 - x$, $3x$ and $4x + 1$, respectively. Calculate the value of x and find the sum of the first eight terms of the progression.

17 Find the sum of the integers from 1 to 200 inclusive which are not divisible by 5.

18 The sum of the first n terms, S_n, of a particular arithmetic progression is given by $S_n = pn + qn^2$. Given that $S_3 = 6$ and $S_5 = 11$. Find

  a   the values of p and q

  b   an expression for the nth term and the common difference.

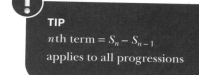

> **TIP**
>
> nth term $= S_n - S_{n-1}$
>
> applies to all progressions

19 Given that both the sum of the first ten terms of an arithmetic progression and the sum of the 11th and 12th terms of the same arithmetic progression are equal to 60, find the first term and the common difference.

20 In an arithmetic progression the nth term is 11, the sum of the first n terms is 72, and the first term is $\frac{1}{n}$. Find the value of n.

11.4 Geometric progressions

 REMINDER

In a geometric progression, each term is a multiple of the preceding term. This constant multiple is called the **common ratio**.

    The notation used for a geometric progression is:

    $a = $ first term $r = $ common ratio

    nth term $= ar^{n-1}$

The sum of a geometric progression, S_n, can be written as:

$$S_n = \frac{a(1 - r^n)}{1 - r} \quad \text{or} \quad S_n = \frac{a(r^n - 1)}{r - 1}$$

> **TIP**
>
> These formulae are not defined when $r = 1$.
>
> Either formula can be used but it is usually easier to:
>
> - use the first formula when $-1 < r < 1$
>
> - use the second formula when $r > 1$ or when $r < -1$.

WORKED EXAMPLE 9

The third term of a geometric progression is 8 and the common ratio is $-\frac{1}{2}$. Find the fifth term and an expression for the nth term.

Answers

nth term $= ar^{n-1}$ use nth term $= 8$ when $n = 3$ and $r = -\frac{1}{2}$

$$8 = a\left(-\frac{1}{2}\right)^2$$

$$a = 32$$

$$5\text{th term} = 32\left(-\frac{1}{2}\right)^4 = 2$$

$$n\text{th term} = ar^{n-1} = 32\left(-\frac{1}{2}\right)^{n-1}$$

WORKED EXAMPLE 10

The third and sixth terms in a geometric progression are 2 and 16 respectively. Given that all the terms are positive, find the first term and the common ratio. Hence, write down an expression for the nth term.

Answers

$16 = ar^5$ ——(1) $\qquad 2 = ar^2$ ——(2)

(1) $\div$ (2) gives $\dfrac{ar^5}{ar^2} = \dfrac{16}{2}$

$\qquad\qquad\qquad r^3 = 8$

$\qquad\qquad\qquad r = 2$

Substituting $r = 2$ into equation (1) gives $a = \dfrac{1}{2}$.

First term $= \dfrac{1}{2}$, common ratio $= 2$, nth term $= \dfrac{1}{2}(2)^{n-1}$.

WORKED EXAMPLE 11

The nth term of a geometric progression is $(3)^{n-2}$. Find the first term and the common ratio.

Answers

1st term $= (3)^{1-2} = \dfrac{1}{3}$

2nd term $= (3)^{2-2} = 1$

Common ratio $= \dfrac{\text{2nd term}}{\text{1st term}} = \dfrac{1}{\frac{1}{3}} = 3$

First term $= \dfrac{1}{3}$, common ratio $= 3$

WORKED EXAMPLE 12

In a geometric sequence the first two terms are 10, 11,… which is the first term to exceed 1000?

Answers

$\qquad n\text{th term} = ar^{n-1}$ $\qquad\qquad$ use $a = 10$ and $r = 1.1$

$\qquad 10 \times 1.1^{n-1} > 1\,000$ $\qquad\qquad$ divide by 10 and take logs

$\qquad \log_{10} 1.1^{n-1} > \log_{10} 100$ $\qquad\qquad$ use the power rule for logs

$\qquad (n-1)\log_{10} 1.1 > 2$ $\qquad\qquad$ divide both sides by $\log_{10} 1.1$

$\qquad\qquad n - 1 > \dfrac{2}{\log_{10} 1.1}$

$\qquad\qquad n - 1 > 48.317\ldots$

$\qquad\qquad\qquad n > 49.317\ldots$

The 50th term is the first to exceed 1000.

WORKED EXAMPLE 13

Find the sum of the first eight terms of the geometric series $1 + 3 + 9 + 27 + ...$

Answers

$$S_n = \frac{a(r^n - 1)}{r - 1}$$ use $a = 1$, $r = 3$ and $n = 8$

$$S_{12} = \frac{1(3^8 - 1)}{3 - 1}$$ simplify

$$= 3280$$

WORKED EXAMPLE 14

The first term of a geometric progression is 15 less than second term. The sum of the second and third terms is 100. Find the two possible values of the first term.

Answers

2nd term = 1st term + 15

$\qquad ar = a + 15$ rearrange to make a the subject

$\qquad a = \dfrac{15}{r - 1}$ ——(1)

2nd term + 3rd term = 100

$\qquad ar + ar^2 = 100$ factorise

$\qquad ar(1 + r) = 100$ ——(2)

(2) ÷ (1) gives $\dfrac{ar(1 + r)}{a} = \dfrac{100(r - 1)}{15}$ simplify

$\qquad 3r^2 - 17r + 20 = 0$ factorise and solve

$\qquad (3r - 5)(r - 4) = 0$

$\qquad r = \dfrac{5}{3}$ or $r = 4$

Substituting $r = 4$ into (1) gives $a = 5$

Substituting $r = \dfrac{5}{3}$ into (1) gives $a = 22.5$

First term could be 5 or 22.5.

Exercise 11.4

1   Identify whether the following sequences are geometric. If they are geometric, write down the common ratio and the eighth term.

 a $2, 6, 18, 54, ...$ b $1, 2, -4, -8, 16, 32...$

 c $1, \dfrac{1}{3}, \dfrac{1}{6}, \dfrac{1}{9}, \dfrac{1}{12} ...$ d $1, \dfrac{1}{2}, \dfrac{1}{4}, \dfrac{1}{8}, \dfrac{1}{16}, ...$

 e $1, 1.1, 1.11, 1.111, ...$ f $1, a, a^2, a^3, ...$

2   The second term in a geometric progression is -12 and the fifth term is 578. Find the common ratio and the first term.

3   Find the value of the common ratio of the geometric progression that has third term equal to 6 and eighth term equal to 1458.

4 The seventh term of a geometric progression equals 8 and the ninth term equals 18. Find the possible values of the common ratio.

5 A geometric progression has the sixth term equal to 24 and the eleventh term equal to 768.
Find the nth term.

6 Find the number of terms in the geometric progression 5, –10, 20, ..., –4096.

7 The three numbers $n-2$, n, $n+3$ are consecutive terms of a geometric progression.
Find n and the term after $n+3$.

8 The first term of a geometric progression is 16 and the fifth term is 9. What is the value of the seventh term?

9 The numbers $x-4$, $x+2$ and $3x+1$ are a geometric progression. Find the two possible values of the common ratio.

10 A nth term of a progression is written as $6\left(\dfrac{1}{2}\right)^{n-1}$.

    a Prove that the progression is geometric.

    b Find the first term and the common ratio.

    c Find the fifth term.

11 Which is the first term of the geometric progression 5, 10, 20, ... to exceed 400000?

12 In a geometric progression, the sum of the second and third terms is 9 and the seventh term is eight times the fourth. Find the first term, the common ratio and the fifth term.

13 Find the sum of each of these geometric series.

    a $4-12+36-...-972$ **b** $36+12+4+.....+\dfrac{4}{27}$

    c $\dfrac{1}{3}-\dfrac{1}{9}+\dfrac{1}{27}-...-\dfrac{1}{729}$ **d** $1+\dfrac{1}{2}+\dfrac{1}{4}+...+\dfrac{1}{2^n}$

14 How many terms of the geometric progression $5-10+20-...$ should be chosen so that the sum equals 215?

15 Find the sum of the first ten terms of a geometric progression that has a sixth term $\dfrac{32}{33}$ and a seventh term $\dfrac{64}{33}$.

16 Find the sum of the first 12 terms of the following geometric progression.
$\sqrt{7}+7+7\sqrt{7}+49+...$. (Give your answer to three significant figures.)

17 Find the values of x given that 4, x and x^2-1 are consecutive geometric terms.

18 Find the first term of the geometric sequence 24, 8, $\dfrac{8}{3}$, $\dfrac{8}{9}$, which is less than 0.001.

19 A geometric progression has the 6th term 24 and the 11th term 768. Find the sum of the first 15 terms.

20 Find the first five terms of a geometric series such that the sum of its first and third terms is 50 and the sum of the second and fourth terms is 150.

11.5 Infinite geometric series

WORKED EXAMPLE 15

The first three terms of a geometric progression are $2, \dfrac{1}{2}, \dfrac{1}{8}, \dfrac{1}{32} \cdots$.

a Write down the common ratio.

b Find the sum to infinity.

Answers

a Common ratio $= \dfrac{\text{second term}}{\text{first term}} = \dfrac{\frac{1}{2}}{2} = \dfrac{1}{4}$

b $S_\infty = \dfrac{a}{1 - r}$ use $a = 2$ and $r = \dfrac{1}{4}$

$= \dfrac{2}{1 - \dfrac{1}{4}}$

$= \dfrac{8}{3}$

WORKED EXAMPLE 16

A geometric progression has a common ratio of $-\dfrac{1}{3}$ and a sum to infinity of 18.
Find the third term of the progression.

Answers

a $S_\infty = \dfrac{a}{1 - r}$ use $S_\infty = 18$ and $r = -\dfrac{1}{3}$

$18 = \dfrac{a}{1 - \left(-\dfrac{1}{3}\right)}$ simplify

$18 = \dfrac{3a}{4}$ solve

$a = 24$

b n^{th} term $= ar^{n-1}$ use $a = 24$ and $r = -\dfrac{1}{3}$

3rd term $= 24\left(-\dfrac{1}{3}\right)^2$

$= 2\dfrac{2}{3}$

Exercise 11.5

1 Find the sum to infinity of each of the following geometric series.

    a $16 + 12 + 9 + \ldots$

    b $2 + \dfrac{1}{2} + \dfrac{1}{8} + \dfrac{1}{32} + \ldots$

    c $0.5 + 0.05 + 0.005 + \ldots$

    d $84 - 42 + 21 - 10\dfrac{1}{2} + \ldots$

2 Find the first term of a geometric progression that has a common ratio of 0.4 and a sum to infinity of 20.

3 Find the common ratio of a geometric progression whose first term is 6 and whose sum to infinity is 60.

4 The sum to infinity of a geometric progression with a positive common ratio is 7 and the sum of the first two terms is $\dfrac{48}{7}$.

Find the common ratio and first term.

5 **a**   Write the recurring decimal $0.\dot{4}\dot{5}$ as the sum of a geometric progression.

    b   Use your answer to **part a** to show that $0.\dot{4}\dot{5}$ can be written as $\dfrac{5}{11}$.

6 The second term of a geometric progression is 6 and the sum to infinity is 24. Find the common ratio and the sum of the first three terms.

7 The second term of a geometric progression is 6 and the sum to infinity is 27. Find the values of the common ratio and the possible values of the first three terms.

8 The sixth term of a geometric progression is $\dfrac{256}{3}$ and the tenth term is $\dfrac{16}{3}$.

    a   Find the nth term.

    b   Find the sum to infinity.

9 Find the least number of terms of the geometric series with first term 50 and second term 47 for which the sum exceeds 800.

10 The first term of a geometric progression is 27 and the fourth term is 8. Find

    a   the common ratio

    b   the sum to infinity.

11 The first three terms of a geometric progression are $k - 8$, $k + 4$ and $3k + 2$ respectively. Where k is a positive constant find

    a   the value of k.

    b   the common ratio.

    c   Explain why it is not possible to find the sum to infinity for this progression.

12 A geometric series has a common ratio r and first term equal to 64.

    The third term minus the second term is 20.

    a   Find the two possible values of r.

    b   Taking the value of r which leads to convergence, find the sum to infinity of the series.

13 A geometric series has a first term 12 and a common ratio $\frac{2}{3}$. Find

   a the fifth term

   b the sum of the first eight terms

   c the sum to infinity. Give your answers to three significant figures where necessary.

14 Find the sum of the first n terms of the following geometric series and find the sum to infinity in cases where the series is convergent.

   a $\frac{3}{10} + \frac{3}{100} + \frac{3}{1000} + \ldots$

   b $16 - 8 + 4 - \ldots$

   c $8 - 12 + 18 - \ldots$

15 The sum to infinity of a geometric series is 5 and the first term is 7. Find the common ratio and the sum of the first 15 terms.

16 By the end of the year the value of a building had increased by 3% of its value at the start of the year. At the start of 2004 the building was valued at $45000. Estimate to the nearest $100 the value of the building at the end of 2210.

11.6 Further arithmetic and geometric series

Some problems may involve more than one progression.

Exercise 11.6

1 The fourth, seventh and 16th terms of an arithmetic progression are in geometric progression. If the first six terms of the arithmetic progression have a sum of 12, find the common difference of the arithmetic progression and the common ratio of the geometric progression.

2 The second, fifth and 11th terms of an arithmetic progression are in geometric progression and the seventh term is 4. Find:

   a the first term and the common difference

   b the common ratio of the geometric progression.

3 The second, third and sixth terms of an arithmetic progression are consecutive terms of a geometric progression. Find the common ratio of the geometric progression.

4 The sum of the first three terms of a geometric progression is $\frac{13}{12}$ and their product is -1.

Find the geometric progression.

5 The product of the first three terms of a geometric progression is 1000. If we add 6 to its second term and 7 to its third term , the three terms form an arithmetic progression. Find the terms of the geometric progression.

6 If $\log 2$, $\log\left(2^x - 1\right)$ and $\log\left(2^x + 3\right)$ are in arithmetic progression, find the value of x to three significant figures.

Summary

Binomial expansions

If n is a positive integer then $(a+b)^n$ can be expanded using the formula

$$(a+b)^n = a^n + {}^nC_1\, a^{n-1}\, b + {}^nC_2\, a^{n-2}\, b^2 + {}^nC_3\, a^{n-3}\, b^3 + \ldots + {}^nC_r\, a^{n-r}\, b^r + \ldots + b^n$$

or

$$(a+b)^n = a^n + \binom{n}{1} a^{n-1}\, b + \binom{n}{2} a^{n-2}\, b^2 + \binom{n}{3} a^{n-3}\, b^3 + \ldots + \binom{n}{r} a^{n-r}\, b^r + \ldots + b^n$$

where ${}^nC_r = \binom{n}{r} = \dfrac{n!}{(n-r)!\,r!}$.

In particular, $(1+x)^n = 1 + nx + \dfrac{n(n-1)}{2!}\, x^2 + \dfrac{n(n-1)(n-2)}{3!}\, x^3 + \dfrac{n(n-1)(n-2)(n-3)}{4!}\, x^4 + \ldots + x^n$

Arithmetic series

For an arithmetic progression with first term a, common difference d and n terms

- the kth term $= a + (k-1)d$
- the last term $= l = a + (n-1)d$
- the sum of the terms $= S_n = \dfrac{n}{2}(a+l) = \dfrac{n}{2}\big[2a+(n-1)d\big]$.

Geometric series

For a geometric progression with first term a, common ratio r and n terms

- the kth term $= ar^{k-1}$
- the last term $= ar^{n-1}$
- the sum of the terms $= S_n = \dfrac{a\left(1-r^n\right)}{1-r} = \dfrac{a\left(r^n-1\right)}{r-1}$.

The sum to infinity $S_\infty = \dfrac{a}{1-r}$ provided that $-1 < r < 1$

The condition for a geometric series to converge is, $-1 < r < 1$.

When a geometric series converges, $S_\infty = \dfrac{a}{1-r}$.

Exercise 11.7

1 Find the coefficient of x^5 in the expansion of $(3x-2)^8$.

2 Simplify $(3+2x)^3 - (3-2x)^3$.

3 a Find the first four terms in the expansion, in ascending powers of x, of $(1+3x)^8$.

   b Show that, if terms involving x^4 and higher powers of x are ignored,
   $(1+3x)^8 + (1-3x)^8 = 2 + 504x^3$.

4 a Expand $(2+3x)^4$ completely, simplifying the coefficients.

   b Find the coefficient of x^2 in the expansion of $(1 - \frac{1}{2}x)^2(2+3x)^4$.

5 a Find the first three terms of the expansion, in ascending powers of x, of $(1-2x)^{12}$.

   b Find the coefficient of x^2 in the expansion of $(1+3x)(1-2x)^{12}$.

6 Find the coefficient of $a^3 b^4$ in the expansion of $(5a + b)^7$.

7 Find the constant term in the expansion of $\left(x - \dfrac{2}{x^2} \right)^9$.

8 Complete this expansion $(3x + 2y)^4 = 81x^4 + 216x^3 y + \ldots$

9 **a** Find the first four terms in ascending powers of x in the binomial expansion $(1 + kx)^6$ where k is a non-zero constant.

   b Given that in this expansion the coefficients of x and x^2 are the same, find the value of k.

10 Find the ratio of the coefficients of the x^5 term to the x^6 term in the expansion of $(2x + 3)^{20}$.

11 The coefficient of x^2 in the expansion of $(1 + kx)^7$ is 525 (k is a positive constant).

   a Find the value of k.

   b Using this value of k, and the fact that the coefficient of x^3 is 4375, find the first three terms in the expansion of $(2 - x)(1 + kx)^7$.

12 **a** Expand $(1 + x)^4$ in ascending powers of x.

   b Using your expansion, express $\left(1 - \sqrt{2}\right)^8$ in the form $a + b\sqrt{2}$.

13 Given that x, 10 and y are consecutive terms of an arithmetic progression and that 1, x and y are consecutive terms of a geometric progression, find the possible values of x and y.

14 The first, second and third terms of an arithmetic progression are x, y and y^2 where x is negative.

   The first, second and third terms of an geometric progression are x, x^2 and y. Find

   a the values of x and y

   b the sum to infinity of the geometric progression

   c the sum of the first 40 terms of the arithmetic progression.

15 A geometric progression has a first term $\sqrt{2}$ and a second term $\sqrt{6}$. Find the exact value of the 12th term and the sum of the first 12 terms to three significant figures.

16 A ball is dropped vertically from a height of $10\,\text{m}$ and bounces to a height of $8\,\text{m}$. On each bounce the height reached is 0.8 times the height reached on the previous bounce. Find the total distance the ball travels before it comes to rest.

17 The first, second and third terms of a geometric progression are the first, seventh and ninth terms of an arithmetic progression. Find the common ratio of the geometric progression.

18 Find the value of x for which the numbers $x + 1$, $x + 3$ and $x + 7$ are in a geometric progression.

19 The second term of a geometric progression is $\dfrac{1}{2}$ and the sum to infinity of the series is 4. Find the first term and the common ratio of the series.

20 The sum of n terms of a series is $4^n - 1$.

    a Find the first three terms and the nth term.

    b Show that the series is a geometric progression.

21 An insect walks 0.6 m east and then 0.36 m west, 0.216 m east and so on. Find its final position and the total distance it has walked to get there.

Chapter 12:
Differentiation 1

This section will show you how to:

- use the notations $f'(x), f''(x), \dfrac{dy}{dx}, \dfrac{d^2y}{dx^2}, \left[\dfrac{d}{dx}\left(\dfrac{dy}{dx}\right)\right]$
- use the derivative of x^n (for any rational n), together with constant multiples, sums and composite functions of these
- differentiate products and quotients of functions
- apply differentiation to gradients, tangents and normals, stationary points, connected rates of change, small increments and approximations, and practical maxima and minima problems
- use the first and second derivative tests to discriminate between maxima and minima.

12.1 The gradient function

 REMINDER

- **Notation**

  This process of finding the gradient of a curve at any point is called **differentiation**.

  There are three different notations that can be used to describe differentiation:

  1. If $y = x^2$, then $\dfrac{dy}{dx} = 2x$.
  2. If $f(x) = x^2$, then $f'(x) = 2x$.
  3. $\dfrac{d}{dx}(x^2) = 2x$.

  1. $\dfrac{dy}{dx}$ is called the **derivative** of y with respect to x.

  2. $f'(x)$ is called the **gradient function** of the curve $y = f(x)$.

  3. $\dfrac{d}{dx}(x^2) = 2x$ means if you differentiate x^2 with respect to x, the result is $2x$.

- **Rules for differentiation**

  The rule for differentiating power functions is:

  If $y = x^n$, then $\dfrac{dy}{dx} = nx^{n-1}$.

  You also need to know and be able to use the following two rules:

  Scalar multiple rule: $\qquad \dfrac{d}{dx}[kf(x)] = k\dfrac{d}{dx}[f(x)]$

  Addition/subtraction rule: $\dfrac{d}{dx}[f(x) \pm g(x)] = \dfrac{d}{dx}[f(x)] \pm \dfrac{d}{dx}[g(x)]$

WORKED EXAMPLE 1

$y = \dfrac{2 - x^2}{\sqrt{x}}$, find $\dfrac{dy}{dx}$ when $x = 4$.

Answer

$y = \dfrac{2 - x^2}{\sqrt{x}}$

$y = \dfrac{2}{\sqrt{x}} - \dfrac{x^2}{\sqrt{x}}$

$y = 2x^{-\frac{1}{2}} - x^{\frac{3}{2}}$ Write in index form.

$\dfrac{dy}{dx} = 2 \times -\dfrac{1}{2} \times x^{-\frac{3}{2}} - \dfrac{3}{2} \times x^{\frac{1}{2}}$

$\dfrac{dy}{dx} = -x^{-\frac{3}{2}} - \dfrac{3}{2}x^{\frac{1}{2}}$

$x = 4 : \dfrac{dy}{dx} = -(4)^{-\frac{3}{2}} - \dfrac{3}{2}(2)^{\frac{1}{2}}$

$= -\dfrac{1}{8} - 3$

$= -\dfrac{25}{8}$

Exercise 12.1

1 Differentiate with respect to x.

a x^7 b x^9 c x^{-2} d x^{-1}

e $\dfrac{3}{x}$ f $\dfrac{1}{2x^5}$ g $\sqrt[3]{x^2}$ h $\sqrt{x^3}$

i $x^{-\frac{1}{2}}$ j $x^{\frac{-2}{3}}$ k $\sqrt[3]{x^4}$ l $\dfrac{1}{2\sqrt{x}}$

m x^0 n $2x^{\frac{1}{2}}$ o $\sqrt[3]{8x^6}$ p $2x^3 \times x^5$

q $\dfrac{1}{2}x^{\frac{1}{2}}$ r $\dfrac{3x^3}{2x^2}$ s $\dfrac{x^2}{2\sqrt{x}}$ t $\dfrac{x^3\sqrt{x}}{x^4}$

TIP

In this exercise take care with manipulating negative and fractional indices,

e.g. $\dfrac{-1}{2x^{\frac{1}{2}}} = -\dfrac{1}{2}x^{-\frac{1}{2}}$.

2 Differentiate with respect to x.

a $4x^3 - 6x + 2$ b $2x^4 - 3x^3 - 2x$ c $5 - 3x^{-1} + x$

d $3x^2 + 2x^{-1} - \dfrac{1}{x^3}$ e $4x - \dfrac{1}{x^2} - \dfrac{1}{\sqrt{4x}}$ f $\dfrac{2x + 5x^2}{2\sqrt{x}}$

g $\dfrac{3x^2 - 3}{2x}$ h $\dfrac{3x^2 - \sqrt{x}}{x^3}$ i $\dfrac{x^3 - x - 2}{\frac{1}{2}\sqrt{x}}$

j $2x^3(2x + 3)$ k $\dfrac{1}{2}x^{-3}(2x - 5)$ l $\dfrac{1}{\sqrt{x}}(x^3 - 2x)$

m $(2x - 1)^2$ n $(1 - 2x^2)^2$ o $(3x - 4)(2x + 1)$

3 Find the value of $\dfrac{dy}{dx}$ at the given point on the curve.

  a $y = 3 - 2x^2$ at the point where $x = 2$.

  b $y = 2x^3 - 2x$ at the point where $x = -2$.

  c $y = (x - 3)(x - 2)$ at the points where $y = 0$.

  d $y = 6x^3 - 2x^{-2} - x$ at the point where the graph crosses the y-axis.

  e $y = \dfrac{x^2 + 5}{x}$ at the point $(1, 6)$.

4 Find the coordinates of the points on the curve $y = x^3 - x^2 + 3$ at which the gradient is 0.

5 Find the gradient of the curve $y = \dfrac{2x - 4}{3x}$ at the point where the curve crosses the x-axis.

6 Find the gradient of the curve $y = 3x^3 - 3x^2 - x + 1$ at the point where the curve crosses the y-axis.

7 The line $y = 4x - 5$ intersects the curve $y = x^2 - 2x$ at two points. Find the gradient of $y = x^2 - 2x$ at these two points.

8 The gradient of $y = x^2 - 4x + 6$ at the point where $x = 3$ is the same as the gradient of $y = 8x - 3x^2$ at the point (p, q). Find the values of p and q.

9 Find the coordinates of the point on the curve $y = x^2 - 6x + 3$ where the tangent is parallel to the line $y = 2x - 1$.

10 Find the coordinates of the point on the curve $y = x - x^2$ where the tangent is parallel to the line $2y + x = 8$.

11 A curve has an equation $y = px^2 + q$ where p and q are constants. Given that the gradient of the curve at the point $(2, -2)$ is 3, find the values of p and q.

12 Given that the function $f(x) = x^3 + 5x^2 - x - 4$ find

  a $f'(-2)$ **b**   the values of a such that $f'(a) = 56$.

13 $f(x) = \dfrac{1}{3}x^3 - \dfrac{1}{2}x^2 - 6x$

  a   Find $f'(x)$.

  b   Find the range of values of x for which $f'(x) > 0$.

12.2 The chain rule

  REMINDER

- The chain rule is used when finding the derivative of a composite function such as $(2x + 5)^7$.

- It is best remembered as $\dfrac{dy}{dx} = \dfrac{dy}{du} \times \dfrac{du}{dx}$.

WORKED EXAMPLE 2

$y = (2x + 5)^7$, find $\dfrac{dy}{dx}$.

Answer

$u = 2x + 5 \quad \dfrac{du}{dx} = 2$ Define u.

$y = u^7 \quad\quad \dfrac{dy}{du} = 7u^6$

$\dfrac{dy}{dx} = \dfrac{dy}{du} \times \dfrac{du}{dx}$ Apply the chain rule.

$\dfrac{dy}{dx} = 7u^6 \times 2$

$\dfrac{dy}{dx} = 14u^6$

$\dfrac{dy}{dx} = 14(2x + 5)^6$ Write $\dfrac{dy}{dx}$ in terms of x.

Exercise 12.2

1 Differentiate with respect to x.

a $(3x + 2)^4$ **b** $(2x - 3)^5$ **c** $(1 - 4x)^7$

d $\left(\dfrac{1}{3}x - 3\right)^6$ **e** $\dfrac{(3x + 1)^3}{6}$ **f** $12(x - 1)^5$

g $4(3 - 2x)^3$ **h** $-\dfrac{3}{2}(2x - 5)^4$ **i** $(3x^2 + 2)^3$

j $(1 - 2x^3)^{-7}$ **k** $(x^2 - 2x)^3$ **l** $\left(x^2 + \dfrac{4}{x}\right)^3$

2 Differentiate with respect to x.

a $\dfrac{1}{(x - 5)}$ **b** $\dfrac{4}{(2x + 1)}$ **c** $\dfrac{6}{(2 - 4x)}$

d $\dfrac{12}{(3x^2 - 2)}$ **e** $\dfrac{1}{(1 + \sqrt{x})}$ **f** $\dfrac{1}{(x - 4)^3}$

g $\dfrac{3}{\sqrt{5x - 2}}$ **h** $\dfrac{1}{2(3 - 2x)^2}$

3 Differentiate with respect to x.

a $\sqrt{2x + 2}$ **b** $\sqrt{1 - 5x}$ **c** $\sqrt{2x^2 + 1}$

d $\sqrt{x^3 - 4x}$ **e** $\sqrt[3]{3x - 2}$ **f** $4\sqrt{2x + 5}$

g $\dfrac{1}{\sqrt{2x + 1}}$ **h** $\dfrac{-4}{\sqrt[3]{1 - 3x}}$

4 Find the gradient of the curve $y = (3x + 5)^3$ at the point $(1, 512)$.

5 Find the gradient of the curve $y = \dfrac{1}{1 + x^2}$ at the point where the curve crosses the y-axis.

6 Find the gradient of the curve $y = 2x + \dfrac{4}{3 - 2x}$ at the points where the curve crosses the x-axis.

7 Given that $y = \sqrt[4]{x^3 + 8}$ find the value of $\dfrac{dy}{dx}$ when $x = 2$.

8 Given that $y = \sqrt{x^3 + 1}$, show that $\dfrac{dy}{dx} > 0$ for all $x > -1$.

9 Given that $\dfrac{1}{3x - 1} + \dfrac{1}{(3x - 1)^2}$ find the exact value of $\dfrac{dy}{dx}$ when $x = 2$.

12.3 The product rule

REMINDER

- To differentiate the product of two functions you can use the **product rule**:

$$\frac{d}{dx}(uv) = u\frac{dv}{dx} + v\frac{du}{dx}$$

- It is easier to remember this rule as:

'(first function × derivative of second function) + (second function × derivative of first function)'

WORKED EXAMPLE 3

$y = 4x^3(x^4 + 2x)$, find $\dfrac{dy}{dx}$.

Answer

$u = 4x^3,\ v = x^4 + 2x$ \qquad\qquad Define u and v.

$\dfrac{dy}{dx} = (4x^3)\dfrac{d}{dx}(x^4 + 2x) + (x^4 + 2x)\dfrac{d}{dx}(4x^3)$ \qquad $\dfrac{d}{dx}(uv) = u\dfrac{dv}{dx} + v\dfrac{du}{dx}$

$\quad = (4x^3)(4x^3 + 2) + (x^4 + 2x)(12x^2)$

$\quad = 16x^6 + 8x^3 + 12x^6 + 24x^3$

$\quad = 28x^6 + 32x^3$

Exercise 12.3

1 Use the product rule to differentiate each of the following with respect to x.

  a $x(2x + 3)$ **b** $2x(x - 5)$ **c** $2x(x + 1)^3$

  d $3x^2(1 - x)^3$ **e** $x^2\sqrt{x + 3}$ **f** $(x + 2)\sqrt{x + 1}$

  g $2x^2\sqrt{2x - 3}$ **h** $2\sqrt{x}\left(1 - x^2\right)^2$ **i** $(3x + 2)\left(x^2 - 1\right)$

  j $(2x - 4)(x + 3)^3$ **k** $(x - 1)^2(x + 1)^2$ **l** $(3x + 1)^2(2x - 3)$

2 Find the gradient of the curve $y = (x + 1)^2\sqrt{x + 3}$ at the point $(1, 8)$.

3 Find the gradient of the curve $y = (2x - 1)^2(x + 1)^2$ at the point where $x = 1$.

4 Find the gradient of the curve $y = (x - 3)(x + 1)^2$ at the points where the curve meets the x-axis.

5 Find the x-coordinates of the points on the curve $y = (2x - 1)^3(x + 2)^2$ where the gradient is zero.

6 Find the x-coordinate of the point on the curve $y = (x + 1)\sqrt{9 - x}$ where the gradient is zero.

7 A curve has equation $y = x^{\frac{3}{2}}(x - 3)^3$ $x > 0$. Show that $\dfrac{dy}{dx} = kx^{\frac{1}{2}}(x - 3)^2$ where k is a constant to be found.

8 If $y = \sqrt{x}\,(3 - x)^2$, find

a $\dfrac{dy}{dx}$

b the x-coordinates of all points on the curve where the tangent is horizontal.

12.4 The quotient rule

REMINDER

- If $y = \dfrac{u}{v}$ where u and v are two functions of x then:

$$\dfrac{d}{dx}\left(\dfrac{u}{v}\right) = \dfrac{v\dfrac{du}{dx} - u\dfrac{dv}{dx}}{v^2}$$

- It is easier to remember this rule as:

$$\dfrac{(\text{denominator} \times \text{derivative of numerator}) - (\text{numerator} \times \text{derivative of denominator})}{(\text{denominator})^2}$$

WORKED EXAMPLE 4

Find the gradient of the curve $y = \dfrac{4x + 2}{x + 5}$ at the point $(1, 1)$.

Answer

$u = 4x + 2,\ v = x + 5$

$$\dfrac{d}{dx}\left(\dfrac{u}{v}\right) = \dfrac{v\dfrac{du}{dx} - u\dfrac{dv}{dx}}{v^2}$$

$$= \dfrac{(x + 5)(4) - (4x + 2)(1)}{(x + 5)^2}$$

$$= \dfrac{4x + 20 - 4x - 2}{(x + 5)^2}$$

$$= \dfrac{18}{(x + 5)^2}$$

When $x = 1$, $\dfrac{dy}{dx} = \dfrac{18}{(1 + 5)^2} = \dfrac{1}{2}$.

Exercise 12.4

1 Use the quotient rule to differentiate each of the following with respect to x.

a $\dfrac{1 - 3x}{5 + x}$

b $\dfrac{4x + 2}{2x + 5}$

c $\dfrac{3x - 2}{2x + 4}$

d $\dfrac{(x + 1)^2}{x + 3}$

e $\dfrac{x^2 + 1}{x^2 - 2}$

f $\dfrac{\sqrt{x}}{x - 4}$

g $\dfrac{\sqrt{x + 1}}{x^2}$

h $\dfrac{x^2 - 4}{2x + 1}$

2 Find the gradient of the curve $y = \dfrac{2x - 5}{x - 3}$ at the point $(2, 1)$.

3 Find the coordinates of the points on the curve $y = \dfrac{x^2 - 3x + 1}{x + 2}$ where the gradient is zero.

4 Find the gradient of the curve $y = \dfrac{6x - 6}{2x + 3}$ at the point where the curve crosses the y-axis.

5 Given $f(x) = \dfrac{2\sqrt{x}}{1 - x}$ find $f'(4)$.

6 Find the gradient of the tangent drawn at $x = -1$ on the curve whose equation is $y = \dfrac{x + 3}{x^2 - 4x + 1}$.

7 Find the coordinates of the points on the curve $y = \dfrac{x - 1}{x^2 + 3}$ where the gradient is zero.

8 Find the coordinates of the two points on the curve $y = \dfrac{x}{1 + x}$ where the gradient is $\dfrac{1}{9}$.

12.5 Tangents and normals

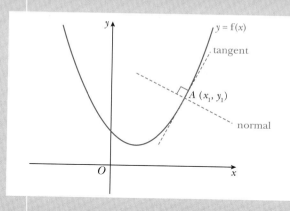

- The line perpendicular to the tangent at the point A is called the **normal** at A.
- If the value of $\dfrac{dy}{dx}$ at the point (x_1, y_1) is m, then the equation of the tangent is given by:

  $y - y_1 = m(x - x_1)$

- The normal at the point (x_1, y_1) is perpendicular to the tangent, so the gradient of the normal is $-\dfrac{1}{m}$ and the equation of the normal is given by:

  $y - y_1 = -\dfrac{1}{m}(x - x_1), m \neq 0$

WORKED EXAMPLE 5

$y = x^2(x-1)^5$, find

a the equation of the tangent to the curve at the point $(2, 4)$

b the equation of the normal to the curve at the point $(2, 4)$.

Answers

a $\dfrac{dy}{dx} = x^2 \times \dfrac{d}{dx}\left((x-1)^5\right) + (x-1)^5 \times \dfrac{d}{dx}(x^2)$ $\qquad \dfrac{d}{dx}(uv) = u\dfrac{dv}{dx} + v\dfrac{du}{dx}$

$\dfrac{dy}{dx} = x^2 \times 5(x-1)^4 + (x-1)^5 \times 2x$

$\dfrac{dy}{dx} = 5x^2(x-1)^4 + 2x(x-1)^5$

When $x = 2$, $\dfrac{dy}{dx} = 24$.

Gradient of the tangent at $(2, 4) = 24$.

Equation of tangent: $y - 4 = 24(x-2)$

$\qquad\qquad\qquad\qquad y = 24x - 44$

b Gradient of the normal at $(2, 4) = -\dfrac{1}{24}$.

Equation of tangent: $y - 4 = -\dfrac{1}{24}(x-2)$

$\qquad\qquad\qquad\qquad y = \dfrac{49}{12} - \dfrac{x}{24}$

Exercise 12.5

1 Find the equation of the tangent to the curve at the given value of x.

a $y = x - 2x^2 + 3$ at $x = 2$ 　　　　b $y = 1 + \sqrt{x}$ at $x = 4$

c $y = x^3 - 5x$ at $x = 1$ 　　　　　　d $y = \dfrac{3}{x} - \dfrac{1}{x^2}$ at $x = -1$

e $y = (x+1)(3x-1)^3$ at $x = 1$ 　　f $y = \dfrac{x^2}{2x+1}$ at $x = -2$

2 Find the equation of the normal to the curve at the given value of x.

a $y = x^3 - 5x + 2$ at $x = -2$ 　　　b $y = 3x^2 - 4x + 1$ at $x = 2$

c $y = 2x^4 - 4x^2 - 2x$ at $x = -1$ 　d $y = \dfrac{5}{\sqrt{x}} - \sqrt{x}$ at $x = 1$

e $y = (3x-1)(x-2)^3$ at $x = 2$ 　　f $y = \dfrac{2x+1}{3x-2}$ at $x = 3$

3 Find where the tangent to the curve $y = -x^3 + 2x^2 + 1$, at the point where $x = -1$, meets the curve again.

4 Find the equations of the horizontal tangents to $y = 2x^3 + 3x^2 - 12x + 1$.

5 The curve $y = 2\sqrt{x} + \dfrac{1}{\sqrt{x}}$ has a horizontal tangent at one point. Find the coordinates of this point of contact.

6 A curve has equation $y = (2x - 3)^5$.

   a Find the equation of the tangent to the curve at $A(1, -1)$.

   b Given that the equation of the tangent at another point B on the curve has the same gradient, find the coordinates of B.

7 The tangent to $y = \dfrac{px + q}{\sqrt{x}}$ at the point where $x = 1$ is $y = 2x - 1$. Find p and q.

8 Find the equation of the tangent to the curve $y = x^2 - 2x$ that is perpendicular to the line $2y - x + 1 = 0$.

9 The normal to the curve $y = px^{\frac{1}{2}} + qx$ at $x = 1$ has gradient 1. It also intersects the y-axis at $(0, -4)$. Find the values of p and q.

12.6 Small increments and approximations

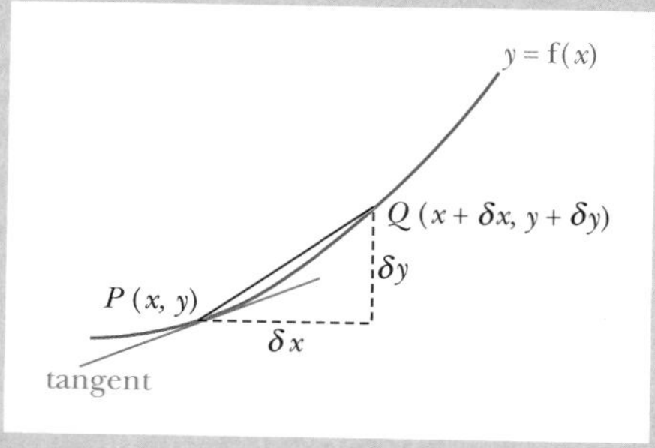

- In the diagram the gradient of the tangent at the point P is $\dfrac{dy}{dx}$.
- The gradient of the chord PQ is $\dfrac{\delta y}{\delta x}$.
- If P and Q are sufficiently close then $\dfrac{\delta y}{\delta x} \approx \dfrac{dy}{dx}$.

WORKED EXAMPLE 6

Variables x and y are connected by the equation $y = 3x^2 - 4x$.

a Find, in terms of p, the approximate change in y as x increases from 5 to $5 + p$, where p is small.

b Find the approximate change in y as x increases from 3 to 3.01.

Answers

a $\dfrac{dy}{dx} = 6x - 4$

When $x = 5$, $\dfrac{dy}{dx} = 6(5) - 4 = 26$.

For small values of p, $\dfrac{\delta y}{\delta x} \approx \dfrac{dy}{dx}$.

$\dfrac{\delta y}{p} = 26$

$\delta y = 26p$

b When $x = 3$, $\dfrac{dy}{dx} = 6(3) - 4 = 14$.

For small values of δx, $\dfrac{\delta y}{\delta x} \approx \dfrac{dy}{dx}$.

$\dfrac{\delta y}{0.01} = 14$

$\delta y = 0.14$

Exercise 12.6

1 Variables x and y are connected by the equation $y = 3x - \dfrac{8}{x^2}$.

Find the approximate change in y as x increases from 3 to 3.02.

2 Variables x and y are connected by the equation $y = x + \dfrac{1}{x}$.

Find the approximate change in y as x increases from 2 to 2.04.

3 Variables x and y are connected by the equation $y = (3x - 2)^3$.

Find, in terms of p, the approximate change in y as x increases from 4 to $4 + p$, where p is small.

4 A curve has equation $y = \dfrac{3 + x}{2x - 1}$.

Find, in terms of p, the approximate change in y as x increases from 5 to $5 + p$, where p is small.

5 Find an approximate value for the increase in the volume of a sphere when the radius increases from 5 to 5.1 cm.

6 A solid circular cylinder has a base radius 5 cm and a height 12.5 cm. Find the approximate increase in the surface area of the cylinder when the radius of the base increases to 5.05 cm.

7

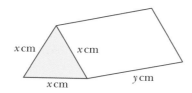

The triangular prism shown has an equilateral triangle as its cross section.

a If its volume V is 420 cm^3 express y in terms of x.

b Find in terms of of p, the approximate change in V as x increases from 3 to $3 + p$, where p is small. State whether the change is an increase or decrease.

12.7 Rates of change

> **REMINDER**
>
> • When two variables x and y both vary with a third variable t, the three variables can be connected using the chain rule:
>
> $$\frac{dy}{dt} = \frac{dy}{dx} \times \frac{dx}{dt}$$
>
> • You may also need to use the rule that $\dfrac{dy}{dx} = \dfrac{1}{\frac{dx}{dy}}$.

WORKED EXAMPLE 7

Variables x and y are connected by the equation $y = 2x^3 + 2x$.

Given that x increases at a rate of 0.02 units per second, find the rate of change of y when $x = 3$.

Answer

$$\frac{dy}{dt} = \frac{dy}{dx} \times \frac{dx}{dt}$$

$$= \left(6x^2 + 2\right) \times 0.02$$

$$= 0.12x^2 + 0.04$$

When $x = 3$, $\dfrac{dy}{dt} = 0.12 \times (3)^2 + 0.04 = 1.12$ units per second.

Exercise 12.7

1 Variables x and y are connected by the equation $y = \dfrac{2x}{\sqrt{x + 1}}$.

Given that x increases at a rate of 0.2 units per second, find the rate of change of y when $x = 8$.

2 Variables x and y are connected by the equation $y = (2x + 1)(3x + 5)^2$.

Given that x increases at a rate of 0.5 units per second, find the rate of change of y when $x = -2$.

3 Variables x and y are connected by the equation $y = \dfrac{\sqrt{x}}{3x + 1}$.

Given that y increases at a rate of 0.2 units per second, find the rate of change of x when $x = 1$.

TIP

Be careful!

4 Variables x and y are connected by the equation $y = 2x^3(x+3)^2$.

Given that x increases at a rate of 3 units per second, find the rate of increase of y when $x = -1$.

5 Variables x and y are connected by the equation $y = \dfrac{4x+5}{1-2x}$.

Given that x increases at a rate of 0.01 units per second, find the rate of change of y when $y = 2$.

6 Variables x and y are connected by the equation $\dfrac{1}{y} = \dfrac{1}{4} - \dfrac{3}{x}$.

Given that x increases at a rate of 0.02 units per second, find the rate of change of y when $x = 8$.

7 Ink is dropped onto paper forming a circular stain which increases in area at a rate of $2.5\,\text{cm}^2\text{s}^{-1}$. Find the rate at which the radius is changing when the area of the stain is $16\pi\,\text{cm}^2$.

8 A spherical balloon is increasing in size at a rate of $1.5\,\text{cm}^3\text{s}^{-1}$. Find the rate of increase of the radius when the volume of the balloon is $56\,\text{cm}^3$.

9 The length of the side of a cube is increasing at a rate of $0.5\,\text{cm}\,\text{s}^{-1}$.

When the length of the edge is $20\,\text{cm}$, what is

a the rate of increase of the surface area?

b the rate of increase of the volume?

10 A circular stain is spreading so that its radius is increasing at a constant rate of $4\,\text{cm}^2\text{s}^{-1}$.

Find the rate at which the area is increasing when the radius is $20\,\text{cm}$.

11 A spherical snowball melts so that its volume decreases at a rate of $2\,\text{cm}^3\text{min}^{-1}$. How fast is the radius changing when the diameter of the snowball is $10\,\text{cm}$?

12 The surface area of a cube is increasing at a rate of $10\,\text{cm}^2\text{s}^{-1}$. Find the rate of increase of volume of the cube when its edge is $12\,\text{cm}$.

12.8 Second derivatives

 REMINDER

- If you differentiate y with respect to x you obtain $\dfrac{\mathrm{d}y}{\mathrm{d}x}$.

- $\dfrac{\mathrm{d}y}{\mathrm{d}x}$ is called the **first derivative** of y with respect to x.

- If you differentiate $\dfrac{\mathrm{d}y}{\mathrm{d}x}$ with respect to x you obtain $\dfrac{\mathrm{d}}{\mathrm{d}x}\left(\dfrac{\mathrm{d}y}{\mathrm{d}x}\right) = \dfrac{\mathrm{d}^2 y}{\mathrm{d}x^2}$.

- $\dfrac{\mathrm{d}^2 y}{\mathrm{d}x^2}$ is called the **second derivative** of y with respect to x. (This can be written $f''(x)$.)

WORKED EXAMPLE 8

Find $\dfrac{d^2y}{dx^2}$ for $y = 3x^3 + \sqrt{x}$.

Answer

$y = 3x^3 + x^{\frac{1}{2}}$ Write in index form.

$\dfrac{dy}{dx} = 9x^2 + \dfrac{1}{2}x^{-\frac{1}{2}}$ Find the first derivative.

$\dfrac{d^2y}{dx^2} = 18x - \dfrac{1}{4}x^{-\frac{3}{2}}$

Exercise 12.8

1 Find the $\dfrac{d^2y}{dx^2}$ for each of the following functions.

   a $y = 3x^4 - 3x + 7$ **b** $y = 0.5x^4 + \dfrac{3}{x^3} - x$ **c** $y = 4\sqrt{x} - \dfrac{3}{x}$

   d $y = (1 - 5x)^5$ **e** $y = \sqrt{5x - 2}$ **f** $y = \dfrac{5}{\sqrt{2x + 4}}$

2 Find the $\dfrac{d^2y}{dx^2}$ for each of the following functions.

   a $y = 2x(4 - x)^3$ **b** $y = \dfrac{1 - 3x}{x^{\frac{1}{2}}}$ **c** $y = \dfrac{2x + 1}{3x + 1}$

   d $y = \dfrac{x^2 + 2}{(x - 1)^2}$ **e** $y = \dfrac{1}{x} + \dfrac{1}{x^2}$ **f** $y = \sqrt{4x + 3}$

3 Given that $f(x) = 2x^3 + 3x^2 - 2x - 1$, find

   a $f(-1)$ **b** $f'(-1)$ **c** $f''(-1)$.

4 A curve has equation $f(x) = 2x^4 - 4x^3 - 9x^2 + 4x + 7$.
   Find the values of x for which $f''(x) = 0$.

5 Given that $y = \dfrac{1}{x^2 + 4}$, find the value of $\dfrac{d^2y}{dx^2}$ at $x = 1$.

6 $x^3y = 2$, find $\dfrac{d^2y}{dx^2}$ when $x = 1$.

7 If $y = 4x^3 - 6x^2 - 9x + 1$, find

   a $\dfrac{dy}{dx}$

   b   the values of $\dfrac{d^2y}{dx^2}$ when the gradient is zero.

12.9 Stationary points

Stationary points (turning points) of a function $y = f(x)$ occur when $\dfrac{dy}{dx} = 0$.

- First derivative test for maximum and minimum points.

  At a maximum point
  - $\dfrac{dy}{dx} = 0$
  - the gradient is positive to the left of the maximum and negative to the right.

  At a minimum point
  - $\dfrac{dy}{dx} = 0$
  - the gradient is negative to the left of the minimum and positive to the right.

- Second derivative test for maximum and minimum points.

  - $\dfrac{dy}{dx} = 0$ and
    - $\dfrac{d^2 y}{dx^2} < 0$, then the point is a maximum point
    - $\dfrac{d^2 y}{dx^2} > 0$, then the point is a minimum point

WORKED EXAMPLE 9

Determine the nature of the stationary points of the curve $y = 2x^3 + 6x^2 - 48x - 10$.

Answers

$\dfrac{dy}{dx} = 6x^2 + 12x - 48$ 　　　　　Stationary values occur when $\dfrac{dy}{dx} = 0$.

$\quad 0 = 6x^2 + 12x - 48$

$\quad 0 = x^2 + 2x - 8$

$\quad 0 = (x + 4)(x - 2)$

$\quad x = -4 \text{ or } x = 2$

When $x = -4$, $y = 2(-4)^3 + 6(-4)^2 - 48(-4) - 10 = 150$.

When $x = 2$, $y = 2(2)^3 + 6(2)^2 - 48(2) - 10 = -66$.

The stationary points are $(-4, 150)$ and $(2, -66)$.

$\dfrac{d^2 y}{dx^2} = 12x + 12$

When $x = -4$, $\dfrac{d^2 y}{dx^2} = -36$ which is < 0.

When $x = 2$, $\dfrac{d^2 y}{dx^2} = 36$ which is > 0.

So $(-4, 150)$ is a maximum point and $(2, -66)$ is a minimum point.

Exercise 12.9

1 Find the coordinates of the stationary points on each of the following curves and determine the nature of each of the stationary points.

   a $y = x^2 - 2x + 5$ **b** $y = 3(3 + x)(2x - 1)$

   c $y = -x^3 + 6x^2 - 9x$ **d** $y = (x - 5)^2$

   e $y = 3 + 15x - 6x^2 - x^3$ **f** $y = 3 + x - x^2$

2 Find the coordinates of the stationary points on each of the following curves and determine the nature of each of the stationary points.

   a $y = \sqrt{x} + \dfrac{2}{\sqrt{x}}$ **b** $y = x^2 + \dfrac{16}{x}$ **c** $y = \dfrac{1}{x} - \dfrac{3}{x^2}$

   d $y = \dfrac{12x^2 - 1}{x^3}$ **e** $y = \dfrac{x}{1 + x^2}$ **f** $y = x^{\frac{1}{3}}(4 - x)$

3 The equation of a curve is $y = \dfrac{2x - 4}{x + 3}$.

   Find $\dfrac{dy}{dx}$ and hence explain why the curve has no turning points.

4 The curve $y = 2x^3 + ax^2 - 24x + 1$ has a maximum point at $x = -4$.

   Find the value of a.

5 The curve $y = x^3 + ax + b$ has a stationary point at $(-2, 3)$.

   a   Find the value of a and the value of b.

   b   Determine the nature of the stationary point $(-2, 3)$.

   c   Find the coordinates of the other stationary point on the curve and determine the nature of this stationary point.

6 A curve has equation $y = 2x^3 + 3x^2 + 4x - 5$. Prove that this curve has no stationary points.

12.10 Practical maximum and minimum problems

WORKED EXAMPLE 10

The sum of two numbers x and y is 12.

a   Express y in terms of x.

b   Given that $P = xy$, write down an expression for P, in terms of x.

c   Find the maximum value of P.

Answers

a $x + y = 12$

       $y = 12 - x$

b $P = xy$

      $= x(12 - x)$

      $= 12x - x^2$

c $\dfrac{dP}{dx} = 12 - 2x$ Stationary values occur when $\dfrac{dP}{dx} = 0$.

     $0 = 12 - 2x$

     $2x = 12$

     $x = 6$

     $P = 12(6) - (6)^2$ Find the value of P when $x = 6$.

       $= 36$

     $\dfrac{d^2P}{dx^2} = -2$ so the stationary value is a maximum.

Exercise 12.10

1 A rectangular box without a lid is made from a sheet of cardboard $25\,\text{cm}$ by $40\,\text{cm}$ by cutting out squares from the corners and folding up the sides. If the squares are side $x\,\text{cm}$,

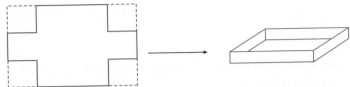

   a write down the volume of the box V

   b find $\dfrac{\mathrm{d}V}{\mathrm{d}x}$

   c what size squares must be cut in order to produce a box of maximum volume?

2 The diagram shows a rectangular animal enclosure of area $100\,\text{m}^2$. It has a fence on three of its sides and a wall on its fourth side. The total length of the fence is L metres.

   a If the length of the shorter side of the enclosure is $x\,\text{m}$, show that the total length of fencing needed is $L = \dfrac{100}{x} + 2x$.

   b Find the minimum value of L and the value of x when this occurs.

3 A running track has two straight sections of length $y\,\text{m}$ and two semi-circular ends of radius $x\,\text{m}$. The perimeter of the track is $400\,\text{m}$.

   a Show that $y = 200 - \pi x$.

   b Show that the area inside the track is $A = 400x - \pi x^2$.

   c What values of x and y give the maximum area?

4 A rectangle with width $x\,\text{cm}$ is drawn inside a semi circle whose radius is $6\,\text{cm}$.

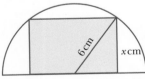

   a Show that the area of the rectangle is $2x\sqrt{36 - x^2}\ \text{cm}^2$.

   b Calculate the maximum value of this area.

5 A rectangle is inscribed in a parabola whose equation is $y = a - x^2$ and the x-axis as shown.

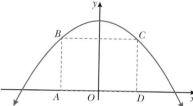

   a If $OD = x$ cm, show that the rectangle $ABCD$ has an area $A = 2ax - 2x^3$.

   b If the area of $ABCD$ is a maximum when $AD = 2\sqrt{3}$, find a.

6 The daily profit Y thousand dollars of an oil company is given by the formula $Y = 5x - 0.02x^2$, where x is the number of barrels produced.

How many barrels will give a maximum profit and what is the maximum profit?

7 The volume of the solid cuboid is $13\,500\,\text{cm}^3$ and the surface area is $A\,\text{cm}^2$.

   a Express y in terms of x.

   b Show that $A = 6x^2 + \dfrac{36000}{x}$.

   c Find the maximum value of A (to 3 sf) and state the value of x for which this occurs.

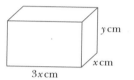

8 An open cylindrical waste bin of radius r cm, height h cm and capacity $V\,\text{cm}^3$, has a surface area $5000\,\text{cm}^2$.

   a Show that $V = \dfrac{1}{2}r\left(5000 - \pi r^2\right)$.

   b Calculate the maximum possible capacity of the bin.

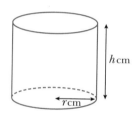

Summary

Rules of differentiation

Power rule:

If $y = x^n$, then $\dfrac{dy}{dx} = nx^{n-1}$.

Scalar multiple rule:

$$\frac{d}{dx}\left[k f(x)\right] = k \frac{d}{dx}\left[f(x)\right]$$

Addition/subtraction rule:

$$\frac{d}{dx}\left[f(x) \pm g(x)\right] = \frac{d}{dx}\left[f(x)\right] \pm \frac{d}{dx}\left[g(x)\right]$$

Chain rule:

$$\frac{dy}{dx} = \frac{dy}{du} \times \frac{du}{dx}$$

Product rule:

$$\frac{d}{dx}(uv) = u\frac{dv}{dx} + v\frac{du}{dx}$$

Quotient rule:

$$\frac{d}{dx}\left(\frac{u}{v}\right) = \frac{v\dfrac{du}{dx} - u\dfrac{dv}{dx}}{v^2}$$

Tangents and normals

If the value of $\dfrac{dy}{dx}$ at the point (x_1, y_1) is m, then:

- the equation of the tangent is given by $y - y_1 = m(x - x_1)$

- the equation of the normal is given by $y - y_1 = -\dfrac{1}{m}(x - x_1)$

Small increments and approximations

If δx and δy are sufficiently small then $\dfrac{\delta y}{\delta x} \approx \dfrac{dy}{dx}$.

Stationary points

Stationary points (turning points) of a function $y = f(x)$ occur when $\dfrac{dy}{dx} = 0$.

First derivative test for maximum and minimum points

At a maximum point:

- $\dfrac{dy}{dx} = 0$
- the gradient is positive to the left of the maximum and negative to the right.

At a minimum point:

- $\dfrac{dy}{dx} = 0$
- the gradient is negative to the left of the minimum and positive to the right.

Second derivative test for maximum and minimum points

If $\dfrac{dy}{dx} = 0$ and
$$\begin{cases} \dfrac{d^2y}{dx^2} < 0, \text{ then the point is a maximum point} \\[2ex] \dfrac{d^2y}{dx^2} > 0, \text{ then the point is a minimum point} \end{cases}$$

Exercise 12.11

1 $f(x) = 54x - 2x^3$

    a Find $f'(x)$.

    b Find the range of values of x for which $f'(x) < 0$.

2 Find the equations of the normals to the curve $y = x^3 - 3x^2 + 4$ which are perpendicular to the line $y = 24x + 1$.

3 The line joining $P(2, 4)$ to $Q(0, 8)$, is a tangent to $y = \dfrac{a}{(x+2)^2}$. Find a.

4 A curve has equation $y = \sqrt{x}\,(2 - 3x)^3$.

    Find, in terms of p, the approximate change in y as x increases from 1 to $1 + p$, where p is small.

5 x and y are connected by the rule: $y = (2x + 3)(x + 2)$.

    When x is increased slightly from an initial value of 7, y increased by 0.7. Find the approximate increase in x that caused this increase in y.

6 A hollow cone is placed with its vertex pointing downwards. Water is poured into it at a rate of $5\,\text{cm}^3\text{s}^{-1}$. After t seconds, the volume of water in the container, $V\,\text{cm}^3$, is given by $V = \dfrac{1}{9}\pi x^3$, where $x\,$cm is the height of the water in the container.

    Find the rate at which the depth of the water in the cone is increasing when the depth is $10\,$cm.

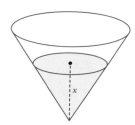

7 The curve $y = ax + \dfrac{b}{x^2}$ has a stationary point at $(1, 3)$.

    a Find the value of a and the value of b.

    b Determine the nature of the stationary point $(1, 3)$.

8 The total profit y in thousands of dollars generated by a company selling x items is given by the formula $y = \dfrac{200\sqrt{x}}{100 + x}$.

    Calculate the value of x which gives the maximum profit and find this maximum profit.

9 A triangular area ABC, next to a river, is fenced off as shown.

    a If $AB = BC = 60\,$m and $AC = 2x\,$m, show that the area A of triangle ABC is $A = x\sqrt{3600 - x^2}$.

    b Find the value of x when the area is a maximum.

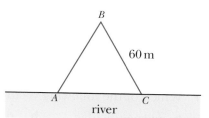

10 A 200 cm length strip of metal is placed around the outside edge of a window which is the shape of a rectangle with a semi-circular top.

    a Using the dimensions shown on the diagram, show that $y = 100 - x - \dfrac{\pi}{2}x$.

    b Find the area of the window in terms of x only.

    c Find the dimensions of the window which gives the maximum area.

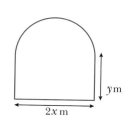

Chapter 13: Vectors

This section will show you how to:

- use vectors in any form, e.g. $\begin{pmatrix} a \\ b \end{pmatrix}$, $\overrightarrow{AB}$, **p**, $a\mathbf{i} + b\mathbf{j}$
- use position vectors and unit vectors
- find the magnitude of a vector; add and subtract vectors and multiply vectors by scalars
- compose and resolve velocities.

13.1 Further vector notation

Exercise 13.1

1 Write each vector in the form $a\mathbf{i} + b\mathbf{j}$.

  a $\overrightarrow{AB}$ **b** $\overrightarrow{AC}$ **c** $\overrightarrow{AD}$

  d $\overrightarrow{AE}$ **e** $\overrightarrow{BE}$ **f** $\overrightarrow{DE}$

  g $\overrightarrow{EA}$ **h** $\overrightarrow{DB}$ **i** $\overrightarrow{DC}$

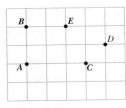

> **TIP**
> **i** is a vector of length 1 unit in the positive *x*-direction and **j** is a vector of length 1 unit in the positive *y*-direction.

2 Find the magnitude of each of these vectors.

  a $-3\mathbf{i}$ **b** $8\mathbf{i} + 6\mathbf{j}$ **c** $10\mathbf{i} - 24\mathbf{j}$ **d** $-4\mathbf{i} - 3\mathbf{j}$

  e $-7\mathbf{i} + 2\mathbf{j}$ **f** $5\mathbf{i} - 8\mathbf{j}$ **g** $-3\mathbf{i} + 3\mathbf{j}$ **h** $3\mathbf{i} - 6\mathbf{j}$

3 The vector $\overrightarrow{AB}$ has a magnitude of 30 units and is parallel to $3\mathbf{i} + 4\mathbf{j}$. Find $\overrightarrow{AB}$.

4 The vector $\overrightarrow{PQ}$ has a magnitude of 52 units and is parallel to $5\mathbf{i} + 12\mathbf{j}$. Find $\overrightarrow{PQ}$.

> **TIP**
> Remember: the magnitude (or modulus) of a vector $\overrightarrow{AB}$ is denoted by $\left| \overrightarrow{AB} \right|$ and is found using Pythagoras' theorem. Give your answers as exact values if necessary.

5 Find the unit vector in the direction of each of these vectors.

  a $9\mathbf{i} + 12\mathbf{j}$ **b** $10\mathbf{i} + 24\mathbf{j}$ **c** $-3\mathbf{i} - 4\mathbf{j}$ **d** $8\mathbf{i} - 5\mathbf{j}$

  e $4\mathbf{i} + 4\mathbf{j}$

6 **a** $4\mathbf{i} - 3\mathbf{j}$, **b** $-3\mathbf{i} + 2\mathbf{j}$ and **c** $= 5\mathbf{i}$

  Find **a** $2\mathbf{b}$,   **b** $2\mathbf{a} + \mathbf{b}$,   **c** $\frac{1}{2}\mathbf{a} - 3\mathbf{c}$,   **d** $\frac{1}{2}\mathbf{c} - \mathbf{a} - \mathbf{b}$.

> **TIP**
> A vector of length 1 unit is called a **unit vector**.

7 Which of the following vectors are

  a perpendicular   **b** parallel?

  A $\mathbf{i} + 2\mathbf{j}$ **B** $2\mathbf{i} + \mathbf{j}$ **C** $-\mathbf{i} + 2\mathbf{j}$ **D** $2\mathbf{i} - \mathbf{j}$

  E $\mathbf{i} - 2\mathbf{j}$ **F** $-2\mathbf{i} + \mathbf{j}$

8 Find the value of x given that these vectors are unit vectors.

  a $\begin{pmatrix} -0.5 \\ x \end{pmatrix}$ **b** $\begin{pmatrix} x \\ 1 \end{pmatrix}$ **c** $\begin{pmatrix} -\frac{1}{3} \\ x \end{pmatrix}$.

48

13.2 Position vectors

REMINDER

If two points A and B have position vectors **a** and **b**.

$\overrightarrow{AB}$ means the position vector of B relative to A.

$\overrightarrow{AB} = \overrightarrow{AO} + \overrightarrow{OB}$ or $\overrightarrow{AB} = -\mathbf{a} + \mathbf{b}$

WORKED EXAMPLE 1

If A is the point $(6, 4)$ and B is the point $(1, -7)$, find $\overrightarrow{AB}$.

Answer

$\overrightarrow{AB} = \overrightarrow{OB} - \overrightarrow{OA}$

$\quad = (\mathbf{i} - 7\mathbf{j}) - (6\mathbf{i} + 4\mathbf{j})$ collect **i**'s and **j**'s

$\overrightarrow{AB} = -5\mathbf{i} - 11\mathbf{j}$

Exercise 13.2

1 Find $\overrightarrow{BA}$, in the form $a\mathbf{i} + b\mathbf{j}$, for each of the following.

   a $A(3, 7)$ and $B(3, -4)$ **b** $A(0, -6)$ and $B(-2, -4)$ **c** $A(4, -3)$ and $B(-6, -2)$.

2 Given $\overrightarrow{BA} = \begin{pmatrix} 2 \\ -3 \end{pmatrix}$ and $\overrightarrow{BC} = \begin{pmatrix} -3 \\ 1 \end{pmatrix}$ find $\overrightarrow{AC}$.

3 If $\overrightarrow{AB} = \begin{pmatrix} -1 \\ 3 \end{pmatrix}$ and $\overrightarrow{CA} = \begin{pmatrix} 2 \\ -1 \end{pmatrix}$, find $\overrightarrow{CB}$.

4 The point A has position vector $-5\mathbf{i} + 3\mathbf{j}$ and B is a point such that $\overrightarrow{AB} = 7\mathbf{i} - \mathbf{j}$. Find the position vector of B.

5 The point A has position vector $3\mathbf{i} - 2\mathbf{j}$ and B is a point such that $\overrightarrow{BA} = 2\mathbf{i} - 3\mathbf{j}$. Find the position vector of B.

6 The point A has position vector $3\mathbf{i} + 2\mathbf{j}$ and the point B has position vector $\mathbf{i} + 3\mathbf{j}$. Find the position vector of the point which divides AB in the ratio $4:3$.

7 The points P, Q and R have position vectors $\mathbf{i} - \mathbf{j}$, $5\mathbf{i} - 3\mathbf{j}$ and $11\mathbf{i} - 6\mathbf{j}$ respectively. Show that that P, Q and R are collinear.

8 Given that $\mathbf{a} = 2\mathbf{i} + \lambda\mathbf{j}$ and $\mathbf{b} = \mu\mathbf{i} - 5\mathbf{j}$, find the values of λ and μ such that $2\mathbf{a} - \mathbf{b} = -3\mathbf{i} + 8\mathbf{j}$

9 O is the origin. The points X and Y have position vectors $\begin{pmatrix} 3 \\ 6 \end{pmatrix}$ and $\begin{pmatrix} -5 \\ 2 \end{pmatrix}$ respectively.

   Find

   a $\overrightarrow{XY}$

   b $\left| \overrightarrow{XY} \right|$

   c   the position vector of the midpoint of XY.

10 O is the origin, P is the point $(2, 5)$ and $\overrightarrow{PQ} = \begin{pmatrix} 3 \\ 6 \end{pmatrix}$. Find $\overrightarrow{OQ}$.

11 Which one of the following vectors represents a unit vector in the same direction as $\begin{pmatrix} -3 \\ 4 \end{pmatrix}$?

   a $\dfrac{-3}{5}\mathbf{i} + \dfrac{4}{5}\mathbf{j}$ **b** $\dfrac{3}{5}\mathbf{i} + \dfrac{4}{5}\mathbf{j}$ **c** $\dfrac{1}{5}\mathbf{i} + \dfrac{1}{5}\mathbf{j}$ **d** $\dfrac{3}{25}\mathbf{i} + \dfrac{-4}{25}\mathbf{j}$

13.3 Vector geometry

Exercise 13.3

1 ABC is a triangle.

M is the midpoint of AB.

N is the midpoint of AC.

$|\overrightarrow{NX}| = \dfrac{2}{3}|\overrightarrow{BC}|$

If $\overrightarrow{AC} = \mathbf{c}$ and $\overrightarrow{AB} = \mathbf{b}$,

   a write $\overrightarrow{BC}$ and $\overrightarrow{MN}$ in terms of $\mathbf{b}$ and $\mathbf{c}$

   b show that $\overrightarrow{NX} = \dfrac{2}{3}(\mathbf{c} - \mathbf{b})$

   c show that M, N and X lie on a straight line.

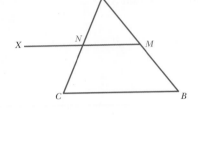

2 In the diagram, $\overrightarrow{AC} = \mathbf{p}$ and $\overrightarrow{AB} = \mathbf{q}$.

Y is the midpoint of AB.

The point X divides the line CB in the ratio $1 : 4$.

   a Express $\overrightarrow{CB}$, $\overrightarrow{CX}$ and $\overrightarrow{AX}$ in terms of $\mathbf{p}$ and $\mathbf{q}$.

   b Show that $\overrightarrow{YX} = \dfrac{4}{5}\mathbf{p} - \dfrac{3}{10}\mathbf{q}$.

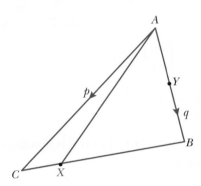

13.4 Constant velocity problems

> **« REMINDER**
>
> If an object has initial position $\mathbf{a}$ and moves with a constant velocity $\mathbf{v}$, the position vector $\mathbf{r}$, at time t, is given by the formula: $\mathbf{r} = \mathbf{a} + t\mathbf{v}$

WORKED EXAMPLE 2

An object travels at a constant velocity from point A to point B.

$\overrightarrow{AB} = (35\mathbf{i} - 84\mathbf{j})$ m and the time taken is $7\,$s. Find:

   a the velocity   **b** the speed.

Answers

   a $\overrightarrow{AB} = \dfrac{35\mathbf{i} - 84\mathbf{j}}{7} = 5\mathbf{i} - 12\mathbf{j}\,\mathrm{m\,s^{-1}}$.

   b speed $= \sqrt{(5)^2 + (-12)^2} = 13\,\mathrm{m\,s^{-1}}$.

Exercise 13.4

1 **a** Displacement = $(16\mathbf{i} + 24\mathbf{j})$ m, time taken = 8 seconds. Find the velocity.

 b Velocity = $(3\mathbf{i} - 5\mathbf{j})$ ms^{-1}, time taken = 5 seconds. Find the displacement.

 c Velocity = $(-2\mathbf{i} + 2\mathbf{j})$ kmh^{-1}, displacement = $(-20\mathbf{i} + 20\mathbf{j})$ km. Find the time taken.

2 A car travels from a point A with position vector $(40\mathbf{i} - 30\mathbf{j})$ km to a point B with position vector $(-25\mathbf{i} + 16\mathbf{j})$ km.

 The car travels with constant velocity and takes 4 hours to complete the journey.

 Find the velocity vector.

3 A helicopter flies from a point P with position vector $(30\mathbf{i} + 80\mathbf{j})$ km to a point Q.

 The helicopter flies with a constant velocity of $(50\mathbf{i} - 20\mathbf{j})$ kmh^{-1} and takes 4 hours to complete the journey. Find the position vector of the point Q.

4 **a** A car travels north-east with a speed of $8\sqrt{2}$ kmh^{-1}.

 Find the velocity vector of the car.

 b A boat sails on a bearing of $060°$ with a speed of 40 kmh^{-1}.

 Find the velocity vector of the boat.

 c A plane flies on a bearing of $300°$ with a speed of 80 ms^{-1}.

 Find the velocity vector of the plane.

5 A particle starts at a point P with position vector $(50\mathbf{i} - 60\mathbf{j})$ m relative to an origin O.

 The particle travels with velocity $(10\mathbf{i} + 24\mathbf{j})$ ms^{-1}.

 a Find the speed of the particle.

 b Find the position vector of the particle after

 i 1 second **ii** 2 seconds **iii** 3 seconds.

 c Find an expression for the position vector of the particle t seconds after leaving P.

6 At 1200 hours, a ship leaves a point Q with position vector $(-20\mathbf{i} + 18\mathbf{j})$ km relative to an origin O. The ship travels with velocity $(8\mathbf{i} - 6\mathbf{j})$ kmh^{-1}.

 a Find the speed of the ship.

 b Find the position vector of the ship at 2 p.m.

 c Find an expression for the position vector of the ship t hours after leaving Q.

 d Find the time when the ship is at the point with position vector $20\mathbf{i} - 12\mathbf{j}$ km.

7 At 1200 hours, a tanker sails from a point P with position vector $(10\mathbf{i} + 6\mathbf{j})$ km relative to an origin O. The tanker sails south-east with a speed of $10\sqrt{3}$ kmh^{-1}.

 a Find the velocity vector of the tanker.

 b Find the position vector of the tanker at

 i 1400 hours **ii** 1230 hours.

 c Find the position vector of the tanker t hours after leaving P.

8 The equation $\mathbf{r} = \begin{pmatrix} 7 \\ 5 \end{pmatrix} + t\begin{pmatrix} 6 \\ -8 \end{pmatrix}$ represents the path of a moving object.

 t is measured in seconds and the distances are measured in metres.

 Find

 a the object's initial position **b** the velocity vector of the object

 c the object's speed.

> **!**
>
> **TIP**
> 'Initial' position is when $t = 0$.

151

9 An object is initially at $-5\mathbf{i} + 0\mathbf{j}$ and is travelling parallel to the vector $2\mathbf{i} + 1\mathbf{j}$. Its speed is $\sqrt{5}$ ms^{-1}. Write down the position vector of the particle t seconds after its initial position.

10 Find a vector equation for a line which passes through a point $5\mathbf{i} - \mathbf{j}$ which is perpendicular to the vector $\mathbf{i} + \mathbf{j}$.

> **!** **TIP**
> There is more than one correct answer!

Summary

Position vectors

$\overrightarrow{AB}$ means the position vector of B relative to A.

$\overrightarrow{AB} = \overrightarrow{OB} - \overrightarrow{OA}$ or $\overrightarrow{AB} = \mathbf{b} - \mathbf{a}$

If an object has initial position $\mathbf{a}$ and moves with a constant velocity $\mathbf{v}$,

the position vector $\mathbf{r}$, at time t, is given by the formula: $\mathbf{r} = \mathbf{a} + t\mathbf{v}$.

Velocity

$$\text{Velocity} = \frac{\text{displacement}}{\text{time taken}}$$

Exercise 13.5

1 $\mathbf{p} = 6\mathbf{i} + 8\mathbf{j}$, $\mathbf{q} = 2\mathbf{i} - 2\mathbf{j}$ and $\mathbf{r} = 7\mathbf{i} + \mathbf{j}$ find

    a $|\mathbf{p} + \mathbf{q}|$ **b** $|\mathbf{p} + \mathbf{q} + \mathbf{r}|$

2 Find a vector that is of magnitude $3\sqrt{5}$ and is parallel to $2\mathbf{i} - \mathbf{j}$.

3 If $\overrightarrow{AB} = \begin{pmatrix} 3 \\ -1 \end{pmatrix}$ and $\overrightarrow{CA} = \begin{pmatrix} -1 \\ 2 \end{pmatrix}$, find $|\overrightarrow{CB}|$.

4 In the diagram, BC is parallel to OA and is twice its length.

    Find

    a $\overrightarrow{AC}$ **b** $\overrightarrow{OM}$

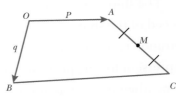

5 If the position vector of A is $\mathbf{i} - 3\mathbf{j}$ and the position vector of B is $2\mathbf{i} + 5\mathbf{j}$, find

    a $|\overrightarrow{AB}|$ **b** the position vector of the midpoint of AB

    c the position vector of the point which divides AB in the ratio 1:3.

6 If A is the point $(2, 5)$ and B is the point $(10, -1)$, find the position vector of a point P on AB such that

    a $|\overrightarrow{AP}| = |\overrightarrow{PB}|$ **b** $2|\overrightarrow{AP}| = |\overrightarrow{PB}|$ **c** $|\overrightarrow{AP}| = 4|\overrightarrow{AB}|$

    d $AP : PB = 2 : 3$

7 In the diagram, X is the midpoint of QR.

    Y is the midpoint of PR.
    $\overrightarrow{PR} = \mathbf{a}$ and $\overrightarrow{PQ} = \mathbf{b}$

    a Express $\overrightarrow{QX}$ and $\overrightarrow{QY}$ in terms of $\mathbf{a}$ and $\mathbf{b}$.

    G is a point on the line PX such that $\overrightarrow{PG} = 2\overrightarrow{GX}$

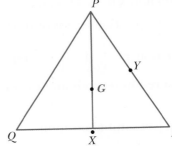

b Write $\overrightarrow{YG}$ in terms and **a** and **b**.

c Show that Q, G and Y are collinear.

8 The position vector of a yacht t hours after 12 noon is given by the equation

$$\mathbf{r} = \begin{pmatrix} 2 \\ 20 \end{pmatrix} + t \begin{pmatrix} 4 \\ -3 \end{pmatrix}$$

Find

a the speed of the yacht

b the position vector of the yacht at 3pm.

9 An object is initially at $5\mathbf{i} + 10\mathbf{j}$ and moves with a velocity vector $3\mathbf{i} - \mathbf{j}$.
Find

a the position of the object at any time t (t is in minutes)

b its position when $t = 3$

c the time when the object is due east of $0\mathbf{i} + 0\mathbf{j}$.

10 Find the velocity vector of a car which is moving parallel to $-3\mathbf{i} + 4\mathbf{j}$ with a speed of $100\,\text{kmh}^{-1}$.

11 An object is initially at the point $-3\mathbf{i} - 2\mathbf{j}$ and moves with a constant velocity $2\mathbf{i} + 4\mathbf{j}$.
If distances are measured in metres and the time in seconds, find

a the position vector of the object at any time t

b the position of the object after 2.5 seconds

c the time when the object is due north of its starting point.

12 The bearing of B from A is 315°. An aircraft whose speed relative to the air is $250\,\text{kmh}^{-1}$ flies from A to B. There is a wind of $60\,\text{kmh}^{-1}$ blowing **from** the SW.

a In what direction must the pilot face the plane?

b Find the resultant speed of the plane.

13 A man is running at $6\,\text{ms}^{-1}$ on a bearing of 155°. A kite appears to be moving at $7\,\text{ms}^{-1}$ on a bearing of 250°. Find the true velocity of the kite.

14 A fish is swimming on a bearing of 036° at a speed of $5\,\text{ms}^{-1}$ relative to the water. If the river current is flowing at $8\,\text{ms}^{-1}$ on a bearing 110°, find

a the true speed of the fish

b the true direction of the fish.

15 Two cyclists A and B are 20 km apart with B due north of A. Cyclist A is travelling at $10\,\text{kmh}^{-1}$ in the direction 060° and cyclist B is travelling at $8\,\text{kmh}^{-1}$ in the direction 135°.
Find

a the speed and direction of the velocity of cyclist A relative to cyclist B

b the time to the nearest minute, taken for cyclist A to be due east of cyclist B.

153

16 At 12 noon, the position vector of aircraft A relative to a control tower is $10\mathbf{i}$ and A's velocity is $12\mathbf{i} + 5\mathbf{j}$.

At the same time another aircraft B whose velocity is $-3\mathbf{i} + 10\mathbf{j}$ is in a position $20\mathbf{i} - 4\mathbf{j}$ relative to the same control tower.

After t hours, find

  a the position of aircraft A relative to the control tower

  b the position of aircraft B relative to the control tower

  c the position of A relative to B

  d the time when A is due north of B.

Chapter 14:
Differentiation 2

This section will show you how to:

■ differentiate sin x, cos x, tan x, e^x, ln x, together with constant multiples, sums and composite functions of these.

14.1 Derivatives of exponential functions

 REMINDER

- $y = e^x$ where $e \approx 2.718$.

  This function has the very special property that the gradient function is identical to the original function, which leads to the rule:

  $$\frac{d}{dx}(e^x) = e^x$$

- $y = e^{f(x)}$

  This function has a gradient function given by the rule:

  $$\frac{d}{dx}\left[e^{ax+b}\right] = a\,e^{ax+b}$$

WORKED EXAMPLE 1

Differentiate

a $\quad e^{x^2+x}$　　　b $\quad x^2e^{-2x}$　　　c $\quad \dfrac{e^{-2x}}{3x}$.

Answers

a $\quad \dfrac{d}{dx}\left(e^{x^2+x}\right) = (2x+1)e^{x^2+x}$　　　　　chain rule

b $\quad \dfrac{d}{dx}\left(x^2e^{-2x}\right) = x^2 \times \dfrac{d}{dx}\left(e^{-2x}\right) + e^{-2x} \times \dfrac{d}{dx}\left(x^2\right)$　　　product rule

$\qquad\qquad\qquad = x^2 \times -2\,e^{-2x} + e^{-2x} \times 2x$

$\qquad\qquad\qquad = -2x^2e^{-2x} + 2xe^{-2x}$

c $\quad \dfrac{d}{dx}\left(\dfrac{e^{-2x}}{3x}\right) = \dfrac{3x \times \dfrac{d}{dx}\left(e^{-2x}\right) - e^{-2x} \times \dfrac{d}{dx}(3x)}{(3x)^2}$　　　quotient rule

$\qquad\qquad\qquad = \dfrac{3x \times -2e^{-2x} - e^{-2x} \times 3}{9x^2}$

$\qquad\qquad\qquad = \dfrac{-6x\,e^{-2x} - 3e^{-2x}}{9x^2}$

$\qquad\qquad\qquad = \dfrac{-2x\,e^{-2x} - e^{-2x}}{3x^2}$

Exercise 14.1

1 Differentiate with respect to x.

a $\quad e^{2x}$ 　　　　　b $\quad e^{8x}$ 　　　　c $\quad 2e^{4x}$ 　　　　d $\quad 3e^{-2x}$

e $\quad 9e^{-\frac{x}{3}}$ 　　　　f $\quad e^{2x+4}$ 　　　g $\quad e^{x^3+3}$ 　　　h $\quad 6x + 2e^{\sqrt{x}}$

i $\quad 3 + \dfrac{1}{e^{2x}}$ 　　　j $\quad 3\left(3 - e^{3x}\right)$ 　　k $\quad \dfrac{2e^x - e^{-x}}{3}$ 　　l $\quad 4\left(2x^2 + e^{x^3}\right)$

2 Differentiate with respect to x.

a $4xe^x$

b $x^3 e^{4x}$

c $4xe^{-2x}$

d $\sqrt{x}e^{2x}$

e $\dfrac{e^{3x}}{x^2}$

f $\dfrac{e^{3x}}{2\sqrt{x}}$

g $\dfrac{e^{3x}+1}{2e^x}$

h $\dfrac{2xe^{-2x}-5}{e^{-2x}+1}$

3 Find the equation of the **i** tangent and **ii** normal to

a $y = xe^x$ at $x = 1$

b $y = 2x - e^{-x}$ at $x = 0$

c $y = x^2 + 2e^{2x}$ at $x = 0$

d $y = e^{-2x}$ at $x = \ln 2$

4 Given $y = x^2 e^{-x}$ show that $\dfrac{dy}{dx} = x(2-x)e^{-x}$. Hence find the coordinates of the two points on the curve where the gradient is zero.

5 Find the coordinates of the stationary points on each of the following curves and determine the nature of each of the stationary points.

a $y = \dfrac{e^x}{x^3}$

b $y = e^x(x-1)^2$

c $y = (2x+1)e^{-2x}$

14.2 Derivatives of logarithmic functions

REMINDER

- $\dfrac{d}{dx}(\ln x) = \dfrac{1}{x}$

- $\dfrac{d}{dx}[\ln(ax+b)] = \dfrac{a}{ax+b}$

WORKED EXAMPLE 2

Differentiate with respect to x.

a $\ln(x^2 + 2)$

b $x^2 \ln x$

c $\dfrac{\ln x}{x^3}$

Answers

a $\dfrac{d}{dx}\left(\ln(x^2+2)\right) = 2x \times \dfrac{1}{x^2+2}$ chain rule

$\qquad\qquad\quad = \dfrac{2x}{x^2+2}$

b $\dfrac{d}{dx}\left(x^2 \ln x\right) = x^2 \times \dfrac{d}{dx}(\ln x) + \ln x \times \dfrac{d}{dx}\left(x^2\right)$ product rule

$\qquad\qquad\quad = x^2 \dfrac{1}{x} + \ln x \times 2x$

$\qquad\qquad\quad = x + 2x \ln x$

c $\dfrac{d}{dx}\left(\dfrac{\ln x}{x^3}\right) = \dfrac{\left(x^3\right) \times \dfrac{d}{dx}(\ln x) - \ln x \times \dfrac{d}{dx}\left(x^3\right)}{\left(x^3\right)^2}$ quotient rule

$\qquad\qquad\quad = \dfrac{\left(x^3\right) \times \dfrac{1}{x} - \ln x \times \left(3x^2\right)}{x^6}$

$\qquad\qquad\quad = \dfrac{x^2 - 3x^2 \ln x}{x^6}$

$\qquad\qquad\quad = \dfrac{1 - 3\ln x}{x^4}$

Exercise 14.2

1 Differentiate with respect to x.

a $\ln 6x$

b $\ln 10x$

c $\ln(3x - 2)$

d $2x + \ln(1 - 2x^2)$

e $\ln(4x + 1)^3$

f $\ln\sqrt{2x + 1}$

g $\ln(2 - 3x)^3$

h $3x - \ln\left(\dfrac{5}{x}\right)$

i $5 - \ln\dfrac{2}{(1 - 2x)}$

j $\ln(\ln 2x)$

k $\ln(\sqrt{x} + 1)^3$

l $\ln(x^3 + \ln 2x)$

2 Differentiate with respect to x.

a $x \ln 2x$

b $3x^3 \ln x$

c $(x^2 - 1)\ln 2x$

d $3x \ln(2x^2)$

e $x^3 \ln(\ln 2x)$

f $\dfrac{2\ln 2x}{3x}$

g $\dfrac{4\sqrt{x}}{\ln x}$

h $x \ln\left[\dfrac{1 - 3x}{4}\right]$

i $\dfrac{\ln(1 - 3x)}{1 - 3x}$

3 A curve has equation $y = 2x^3 \ln 2x$. Find the value of $\dfrac{dy}{dx}$ and $\dfrac{d^2y}{dx^2}$ at the point where $x = 1$.

4 Use the laws of logarithms to help differentiate these expressions with respect to x.

a $\ln\sqrt{2x - 1}$

b $\ln\dfrac{1}{(3 - 2x)}$

c $\ln\left[x(x + 1)^3\right]$

d $\ln\left(\dfrac{3x + 1}{x + 1}\right)$

e $\ln\left(\dfrac{2 - 3x}{x^3}\right)$

f $\ln\left[\dfrac{x(1 - x)}{x - 2}\right]$

g $\ln\left[\dfrac{3x - 2}{(x - 1)(x + 1)}\right]$

h $\ln\left[\dfrac{3}{(x - 3)^2(x + 1)}\right]$

i $\ln\left[\dfrac{(x - 1)(x + 3)}{x(x + 1)}\right]$

> **!**
> **TIP**
> Use change of base of logarithms before differentiating.

5 Find $\dfrac{dy}{dx}$ for each of the following.

a $y = \log_4(2x)$

b $y = \log_3 x^3$

c $y = \log_2(1 - 2x)$

6 Find $\dfrac{dy}{dx}$ for each of the following.

a $e^y = 2x^3 - 1$

b $e^y = 5\sqrt{x} - 2x^2$

c $e^y = (x + 4)(x - 5)$

> **!**
> **TIP**
> Take the natural logarithm of both sides of the equation before differentiating.

14.3 Derivatives of trigonometric functions

REMINDER

If x is measured in radians then:

$$\frac{d}{dx}(\sin x) = \cos x$$

$$\frac{d}{dx}(\cos x) = -\sin x$$

$$\frac{d}{dx}(\tan x) = \sec^2 x$$

$$\frac{d}{dx}[\sin(ax + b)] = a\cos(ax + b)$$

$$\frac{d}{dx}[\cos(ax + b)] = -a\sin(ax + b)$$

$$\frac{d}{dx}[\tan(ax + b)] = a\sec^2(ax + b)$$

WORKED EXAMPLE 3

Differentiate with respect to x.

a $\tan(3 - 2x)$ b $4\sin\left(2x + \dfrac{\pi}{4}\right)$ c $-3\cos\left(2x + \dfrac{\pi}{3}\right)$

Answers

a $\dfrac{d}{dx}(\tan(3 - 2x)) = -2\sec^2(3 - 2x)$

b $\dfrac{d}{dx}\left(4\sin\left(2x + \dfrac{\pi}{4}\right)\right) = 4 \times 2\cos\left(2x + \dfrac{\pi}{4}\right)$

$$= 8\cos\left(2x + \dfrac{\pi}{4}\right)$$

c $\dfrac{d}{dx}\left(-3\cos\left(2x + \dfrac{\pi}{3}\right)\right) = -3 \times -2\sin\left(2x + \dfrac{\pi}{3}\right)$

$$= 6\sin\left(2x + \dfrac{\pi}{3}\right)$$

Exercise 14.3

1 Differentiate with respect to x.

   a $\tan 3x$

   b $-3\sin x - 3\tan x$

   c $2\cos 2x - \sin 2x$

   d $8\sin 3x$

   e $2\tan 3x$

   f $2\cos\dfrac{1}{2}x - \sin\dfrac{1}{2}x$

2 Differentiate with respect to x.

   a $2\sin^2 x$

   b $-2\cos^2(4x)$

   c $2\sin^2 x - 2\cos^3 x$

   d $(x + \cos x)^3$

   e $3\sin^2\left(4x + \dfrac{\pi}{3}\right)$

   f $4\cos^4 x + 3\tan^3 2x$

3 Differentiate with respect to x.

   a $x \cos x$ **b** $\sin 3x \cos x$ **c** $2x^3 \tan x$

   d $2x \tan^2\left(\dfrac{x}{3}\right)$ **e** $\dfrac{5}{\sin 2x}$ **f** $\dfrac{2x}{3 \cos x}$

   g $\dfrac{\tan^2 x}{2x}$ **h** $\dfrac{3\cos x}{1 - \sin 2x}$ **i** $\dfrac{\sin x^2}{2x + 1}$

   j $\dfrac{1}{\cos^2 2x}$ **k** $\dfrac{\sin^2 x}{\sin 2x}$ **l** $\dfrac{\sin x - \cos x}{\sin x + \cos x}$

> **!**
>
> **TIP**
> You may need to review trigonometric identities in Chapter 9.

4 Differentiate with respect to x.

   a $e^{\sin x}$ **b** $e^{\cos 3x}$ **c** $e^{\tan 2x}$

   d $e^{(\sin x - \cos x)}$ **e** $e^x \cos 2x$ **f** $e^{2x} \cos \dfrac{1}{3} x$

   g $e^x (\cos 2x - \sin x)$ **h** $x^3 e^{-\sin x}$ **i** $\ln(\sin 2x)$

   j $x^3 \ln(\cos x)$ **k** $\dfrac{\sin 2x}{e^{(1-x)}}$ **l** $\dfrac{x \sin x}{e^{3x}}$

5 Find the gradient of the tangent to

   a $y = x^2 \cos 2x$ when $x = \dfrac{\pi}{6}$ **b** $y = \dfrac{2 - \sin x}{4 - \cos x}$ when $x = \dfrac{\pi}{3}$.

6 **a**   Given that $y = \sin x(1 - \cos x)$ show that $\dfrac{dy}{dx} = (1 + 2\cos x)(1 - \cos x)$.

   b   Find the coordinates of the points on the curve in the range $0 \leqslant x \leqslant \pi$ where the gradient is zero.

7 Find $\dfrac{dy}{dx}$ for each of the following.

   a $e^y = \tan 2x$ **b** $e^{2y} = 3 \sin 4x$

15

14.4 Further applications of differentiation

You need to be able to answer questions that involve the differentiation of exponential, logarithmic and trigonometric functions.

WORKED EXAMPLE 4

Variables x and y are connected by the equation $y = \ln\left(\dfrac{x+3}{x^2}\right)$. Find the approximate change in y as x increases from 2 to $2 + p$, where p is small.

Answers

$$\frac{dy}{dx} = \frac{d}{dx}\left(\frac{x+3}{x^2}\right) \times \frac{1}{\dfrac{x+3}{x^2}}$$

$$= \frac{d}{dx}\left(\frac{1}{x} + \frac{3}{x^2}\right) \times \frac{x^2}{x+3}$$

$$= \left(-\frac{1}{x^2} - \frac{6}{x^3}\right) \times \frac{x^2}{x+3}$$

$$= \left(-\frac{1}{x^2} - \frac{6}{x^3}\right) \times \frac{x^2}{x+3}$$

$$= -\frac{1}{x+3} - \frac{6}{x(x+3)}$$

When $x = 2$, $\dfrac{dy}{dx} = \dfrac{-1}{2+3} - \dfrac{6}{2(2+3)}$

$$= -\frac{4}{5}$$

Using $\dfrac{\delta y}{\delta x} \approx \dfrac{dy}{dx}$

$$\frac{\delta y}{p} \approx -\frac{4}{5}$$

$$\delta y \approx -\frac{4}{5}p$$

Exercise 14.4

1 A curve has the equation $y = e^{-x} \sin x$.

  a Find $\dfrac{dy}{dx}$.

  b Find the exact coordinates of the stationary points of the curve in the interval $-\pi \leqslant x \leqslant \pi$ and determine their nature.

2 The tangent to $y = x^2 e^x$ at $x = 1$ cuts the x- and y-axes at P and Q respectively. Find the coordinates of P and Q.

3 Find the minimum value of the function $y = \dfrac{1}{2}\tan x - 4\sin x$.

4 Given that $y = \dfrac{2x^2}{\cos 3x}$, find:

  a $\dfrac{dy}{dx}$

  b the approximate change in y when x increases from $\dfrac{\pi}{3}$ to $\dfrac{\pi}{3} + p$.

5 Given $y = \dfrac{x}{e^x}$:

  a does the graph of $y = \dfrac{x}{e^x}$ have any x- or y-intercepts?

  b find the stationary points on the curve and determine their nature

  c find the equation to the normal to the curve at $x = 2$.

TIP

This exercise requires knowledge of previous work studied in Chapters 6, 9 and 12.

6 The average cost per refrigerator (C) of producing x refrigerators is given by the equation

$$C = 4\ln x + \left(\frac{30 - x}{10}\right)^2 \text{ hundred dollars.}$$

The company needs to produce a minimum 10 refrigerators per day to stay in business. How many should be produced in order to keep the cost per refrigerator a minimum?

7 The curve $y = axe^{bx^2}$ has a maximum value of 1 when $x = 2$. Find the values of a and b given that they are non-zero constants.

8 A curve has equation $y = 3\cos\left(3x + \frac{\pi}{3}\right)$. Find the equation of the normal to the curve at the point on the curve where $x = \frac{\pi}{2}$.

9 Variables x and y are connected by the equation $y = 2\cos 2x$. Find the approximate increase in y as x increases from $\frac{\pi}{3}$ to $\frac{\pi}{3} + p$, where p is small.

10 A metal tube, which cannot be bent, must be kept horizontal as it moves around the corner of an L-shaped room from one part of the room to the next (see diagram).

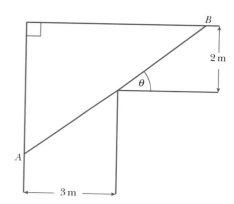

  a Show that the length of the tube is
$$L = \frac{3}{\cos\theta} + \frac{2}{\sin\theta}$$

  b Show that $\frac{dL}{d\theta} = 0$ when $\theta = \tan^{-1}\sqrt[3]{\frac{2}{3}}$.

  c Find L when $\theta = \tan^{-1}\sqrt[3]{\frac{2}{3}}$.

11 Find the coordinates of the stationary points on these curves and determine their nature.

  a $y = \sin x + \cos x$ for $0 \leqslant x \leqslant 2\pi$ **b** $y = \sin^2 x + 2\cos x$ for $0 \leqslant x \leqslant 2\pi$

  c $y = \cos\left(\frac{\pi}{6} - 3x\right)$ for $0 \leqslant x \leqslant \pi$ **d** $y = \dfrac{x^2 - 3}{e^x}$ for $-2 \leqslant x \leqslant 1$

  e $y = 2\ln x - \sqrt{x}$ for $0 \leqslant x \leqslant 20$

12 The curve with equation $4 - e^x$ crosses the x-axis at A and the y-axis at B. Find

  a the equation of the tangent to the curve at B

  b the equation of the normal to the curve at A.

  c The normal line and the tangent line intersect at C.

    The x-coordinate of C is $p\ln 2 + q$ (p and q are constants).

    Find the values of p and q.

16.

Summary

Exponential functions

$$\frac{d}{dx}(e^x) = e^x \qquad \frac{d}{dx}\left[e^{ax+b}\right] = ae^{ax+b} \qquad \frac{d}{dx}\left[e^{f(x)}\right] = f'(x) \times e^{f(x)}$$

Logarithmic functions

$$\frac{d}{dx}(\ln x) = \frac{1}{x} \qquad \frac{d}{dx}\left[\ln(ax+b)\right] = \frac{a}{ax+b} \qquad \frac{d}{dx}\left[\ln(f(x))\right] = \frac{f'(x)}{f(x)}$$

Trigonometric functions

$$\frac{d}{dx}(\sin x) = \cos x \qquad \frac{d}{dx}\left[\sin(ax+b)\right] = a\cos(ax+b)$$

$$\frac{d}{dx}(\cos x) = -\sin x \qquad \frac{d}{dx}\left[\cos(ax+b)\right] = -a\sin(ax+b)$$

$$\frac{d}{dx}(\tan x) = \sec^2 x \qquad \frac{d}{dx}\left[\tan(ax+b)\right] = a\sec^2(ax+b)$$

Exercise 14.5

1 Find the equation of the tangent to $y = \cos^2 x - \sin^2 x$ at $x = \frac{\pi}{6}$.

2 Find the equation of the normal to the curve $y = 3 + x\cos x$ at the point where it crosses the x-axis.

3 Find $\frac{dy}{dx}$ for the following.

   a $y = \ln(e^x + 3)$ b $y = \left[\dfrac{(x+2)^3}{x}\right]$ c $y = \ln(x^3 - 3x)$

4 Find $\frac{dy}{dx}$ given that

   a $y = x\ln(\sin x)$ b $y = \sqrt{e^{\tan x}}$

5 A curve has equation $x = 4 - 3\left[e^{y(4-2x)}\right]$. Find the value of $\frac{dy}{dx}$ when $x = 1$.

6 Variables x and y are connected by the equation $y = 3x - 4e^{-2x} + 1$. Find the approximate change in y as x increases from $\ln 2$ to $\ln 2 + p$, where p is small.

7 The curve with equation $y = 2x - \ln x - 2$ passes through the point $P(1, 0)$. The tangent to the curve at P crosses the y-axis at Q and the normal to the curve at P crosses the y-axis at R.

   a Find the equation of the tangent to the curve at P.

   b Find the midpoint of QR.

   c Find the y-coordinate of the minimum point of the curve.

8 A circular piece of metal of radius 10 cm has 3 segments removed (see diagram).

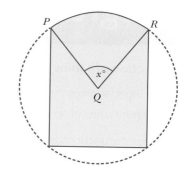

    a If angle $PQR = x°$, show that the remaining area is given by $A = 50(x + 3\sin x)$.

    b Find the value of x which gives the largest area.

9 A piece of metal 30 cm wide is bent into a shape whose cross section is shown in the diagram.

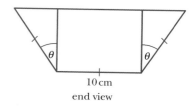

10 cm

end view

    a Show that the cross sectional area of the metal is given by the equation
$$A = 100\cos\theta\,(1 + \theta)$$

    b Show that $\dfrac{\mathrm{d}A}{\mathrm{d}\theta} = 0$ when $\sin x = \dfrac{1}{2}$ or -1.

    c Find the value of θ which would give the maximum capacity?

Chapter 15:
Integration

This section will show you how to:

- use integration as the reverse process of differentiation
- integrate sums of terms in powers of x including $\dfrac{1}{x}$ and $\dfrac{1}{ax+b}$
- integrate functions of the form $(ax+b)^n$ for any rational n, $\sin(ax+b)$, $\cos(ax+b)$, e^{ax+b}
- evaluate definite integrals and apply integration to the evaluation of plane areas.

15.1 Differentiation reversed

REMINDER

Differentiation
- If $y = x^n$, then $\dfrac{dy}{dx} = nx^{n-1}$.

Integration
- If $\dfrac{dy}{dx} = x^n$ then $y = \dfrac{1}{n+1}x^{n+1} + c$, where c is an arbitrary constant and $n \neq -1$.

WORKED EXAMPLE 1

A curve is such that $\dfrac{dy}{dx} = x - \dfrac{2}{\sqrt{x}}$. Given that the curve passes through point $(1, 2)$, find the equation of the curve.

Answer

$\dfrac{dy}{dx} = x - \dfrac{2}{\sqrt{x}}$

$\dfrac{dy}{dx} = x - 2x^{-\frac{1}{2}}$ Write in index form.

$y = \dfrac{1}{2} \times x^2 - 2 \times 2x^{\frac{1}{2}} + c$

$y = \dfrac{1}{2}x^2 - 4x^{\frac{1}{2}} + c$ Remember to include the constant term 'c'.

When $x = 1$, $y = 2$:

$2 = \dfrac{1}{2}(1)^2 - 4(1)^{\frac{1}{2}} + c$ Use the point $(1, 2)$ to find the value of c.

$2 = -\dfrac{7}{2} + c$

$c = \dfrac{11}{2}$

$y = \dfrac{x^2}{2} - 4\sqrt{x} + \dfrac{11}{2}$

Exercise 15.1

1 Find y in terms of x for each of the following.

a $\dfrac{dy}{dx} = 5x^6$ **b** $\dfrac{dy}{dx} = 3x^4$ **c** $\dfrac{dy}{dx} = 4x^4$

d $\dfrac{dy}{dx} = \dfrac{2}{x^4}$ **e** $\dfrac{dy}{dx} = \dfrac{-1}{3x^2}$ **f** $\dfrac{dy}{dx} = \dfrac{4}{2\sqrt{x}}$

2 Find y in terms of x for each of the following.

a $\dfrac{dy}{dx} = 5x^4 + 3x^4 - 1$ **b** $\dfrac{dy}{dx} = 6x^5 - 3x^2 + 2x$

c $\dfrac{dy}{dx} = \dfrac{6}{x^3} - \dfrac{2}{x^5} + 2x$ **d** $\dfrac{dy}{dx} = \dfrac{1}{x^5} + \dfrac{11}{4x^3} - 6$

3 Find y in terms of x for each of the following.

a $\dfrac{dy}{dx} = 2x(3x - 2)$ **b** $\dfrac{dy}{dx} = x^3\left(2x^2 - 1\right)$ **c** $\dfrac{dy}{dx} = \left(3x - \sqrt{x}\right)^2$

d $\dfrac{dy}{dx} = x(2x - 1)(3x + 3)$ **e** $\dfrac{dy}{dx} = \dfrac{x^4 - 2x}{3x^3}$ **f** $\dfrac{dy}{dx} = \dfrac{(2 - 2x)(x + 1)}{x^2}$

g $\dfrac{dy}{dx} = \dfrac{2x^5 - x^2 + 2}{3x^2}$ **h** $\dfrac{dy}{dx} = \dfrac{(5 - 3x) + (x + 1)}{\sqrt{x}}$

4 A curve is such that $\dfrac{dy}{dx} = x^3 - 2x^2 + 3$. Given that the curve passes through the point $(0, 2)$, find the equation of the curve.

5 A curve is such that $\dfrac{dy}{dx} = x(3x + 2)$. Given that the curve passes through the point $(2, 5)$, find the equation of the curve.

6 A curve is such that $\dfrac{d^2y}{dx^2} = 15\sqrt{x} + \dfrac{3}{\sqrt{x}}$. The curve passes through $(0, 5)$ and the gradient of the curve at the point $x = 1$ is 12. Find the equation of the curve.

7 A curve is such that $\dfrac{d^2y}{dx^2} = 2x$ where k is a constant. Given that the curve passes through the points $(1, 0)$ and $(0, 5)$, find the equation of the curve.

15.2 Indefinite integrals

REMINDER

- Notation

$$\int x^n \, dx = \frac{1}{n + 1}x^{n+1} + c, \text{ where } c \text{ is a constant and } n \neq -1$$

- This section provides you with practice in using this new notation together with the following rules:

$$\int k\mathrm{f}(x)\,dx = k\int \mathrm{f}(x)\,dx, \text{ where } k \text{ is a constant}$$

$$\int \left[\mathrm{f}(x) \pm \mathrm{g}(x)\right]dx = \int \mathrm{f}(x)\,dx \pm \int \mathrm{g}(x)\,dx$$

TIP

In this exercise remember to …

- expand brackets
- write in index form … ready for integration.

TIP

Use the coordinate of the point to find the value of 'c'.

165

WORKED EXAMPLE 2

Find $\int \dfrac{x^2 + 5}{\sqrt{x}}\,dx$

Answer

$\int \left(\dfrac{x^2}{\sqrt{x}} + \dfrac{5}{\sqrt{x}} \right) dx$

$\int \left(x^{\frac{3}{2}} + 5x^{-\frac{1}{2}} \right) dx$ Write in index form.

$\dfrac{2}{5} \times x^{\frac{5}{2}} + 5 \times 2x^{\frac{1}{2}} + c$ Remember to include the constant term 'c'.

$\dfrac{2}{5}x^{\frac{5}{2}} + 10x^{\frac{1}{2}} + c$

Exercise 15.2

1 Find each of the following.

  a $\displaystyle\int 8x^7\,dx$ **b** $\displaystyle\int 2x^5\,dx$ **c** $\displaystyle\int 2x^{-4}\,dx$

  d $\displaystyle\int \dfrac{4}{x^5}\,dx$ **e** $\displaystyle\int \dfrac{3}{4\sqrt{x}}\,dx$ **f** $\displaystyle\int \dfrac{1}{x^3\sqrt{x}}\,dx$

2 Find each of the following.

  a $\displaystyle\int (2-x)(5-x)\,dx$ **b** $\displaystyle\int (2x-1)(3x+3)\,dx$ **c** $\displaystyle\int (4x-5)^2\,dx$

  d $\displaystyle\int \left(\sqrt{x}+1\right)^3\,dx$ **e** $\displaystyle\int 2x(2x+6)^2\,dx$ **f** $\displaystyle\int \sqrt[3]{x}\,(2x-1)\,dx$

3 Find each of the following.

  a $\displaystyle\int \dfrac{x^3-2}{x^3}\,dx$ **b** $\displaystyle\int \dfrac{x^4+8}{4x^2}\,dx$ **c** $\displaystyle\int \dfrac{(x-1)^2}{4x^{-2}}\,dx$

  d $\displaystyle\int \dfrac{x^2-2\sqrt{x}}{x^2}\,dx$ **e** $\displaystyle\int \dfrac{x^4+1}{x^3\sqrt{x}}\,dx$ **f** $\displaystyle\int \left(2\sqrt{x} - \dfrac{3}{x^3\sqrt{x}}\right)^2\,dx$

15.3 Integration of functions of the form $(ax+b)^n$

 REMINDER

The general rule:

$\displaystyle\int (ax+b)^n\,dx = \dfrac{1}{a(n+1)}(ax+b)^{n+1} + c,\ \ n \neq -1 \text{ and } a \neq 0$

WORKED EXAMPLE 3

A curve is such that $\dfrac{dy}{dx} = \sqrt{2x - 7}$. Given that the curve passes through the point $(8, 11)$, find the equation of the curve.

Answer

$y = \displaystyle\int (2x - 7)^{\frac{1}{2}} \, dx$ Write in index form.

$y = \dfrac{1}{2\left(\frac{3}{2}\right)}(2x - 7)^{\frac{3}{2}} + c$ $\displaystyle\int (ax + b)^n \, dx = \dfrac{1}{a(n + 1)}(ax + b)^{n+1} + c$, where $a = 2$, $n = \dfrac{1}{2}$

$y = \dfrac{1}{3}(2x - 7)^{\frac{3}{2}} + c$

$11 = \dfrac{1}{3}(2(8) - 7)^{\frac{3}{2}} + c$ Use the point $(8, 11)$ to find the value of c.

$11 = 9 + c$

$c = 2$

$y = \dfrac{1}{3}(2x - 7)^{\frac{3}{2}} + 2$

Exercise 15.3

1 Find.

   a $\displaystyle\int (x + 3)^3 \, dx$ **b** $\displaystyle\int (2x - 1)^4 \, dx$ **c** $\displaystyle\int 2(2x + 5)^6 \, dx$

   d $\displaystyle\int 2(3 - 2x)^4 \, dx$ **e** $\displaystyle\int (3x + 2)^{\frac{2}{3}} \, dx$ **f** $\displaystyle\int \sqrt{(2x + 1)^3} \, dx$

   g $\displaystyle\int \dfrac{-2}{\sqrt{x + 1}} \, dx$ **h** $\displaystyle\int \left(\dfrac{5}{3x + 2}\right)^2 \, dx$ **i** $\displaystyle\int \dfrac{2}{3(1 - 3x)^5} \, dx$

2 A curve is such that $\dfrac{dy}{dx} = 3\sqrt{x} - \dfrac{2}{\sqrt{x}}$, $x > 0$. Given that the curve passes through the point $(4, 7)$, find the equation of the curve.

3 A curve is such that $\dfrac{dy}{dx} = 10x^{\frac{3}{2}} - \dfrac{2}{\sqrt{x}}$. Given that the curve passes through the point $(0, 7)$, find the equation of the curve.

4 A curve is such that $\dfrac{dy}{dx} = 3x^2 + kx$ where k is a constant. Given that the curve passes through the points $(1, 6)$ and $(2, 1)$, find

   a the value of k

   b the equation of the curve.

15.4 Integration of exponential functions

 REMINDER

The rules for integrating exponential functions are:

$\displaystyle\int e^x \, dx = e^x + c$ $\displaystyle\int e^{ax+b} \, dx = \dfrac{1}{a}e^{ax+b} + c$

WORKED EXAMPLE 4

A curve is such that $\dfrac{dy}{dx} = \dfrac{4x^2 e^x - e^{3x}}{2e^x}$. The curve passes through the point $\left(0, \dfrac{1}{4}\right)$. Find the equation of the curve.

Answer

$y = \displaystyle\int \dfrac{4x^2 e^x - e^{3x}}{2e^x}\, dx$

$y = \displaystyle\int \left(2x^2 - \dfrac{1}{2}e^{2x}\right) dx$ Write in exponential form.

$y = \dfrac{2}{3}x^3 - \dfrac{1}{4}e^{2x} + c$

$\dfrac{1}{4} = \dfrac{2}{3}(0)^3 - \dfrac{1}{4}e^0 + c$ Use the point $\left(0, \dfrac{1}{4}\right)$ to find the value of c.

$\dfrac{1}{4} = -\dfrac{1}{4} + c$

$c = \dfrac{1}{2}$

$y = \dfrac{2}{3}x^3 - \dfrac{1}{4}e^{2x} + \dfrac{1}{2}$

Exercise 15.4

1 Find.

  a $\displaystyle\int e^{6x}\, dx$ **b** $\displaystyle\int e^{-3x}\, dx$ **c** $\displaystyle\int e^{\frac{1}{3}x}\, dx$

  d $\displaystyle\int e^{-4x}\, dx$ **e** $\displaystyle\int 2e^{3x}\, dx$ **f** $\displaystyle\int 24e^{4x}\, dx$

  g $\displaystyle\int \dfrac{1}{2}e^{x+1}\, dx$ **h** $\displaystyle\int 3e^{5-3x}\, dx$ **i** $\displaystyle\int \dfrac{1}{4}e^{4x-1}\, dx$

2 Find.

  a $\displaystyle\int e^x\left(2 - e^{3x}\right) dx$ **b** $\displaystyle\int \left(e^{3x} + 3\right)^2 dx$ **c** $\displaystyle\int \left(3e^{2x} + e^{-x}\right)^3 dx$

  d $\displaystyle\int \dfrac{e^{3x} + 1}{e^x}\, dx$ **e** $\displaystyle\int \dfrac{3e^{3x} - e^{2x}}{3e^{-x}}\, dx$ **f** $\displaystyle\int \dfrac{e^{2x} - e^x}{e^{4x}}\, dx$

3 Find.

  a $\displaystyle\int \left(4e^{2x} - \dfrac{2}{\sqrt{x}}\right) dx$ **b** $\displaystyle\int \left(x^3 - 2e^{3x+1}\right) dx$

4 A curve is such that $\dfrac{dy}{dx} = e^x + \dfrac{1}{\sqrt{x}}$. Given that the curve passes through the point $(1, 1)$, find the equation of the curve.

5 A curve is such that $\dfrac{dy}{dx} = \dfrac{e^x}{2} - 3x$. The curve passes through the point $(0, 5.5)$. Find the equation of the curve.

6 A curve is such that $\dfrac{d^2 y}{dx^2} = 45e^{-3x}$. Given that $\dfrac{dy}{dx} = -15$ when $x = 0$ and that the curve passes through the point $(0, 23)$, find the equation of the curve.

15.5 Integration of sine and cosine functions

The rules for integrating sine and cosine functions are:

$$\int \cos x \, dx = \sin x + c \qquad \int [\cos(ax+b)] \, dx = \frac{1}{a}\sin(ax+b) + c$$

$$\int \sin x \, dx = -\cos x + c \qquad \int [\sin(ax+b)] \, dx = -\frac{1}{a}\cos(ax+b) + c$$

WORKED EXAMPLE 5

Find: $\displaystyle\int (4\cos 3x + 2\sin(4x-5)) \, dx$

Answer

$$\int (4\cos 3x + 2\sin(4x-5)) \, dx = 4\int \cos 3x \, dx + 2\int \sin(4x-5) \, dx$$

$$= 4 \times \left(\frac{1}{3}\sin 3x\right) + 2 \times \left(-\frac{1}{4}\cos(4x-5)\right)$$

$$= \frac{4}{3}\sin 3x - \frac{1}{2}\cos(4x-5) + c$$

Exercise 15.5

1 Find.

a $\displaystyle\int \sin 6x \, dx$ **b** $\displaystyle\int \cos 4x \, dx$ **c** $\displaystyle\int \sin \frac{x}{4} \, dx$

d $\displaystyle\int 3\cos 3x \, dx$ **e** $\displaystyle\int 5\sin 2x \, dx$ **f** $\displaystyle\int 4\cos(3x+2) \, dx$

g $\displaystyle\int 2\sin(1-5x) \, dx$ **h** $\displaystyle\int 6\cos(3x+1) \, dx$ **i** $\displaystyle\int 2\sin\left(3 - \frac{1}{2}x\right) \, dx$

2 Find.

a $\displaystyle\int (3 - 2\sin x) \, dx$ **b** $\displaystyle\int \left(\sqrt{x} + 3\cos 2x\right) \, dx$ **c** $\displaystyle\int \left(2\cos 4x + \pi \sin \frac{4x}{3}\right) \, dx$

d $\displaystyle\int \left(\frac{2}{x^3} - \cos \frac{2x}{3}\right) \, dx$ **e** $\displaystyle\int \left(e^{-x} - 3\sin 4x\right) \, dx$ **f** $\displaystyle\int \left(-\frac{3}{\sqrt{x}} + \sin \frac{3x}{4}\right) \, dx$

3 A curve is such that $\dfrac{dy}{dx} = x^2 - 4\cos x$. Given that the curve passes through the point (0, 3), find the equation of the curve.

4 A curve is such that $\dfrac{dy}{dx} = 2\cos x - 3\sin x$. Given that the curve passes through the point $\left(\dfrac{\pi}{4}, \dfrac{1}{\sqrt{2}}\right)$, find the equation of the curve.

5 A curve is such that $\dfrac{dy}{dx} = \sqrt{x} - 6\sin \dfrac{1}{3}x$. Given that the curve passes through the point (0, 20), find the equation of the curve.

6 A curve is such that $\dfrac{d^2y}{dx^2} = -15\cos 2x + \sin 3x$. Given that $\dfrac{dy}{dx} = \dfrac{1}{3}$ when $x = 0$ and that the curve passes through the point $\left(0, -\dfrac{3}{4}\right)$, find the equation of the curve.

15.6 Integration of functions of the form $\frac{1}{x}$ and $\frac{1}{ax+b}$

REMINDER

The rules for integration are:

$$\int \frac{1}{x}\,dx = \ln x + c,\ x > 0 \qquad \int \frac{1}{ax+b}\,dx = \frac{1}{a}\ln(ax+b) + c,\ ax+b > 0$$

WORKED EXAMPLE 6

Find each of these integrals and state the values of x for which the integral is valid.

a $\int \dfrac{3}{x}\,dx$ **b** $\int \dfrac{2}{4x+5}\,dx$ **c** $\int \dfrac{9}{2-3x}\,dx$

Answers

a $\int \dfrac{3}{x}\,dx = 3\int \dfrac{1}{x}\,dx$

$= 3\ln x + c,\ x > 0$ valid for $x > 0$

b $\int \dfrac{2}{4x+5}\,dx = 2\int \dfrac{1}{4x+5}\,dx$

$= 2\left(\dfrac{1}{4}\right)\ln(4x+5) + c$ valid for $4x+5 > 0$

$= \dfrac{1}{2}\ln(4x+5) + c,\ x > -\dfrac{5}{4}$

c $\int \dfrac{9}{2-3x}\,dx = 9\int \dfrac{1}{2-3x}\,dx$

$= 9\left(\dfrac{1}{-3}\right)\ln(2-3x) + c$ valid for $2-3x > 0$

$= -3\ln(2-3x) + c,\ x < \dfrac{2}{3}$

Exercise 15.6

In questions 1 and 2 below, the denominator of the fractions in each part is positive.

1 Find.

a $\int \dfrac{7}{x}\,dx$ **b** $\int \dfrac{12}{x}\,dx$ **c** $\int \dfrac{1}{3x}\,dx$

d $\int \dfrac{4}{3x}\,dx$ **e** $\int \dfrac{1}{2x+2}\,dx$ **f** $\int \dfrac{1}{1-7x}\,dx$

g $\int \dfrac{3}{4x-1}\,dx$ **h** $\int \dfrac{5}{2-x}\,dx$ **i** $\int \dfrac{-2}{5(3x-1)}\,dx$

2 Find.

a $\int \left(2x + \dfrac{3}{x}\right)dx$ **b** $\int \left(4 + \dfrac{1}{x}\right)^2 dx$ **c** $\int \left(1 - \dfrac{2}{x}\right)^2 dx$

d $\int \dfrac{2x+1}{x}\,dx$ **e** $\int \dfrac{1-2x^3}{3x^4}\,dx$ **f** $\int \left(x - \dfrac{3}{x^2}\right)^2 dx$

g $\int \dfrac{2x + 3\sqrt{x}}{x^2}\,dx$ **h** $\int \dfrac{x^2 - 2\sqrt{x}}{x\sqrt{x}}\,dx$ **i** $\int \dfrac{2xe^{3x} - 4e^x}{4xe^x}\,dx$

3 A curve is such that $\dfrac{dy}{dx} = \dfrac{2}{4x-1}$ for $x > 0.25$.

Given that the curve passes through the point $(0.5, 3)$, find the equation of the curve.

4 A curve is such that $\dfrac{dy}{dx} = \dfrac{4}{x} - 3$ for $x > 0$.

Given that the curve passes through the point $(1, 5)$, find the equation of the curve.

5 A curve is such that $\dfrac{dy}{dx} = \dfrac{1}{e^x} + \dfrac{2}{x+1}$ for $x > -1$.

Given that the curve passes through the point $(1, 2\ln 2)$, find the equation of the curve.

15.7 Further indefinite integration

 REMINDER

In this section you will practise using the concept that integration is the reverse process of differentiation to help integrate complicated expressions.

If $\dfrac{d}{dx}[F(x)] = f(x)$, then $\displaystyle\int f(x)\,dx = F(x) + c$

WORKED EXAMPLE 7

a Differentiate $(3x^2 + 6)^5$ with respect to x.

b Hence find $\displaystyle\int x(3x^2 + 6)^4\,dx$.

Answers

a $y = (3x^2 + 6)^5$

$\dfrac{dy}{dx} = 5 \times 6x \times (3x^2 + 6)^4$ Differentiate using the chain rule.

$\dfrac{dy}{dx} = 30x(3x^2 + 6)^4$

b $\displaystyle\int 30x(3x^2 + 6)^4\,dx = (3x^2 + 6)^5$

$\displaystyle\int x(3x^2 + 6)^4\,dx = \dfrac{1}{30}(3x^2 + 6)^5 + c$

Exercise 15.7

1 a $y = \dfrac{\sqrt{x-4}}{2x^2}$, show that $\dfrac{dy}{dx} = \dfrac{16-3x}{4x^3\sqrt{x-4}}$.

b Hence find $\displaystyle\int \dfrac{16-3x}{4x^3\sqrt{x-4}}\,dx$.

2 a Differentiate $(2x^2 + 2)^4$ with respect to x.

b Hence find $\displaystyle\int 8x(2x^2 + 2)^3\,dx$.

 TIP

In this exercise you will need to be able to use the product and quotient rules which you met in Chapter 14.

171

3 a Find $\dfrac{\mathrm{d}}{\mathrm{d}x}(\ln x)^2$.

b Hence find $\displaystyle\int \dfrac{\ln x}{x}\,\mathrm{d}x$.

4 a Given that $y = \left(x^2 + 4x - 1\right)^4$, find $\dfrac{\mathrm{d}y}{\mathrm{d}x}$.

b Hence find $\displaystyle\int (x + 2)\left(x^2 + 4x - 1\right)^3 \mathrm{d}x$.

5 a Given that $y = e^{x^4}$, find $\dfrac{\mathrm{d}y}{\mathrm{d}x}$.

b Hence find $\displaystyle\int x^3 e^{x^4}\,\mathrm{d}x$.

6 a Given that $y = (\sin 2x + 3)^3$, find $\dfrac{\mathrm{d}y}{\mathrm{d}x}$.

b Hence find $\displaystyle\int \cos 2x\,(\sin 2x + 3)^2\,\mathrm{d}x$.

7 a Given that $y = \sin^5 x$, find $\dfrac{\mathrm{d}y}{\mathrm{d}x}$.

b Hence find $\displaystyle\int \cos x\,\sin^4 x\,\mathrm{d}x$.

8 a Given that $y = \left(\sqrt{x^3 + 5}\right)^3$, find $\dfrac{\mathrm{d}y}{\mathrm{d}x}$.

b Hence find $\displaystyle\int x^2 \sqrt{x^3 + 5}\,\mathrm{d}x$.

9 a Given that $y = \left(x^2 + 3\right)^{\frac{1}{2}}$, find $\dfrac{\mathrm{d}y}{\mathrm{d}x}$.

b Hence find $\displaystyle\int \dfrac{x}{\sqrt{x^2 + 3}}\,\mathrm{d}x$.

10 a Given that $y = \dfrac{1}{x^2 + 3}$, show that $\dfrac{\mathrm{d}y}{\mathrm{d}x} = \dfrac{kx}{\left(x^2 + 3\right)^2}$ and state the value of k.

b Hence find $\displaystyle\int \dfrac{6x}{\left(x^2 + 3\right)^2}\,\mathrm{d}x$.

15.8 Definite integration

《 REMINDER

The evaluation of a definite integral can be written as:

$$\int_a^b f(x)\,\mathrm{d}x = \big[F(x)\big]_a^b = F(b) - F(a)$$

The following rules for definite integrals may also be used.

$$\int_a^b k\,f(x)\,\mathrm{d}x = k\int_a^b f(x)\,\mathrm{d}x, \text{ where } k \text{ is a constant}$$

$$\int_a^b \big[f(x) \pm g(x)\big]\,\mathrm{d}x = \int_a^b f(x)\,\mathrm{d}x \pm \int_a^b g(x)\,\mathrm{d}x$$

WORKED EXAMPLE 8

Evaluate $\displaystyle\int_0^2 \frac{4 + 3e^{4x}}{2e^{2x}}\,dx$.

Answer

$$\int_0^2 \left(2e^{-2x} + \frac{3}{2}e^{2x}\right)dx$$

$$\int_0^2 2e^{-2x}\,dx + \int \frac{3}{2}e^{2x}\,dx$$

$$\left[\frac{2}{-2}e^{-2x} + \frac{3}{2} \times \frac{1}{2}e^{2x}\right]_0^2$$

$$\left[-e^{-2x} + \frac{3}{4}e^{2x}\right]_0^2$$

$$\left[-e^{-4} + \frac{3}{4}e^4\right] - \left[-e^0 + \frac{3}{4}e^0\right]$$

$$-e^{-4} + \frac{3}{4}e^4 + e^0 - \frac{3}{4}e^0$$

$$-e^{-4} + \frac{3}{4}e^4 + 1 - \frac{3}{4}$$

$$-e^{-4} + \frac{3}{4}e^4 + \frac{1}{4}$$

REMINDER

$$\int \frac{1}{x}\,dx = \ln|x| + c \qquad \int \frac{1}{ax + b}\,dx = \frac{1}{a}\ln|ax + b| + c$$

WORKED EXAMPLE 9

a Find the value of $\displaystyle\int_2^4 \frac{6}{3x + 1}\,dx$.

Answer

$$\int_2^4 \frac{6}{3x + 1}\,dx = \left[\frac{6}{3}\ln|3x + 1|\right]_2^4 \qquad \text{substitute limits}$$

$$= (2\ln|13|) - (2\ln|7|) \qquad \text{simplify}$$

$$= 2(\ln 13 - \ln 7)$$

$$= 2\ln\frac{13}{7}$$

b Find the value of $\displaystyle\int_3^4 \frac{6}{3 - 2x}\,dx$.

Answer

$$\int_3^4 \frac{6}{3 - 2x}\,dx = \left[\frac{6}{-2}\ln|3 - 2x|\right]_3^4 \qquad \text{substitute limits}$$

$$= (-3\ln|-5|) - (-3\ln|-3|) \qquad \text{simplify}$$

$$= -3\ln 5 + 3\ln 3$$

$$= 3(\ln 3 - \ln 5)$$

$$= 3\ln\frac{3}{5}$$

Exercise 15.8

1 Evaluate.

a $\displaystyle\int_{1}^{2} 3x^6\,dx$

b $\displaystyle\int_{1}^{3} \frac{2}{x^4}\,dx$

c $\displaystyle\int_{1}^{5} (3x+2)\,dx$

d $\displaystyle\int_{0}^{4} \left(2x^2+1\right)dx$

e $\displaystyle\int_{-1}^{2} \left(2x^2-2x\right)dx$

f $\displaystyle\int_{2}^{4} \left(3+\frac{2}{x^2}\right)dx$

g $\displaystyle\int_{1}^{4} \left(x^2-\frac{2}{x^3}\right)dx$

h $\displaystyle\int_{1}^{3} \left(\frac{4x^2+1}{x^4}\right)dx$

i $\displaystyle\int_{-3}^{-2} (3x-1)(1-2x)\,dx$

j $\displaystyle\int_{1}^{4} \sqrt{x}\,(2x+1)\,dx$

k $\displaystyle\int_{-2}^{-0.5} \frac{(1-x)(3+x)}{x^2}\,dx$

l $\displaystyle\int_{1}^{4} \left(4\sqrt{x}-\frac{3}{\sqrt{x}}\right)dx$

2 Evaluate.

a $\displaystyle\int_{1}^{3} (3x-1)^2\,dx$

b $\displaystyle\int_{0}^{5} \sqrt{3x+1}\,dx$

c $\displaystyle\int_{-1}^{6} \sqrt{(x+2)^5}\,dx$

d $\displaystyle\int_{1}^{3} \frac{22}{(2x+1)^3}\,dx$

e $\displaystyle\int_{-3}^{-1} \frac{3}{(2x-3)^2}\,dx$

f $\displaystyle\int_{-2}^{0} \frac{10}{\sqrt{4-x}}\,dx$

3 Evaluate.

a $\displaystyle\int_{0}^{2} e^{3x}\,dx$

b $\displaystyle\int_{0}^{0.25} e^{2x}\,dx$

c $\displaystyle\int_{0}^{3} 7e^{-3x}\,dx$

d $\displaystyle\int_{0}^{\frac{3}{2}} e^{2-4x}\,dx$

e $\displaystyle\int_{0}^{2} \frac{2}{e^{3x-2}}\,dx$

f $\displaystyle\int_{0}^{3} \left(e^{2x}+1\right)^3\,dx$

g $\displaystyle\int_{0}^{1} \left(2e^x+e^{2x}\right)^2\,dx$

h $\displaystyle\int_{0}^{1} \left(2e^x-\frac{1}{2e^x}\right)^2\,dx$

i $\displaystyle\int_{0}^{4} \frac{1+3e^{2x}}{3e^x}\,dx$

4 Evaluate.

a $\displaystyle\int_{0}^{\frac{\pi}{2}} \cos x\,dx$

b $\displaystyle\int_{0}^{\frac{3\pi}{2}} (1+\cos 3x)\,dx$

c $\displaystyle\int_{0}^{\frac{\pi}{4}} \sin\left(3x-\frac{\pi}{2}\right)dx$

d $\displaystyle\int_{\frac{\pi}{6}}^{\frac{\pi}{2}} (3\cos x-2\sin 3x)\,dx$

e $\displaystyle\int_{0}^{\frac{\pi}{2}} (4x+\sin 3x)\,dx$

f $\displaystyle\int_{\frac{\pi}{4}}^{\frac{\pi}{2}} (\sin 4x-\cos 3x)\,dx$

5 Evaluate.

a $\displaystyle\int_{1}^{5} \frac{3}{2x+1}\,dx$

b $\displaystyle\int_{0}^{4} \frac{1}{4x+1}\,dx$

c $\displaystyle\int_{3}^{5} \frac{1}{2x-5}\,dx$

d $\displaystyle\int_{-1}^{2} \frac{3}{2x+3}\,dx$

e $\displaystyle\int_{1}^{4} \frac{-2}{1-2x}\,dx$

f $\displaystyle\int_{-3}^{-1} \frac{2}{2-3x}\,dx$

6 Evaluate.

a $\displaystyle\int_1^4 \left(2 + \frac{3}{2x-1} \right)$ **b** $\displaystyle\int_1^4 \left(\frac{1}{x} - \frac{2}{2x-1} \right) dx$ **c** $\displaystyle\int_{-1}^2 \left(1 + \frac{1}{5+2x} - 3x \right) dx$

7 Given that $\displaystyle\int_3^k \frac{3}{x-2}\, dx = 3\ln 3$, find the value of k.

8 a Divide $x^2 + 4x + 7$ by $x+2$, expressing your answer in the form $A + \dfrac{B}{x+2}$

b Using your answer to part a, evaluate $\displaystyle\int_1^4 \left(A + \frac{B}{x+2} \right)$.

9 a Find the quotient and remainder when $9x^2 + 6$ is divided by $3x+1$.

b Hence show that $\displaystyle\int_0^2 \frac{9x^2 + 6x}{3x+1}\, dx = 8 - \frac{1}{3}\ln 7$.

10 Find the value of $\displaystyle\int_0^2 \frac{4x^2 - 6x}{2x+1}\, dx$.

15.9 Further definite integration

WORKED EXAMPLE 10

a Given that $y = \dfrac{3\ln\left(x^2 + 4\right)}{2}$, find $\dfrac{dy}{dx}$. **b** Hence evaluate $\displaystyle\int_1^2 \frac{3x}{x^2+4}\, dx$.

Answers

a $\dfrac{dy}{dx} = \dfrac{3}{2} \times 2x \times \dfrac{1}{x^2+4}$

$\qquad = \dfrac{3x}{x^2+4}$

b $\displaystyle\int_1^2 \frac{3x}{x^2+4}\, dx = \left[\frac{3\ln\left(x^2+4\right)}{2} \right]_1^2$

$\qquad = \dfrac{3\ln\left((2)^2 + 4\right)}{2} - \dfrac{3\ln\left((1)^2 + 4\right)}{2}$

$\qquad = \dfrac{3\ln(8)}{2} - \dfrac{3\ln(5)}{2}$

$\qquad = \dfrac{3}{2}\ln\dfrac{8}{5}$

Exercise 15.9

1 a Given that $y = \left(x^4 + 4\right)^3$, find $\dfrac{dy}{dx}$. **b** Hence evaluate $\displaystyle\int_1^3 x^3\left(x^4 + 4\right)^2 dx$.

2 a Given that $y = \left(1 + e^x\right)^4$, find $\dfrac{dy}{dx}$. **b** Hence evaluate $\displaystyle\int_1^2 e^x\left(1 + e^x\right)^3 dx$.

3 a Given that $y = x\sqrt{2x^2 + 1}$, find $\dfrac{dy}{dx}$. **b** Hence evaluate $\displaystyle\int_0^2 \frac{4x^2 + 1}{\sqrt{2x^2 + 1}}\, dx$.

4 **a** Given that $y = \dfrac{1}{\sqrt{3x+1}}$, show that $\dfrac{dy}{dx} = \dfrac{3}{2\sqrt{(3x+1)^{\frac{3}{2}}}}$.

b Hence evaluate $\displaystyle\int_0^2 \dfrac{1}{\sqrt{(3x+1)^{\frac{3}{2}}}}\,dx$.

5 **a** Find $\dfrac{d}{dx}\left[\ln\left(5+3x+x^2\right)\right]$.

b Hence evaluate $\displaystyle\int_0^2 \dfrac{4x+6}{5+3x+x^2}\,dx$.

15.10 Area under a curve

 REMINDER

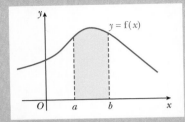

The area of the region bounded by the curve $y = f(x)$, the lines $x = a$ and $x = b$ and the x-axis is given by the definite integral:

$$\int_a^b f(x)\,dx, \text{ where } f(x) \geqslant 0$$

WORKED EXAMPLE 11

The diagram shows part of the curve whose equation is $y = x(x-1)(x-3)$.
Find the total shaded region shown.

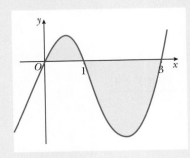

Answer

The required region consists of a section above the *x*-axis and a section below the *x*-axis.
Evaluate each area separately.

$$y = x(x - 1)(x - 3) = x^3 - 4x^2 + 3x$$

$$\int_0^1 x^3 - 4x^2 + 3x \, dx = \left[\frac{1}{4}x^4 - \frac{4}{3}x^3 + \frac{3}{2}x^2\right]_0^1$$

$$= \left(\frac{1}{4}(1)^4 - \frac{4}{3}(1)^3 + \frac{3}{2}(1)^2\right) - \left(\frac{1}{4}(0)^4 - \frac{4}{3}(0)^3 + \frac{3}{2}(0)^2\right)$$

$$= \left(\frac{1}{4} - \frac{4}{3} + \frac{3}{2}\right) - (0)$$

$$= \frac{5}{12}$$

$$\int_1^3 x^3 - 4x^2 + 3x \, dx = \left[\frac{1}{4}x^4 - \frac{4}{3}x^3 + \frac{3}{2}x^2\right]_1^3$$

$$= \left(\frac{1}{4}(3)^4 - \frac{4}{3}(3)^3 + \frac{3}{2}(3)^2\right) - \left(\frac{1}{4}(1)^4 - \frac{4}{3}(1)^3 + \frac{3}{2}(1)^2\right)$$

$$= \left(\frac{81}{4} - 36 + \frac{27}{2}\right) - \left(\frac{5}{12}\right)$$

$$= \left(\frac{-9}{4}\right) - \left(\frac{5}{12}\right)$$

$$= -\frac{8}{3}$$

The total area of the shaded regions $= \dfrac{5}{12} + \dfrac{8}{3} = \dfrac{37}{12}$ units^2

Exercise 15.10

1 Find the area of each shaded region.

a

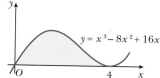

$y = x^3 - 8x^2 + 16x$

b

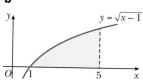

$y = \sqrt{x - 1}$

c

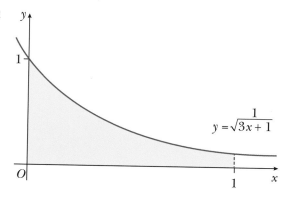

$y = \dfrac{1}{\sqrt{3x + 1}}$

d

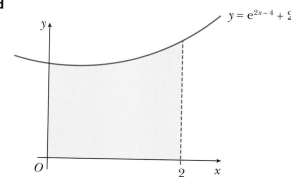

$y = e^{2x - 4} + 2$

e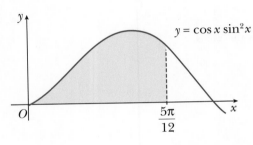

f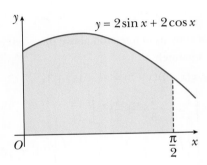

2 Find the area of each shaded region.

a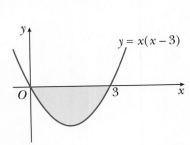

b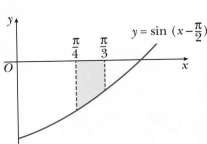

TIP

If the required area between $y = f(x)$ and the x-axis lies below the x-axis, then the result of the

$$\int_a^b f(x)\,dx \text{ calculation will be}$$

negative. The area however, is **positive**.

c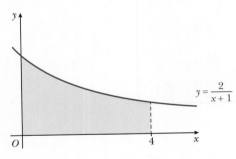

d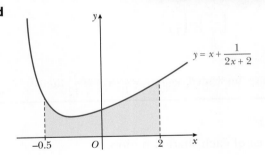

3 Sketch the following curves and find the area of the finite region or regions bounded by the curves and the x-axis.

a $y = x(x + 4)$

b $y = x(x + 3)(4 - x)$

c $y = x(x^2 - 9)$

d $y = x(x - 3)(x + 2)$

e $y = -x(x + 4)(x - 8)$

f $y = x^2(6 - 2x)$

4 Find the area enclosed by the curve $y = \dfrac{1}{x^2}$, the x-axis and the lines $x = -2$ and $x = -3$.

5 Find as an exact value, the area of the region enclosed by the curve $y = e^{\frac{x}{2}}$, the x-axis and the lines $x = 0$ and $x = \ln 2$.

6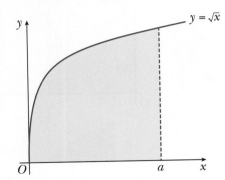

The shaded area in the figure shown is 1 unit². Find 'a' correct to 3 sf.

7 Find the area under the curve between $x = 0$ and $x = 4$. (Give your answer to 3 sf.)

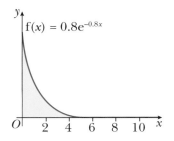

8

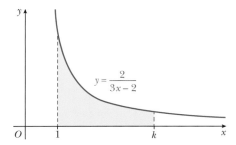

The diagram shows part of the curve $y = \dfrac{2}{3x - 2}$. Given that the shaded region has area 6, find the exact value of k.

15.11 Area of regions bounded by a line and a curve

REMINDER

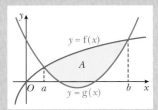

If two functions $f(x)$ and $g(x)$ intersect at $x = a$ and $x = b$, then the area, A, enclosed between the two curves is given by:

$$A = \int_{a}^{b} f(x)\,dx - \int_{a}^{b} g(x)\,dx$$

WORKED EXAMPLE 12

Find the area of the region bounded by the curve $y = 2x^2 + 3$, the line $y = 21$ and the y-axis.

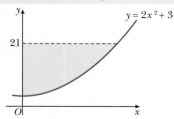

Answer

Find the x coordinate when $y = 21$.

$21 = 2x^2 + 3$

$18 = 2x^2$

$9 = x^2$

$x = 3$

Area = area of rectangle − area under curve

$$= 3 \times 21 - \int_0^3 2x^2 + 3 \, dx$$

$$= 63 - \left[\frac{2}{3}x^3 + 3x \right]_0^3$$

$$= 63 - \left(\left(\frac{2}{3} \times (3)^3 + 3(3) \right) - \left(\frac{2}{3} \times (0)^2 + 3(0) \right) \right)$$

$$= 63 - (27 - 0)$$

$$= 36$$

Exercise 15.11

1 Find the area of the shaded region in the interval $0 \leqslant x < \dfrac{\pi}{2}$.

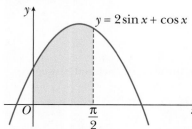

2 Sketch the following curves and lines and find the area enclosed between their graphs.

a $y = x^2 - 2x$ and $y = 2x$ **b** $y = -x^2 + 3x + 10$ and $y = 6$

c $y = x^2 + 1$ and $y = 7 - x$ **d** $y = x^2 - 4x + 5$ and $y = 5$

e $y = (x - 2)(x - 4)$ and $y = x - 2$ **f** $y = 6x - x^2$ and $y = 2x$

3 Sketch the following pairs of curves and find the area enclosed between their graphs.

a $y = 2x^2 - 7$ and $y = 5 - x^2$ **b** $y = (x - 1)^2$ and $y = 8 - (x - 1)^2$

TIP

You will need to find the x-coordinates of the points of intersection.

4 Find the shaded area enclosed by the curve $y = 2\sqrt{x}$, the line $y = 3 - x$ and the x-axis.

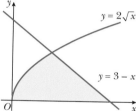

5 The parabolas $y = x^2 - 4x + 8$ and $y = 8 + 4x - x^2$ intersect at P and Q.

  a Find the coordinates of P and Q.

  b Calculate the shaded area.

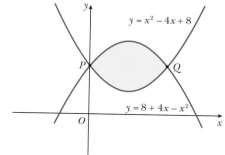

6 The curves with equations $y = 2x^2 - 6$ and $y = 10 - 2x^2$ intersect at A and B.

  a Write down the coordinates of A and B.

  b Calculate the area enclosed by these two curves.

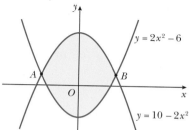

7 The diagram shows the curves $y = x^3 + x^2$ and $y = 2x^2 + 2x$. Calculate the shaded area.

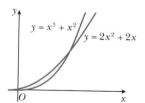

18

Summary

Integration as the reverse of differentiation

If $\dfrac{d}{dx}\big[F(x)\big] = f(x)$, then $\displaystyle\int f(x)\,dx = F(x) + c.$

Integration formulae

$$\int x^n\,dx = \frac{1}{n+1}x^{n+1} + c, \text{ where } c \text{ is a constant and } n \neq -1$$

$$\int (ax+b)^n\,dx = \frac{1}{a(n+1)}(ax+b)^{n+1} + c,\; n \neq -1 \text{ and } a \neq 0$$

$$\int e^x\,dx = e^x + c \qquad\qquad \int e^{ax+b}\,dx = \frac{1}{a}e^{ax+b} + c$$

$$\int \cos x\,dx = \sin x + c \qquad\qquad \int \big[\cos(ax+b)\big]\,dx = \frac{1}{a}\sin(ax+b) + c$$

$$\int \sin x\,dx = -\cos x + c \qquad\qquad \int \big[\sin(ax+b)\big]\,dx = -\frac{1}{a}\cos(ax+b) + c$$

$$\int \frac{1}{x}\,dx = \ln|x| + c \qquad\qquad \int \frac{1}{ax+b}\,dx = \frac{1}{a}\ln|ax+b| + c$$

Rules for indefinite integration

$$\int k f(x)\,dx = k\int f(x)\,dx, \text{ where } k \text{ is a constant}$$

$$\int \left[f(x) \pm g(x)\right]\,dx = \int f(x)\,dx \pm \int g(x)\,dx$$

Rules for definite integration

If $\int f(x)\,dx = F(x) + c$, then $\int_{a}^{b} f(x)\,dx = \left[F(x)\right]_{a}^{b} = F(b) - F(a)$.

$$\int_{a}^{b} k f(x)\,dx = k\int_{a}^{b} f(x)\,dx, \text{ where } k \text{ is a constant}$$

$$\int_{a}^{b} \left[f(x) \pm g(x)\right]\,dx = \int_{a}^{b} f(x)\,dx \pm \int_{a}^{b} g(x)\,dx$$

Area under a curve

The area, A, bounded by the curve $y = f(x)$, the x-axis and the lines $x = a$

and $x = b$ is given by the formula $A = \int_{a}^{b} f(x)\,dx$ if $f(x) \geqslant 0$.

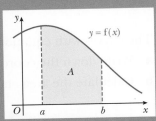

Area bounded by the graphs of two functions

If two functions $f(x)$ and $g(x)$ intersect at $x = a$ and $x = b$, then the area, A, enclosed between the two curves is given by the formula

$$A = \int_{a}^{b} f(x)\,dx - \int_{a}^{b} g(x)\,dx.$$

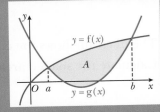

Exercise 15.12

1 A curve is such that $\dfrac{d^2 y}{dx^2} = 12x^2 - 4$. The curve passes through $(1, 4)$ and the gradient of the curve at the point $x = 0$ is -1. Find the equation of the curve.

2 A curve has equation $\dfrac{dy}{dx} = 2\sqrt{x} + \dfrac{p}{\sqrt{x}}$ and passes through the points $(0, 2)$ and $(1, 4)$. Find the value of p.

3 A curve is such that $\dfrac{dy}{dx} = 3x^2 - 4x - 1$. Given that the tangent to the curve at $x = 2$ passes through the origin, find the equation of the curve.

4 The point $P\left(1\dfrac{3}{4} + \dfrac{e}{4}\right)$ lies on the curve for which $\dfrac{dy}{dx} = \dfrac{x^3 + xe^x}{4x}$.
   a Find the equation of the curve.
   b Find the equation of the tangent to the curve at $x = 0$.

5 A curve is such that $\dfrac{dy}{dx} = k\sin 2x - 4$, where k is a constant. The curve passes through the point $(0, 5)$. The gradient of the curve at $x = \dfrac{\pi}{4}$ is -12.
   a Find the value of k.   b Find the equation of the curve.

6 The point $\left(0, -\dfrac{\sqrt{3}}{3}\right)$ lies on the curve for which $\dfrac{dy}{dx} = 2\cos\left(3x - \dfrac{\pi}{3}\right)$.

   a Find the equation of the curve.

   b Find the equation of the tangent to the curve at the point where $x = \dfrac{\pi}{3}$.

7 **a** Differentiate $e^{\cos x}$ with respect to x.

   b Hence find $\displaystyle\int 3\sin x \, e^{\cos x} \, dx$.

8 **a** Find $\dfrac{d}{dx}\left(1 - x^2\right)^{\frac{3}{2}}$.   **b** Hence find $\displaystyle\int x\sqrt{1 - x^2} \, dx$.

9 **a** Find $\dfrac{d}{dx}\left[\ln\left(1 + x^3\right)\right]$.   **b** Hence evaluate $\displaystyle\int_{1}^{e} \dfrac{x^2}{\left(1 + x^3\right)}$.

10 a Given that $y = \cos^3 x$, find $\dfrac{dy}{dx}$.   **b** Hence evaluate $\displaystyle\int_{0}^{\frac{\pi}{6}} \sin x \cos^2 x \, dx$.

11 The shaded area in the diagram below is $3p$ units^2, find p.

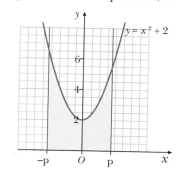

12 $OPQR$ is a rectangle. The two shaded regions are equal in area. Find k.

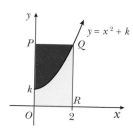

13 The equation of this curve is $y = x^2 + ax + b$. The x-coordinate of $A = 1$.
The curve crosses the y-axis at $(0, 3)$. The x-coordinate of $C = 4$.
Find the shaded area.

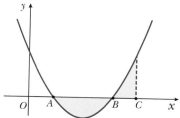

14 The tangent to the curve $y = x(4 - x)$ at the point $(1, 3)$ cuts the x-axis at the point P.

a Find the coordinates of P.

b Find the area of the shaded region.

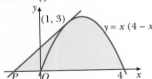

15 The curve $y = \sqrt{3x + 3}$ meets the y-axis at the point P. The tangent at the point $Q(2, 3)$ to this curve meets the y-axis at the point R. Find the exact area of the shaded region PQR.

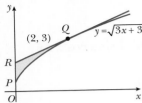

16

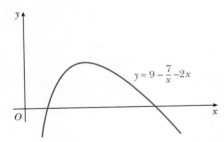

The diagram shows the curve with equation $y = 9 - \dfrac{7}{x} - 2x$, $x > 0$.

a Find the x intercepts of the curve.

b Calculate the area of the region bounded by the curve and the x axis.

17

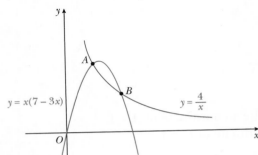

The diagram shows curves $y = x(7 - 3x)$ and $y = \dfrac{4}{x}$, $x > 0$.

The curves intersect at the points A and B.

Given that the coordinates of A are $(1, 4)$, find

a the coordinates of B,

b the area of the region enclosed by the two curves, giving your answer in an exact form.

Chapter 16:
Kinematics

This section will show you how to:

■ apply differentiation to kinematics problems that involve displacement, velocity and acceleration of a particle moving in a straight line with variable or constant acceleration.

16.1 Applications of differentiation in kinematics

 REMINDER

Displacement
Distance is a scalar quantity that refers to 'how much ground an object has covered' during its motion. Displacement is a vector quantity that refers to 'how far out of place an object is'; it is the object's overall change in position.

Velocity and acceleration
- If a particle moves in a straight line, with displacement function $s(t)$, then the rate of change of displacement with respect to time, $\dfrac{ds}{dt}$, is the **velocity**, v, of the particle at time t.

$$v = \frac{ds}{dt}$$

- If the velocity function is $v(t)$, then the rate of change of velocity with respect to time, $\dfrac{dv}{dt}$, is the **acceleration**, a, of the particle at time t.

$$a = \frac{dv}{dt} = \frac{d^2 s}{dt^2}$$

WORKED EXAMPLE 1

A particle starts from rest and moves in a straight line so that, t seconds after leaving a fixed point O, its displacement, s metres, is given by $s = 2t^3 - 15t^2 + 6t + 5$.

a Find the velocity of the particle when $t = 0$.

b Find the acceleration of the particle when $t = 2$.

Answers

a $v = \dfrac{ds}{dt}$

  $v = 6t^2 - 30t + 6$

  $t = 0$ when the particle passes through O.

  $t = 0$: $v = 6(0)^2 - 30(0) + 6$

  velocity $= 6 \text{ ms}^{-1}$

b $a = \dfrac{dv}{dt}$

  $a = 12t - 30$

  $t = 2$: $a = 12(2) - 30$

  $a = -6 \text{ ms}^{-2}$

  acceleration $= -6 \text{ ms}^{-2}$

Exercise 16.1

1 A particle, moving in a straight line, passes through a fixed point O. Its velocity $v\,\text{ms}^{-1}$, t seconds after passing through O, is given by $v = 4t^3 - 5t^2 + 7t + 6$.

  a Find the velocity of the particle as it passes through O.

  b Find the acceleration of the particle when $t = 3$.

2 A particle, moving in a straight line, passes through a fixed point O. Its velocity $v\,\text{ms}^{-1}$, t seconds after passing through O, is given by $v = 6e^{2t} - 2t$.

  a Find the initial velocity of the particle.

  b Find the initial acceleration of the particle.

3 A particle moves in a straight line such that its displacement, s metres, from a fixed point O on the line at time t seconds is given by $s = 4t^2 - t^3$.

  a Find the value of t when the displacement of the particle is again $0\,\text{m}$ from O.

  b Find the velocity of the particle when $t = 2$.

  c Show that the particle is decelerating for $t > \dfrac{4}{3}$ seconds.

4 A particle moves in a straight line so that, t seconds after passing through a fixed point O, its displacement, s metres, from O is given by $s = \ln(2 + 5t)$.

  a Find the value of t when the velocity of the particle is $0.1\,\text{ms}^{-1}$.

  b Find the distance travelled by the particle during the third second.

  c Find the acceleration of the particle when $t = 2$.

TIP

Remember 'in the third second' means between $t = 2$ and $t = 3$.

5 A particle travels in a straight line so that, t seconds after passing through a fixed point O, its velocity $v\,\text{ms}^{-1}$, is given by $v = 6\cos\left(\dfrac{2t}{3}\right)$.

  a Find the value of t when the velocity of the particle first equals $3\,\text{ms}^{-1}$.

  b Find the acceleration of the particle when $t = 6$.

6 A particle starts from rest and moves in a straight line so that, t seconds after leaving a fixed point O, its displacement, s metres, is given by $s = t^2 + t^3 + 12t - 23$.

  a Find the velocity of the particle when $t = 2$.

  b Explain why the motion is always in the same direction.

7 A particle P which is moving in a straight line, is initially at a point O on a line. After t seconds its velocity is $(t^2 - 6t + 2)\,\text{ms}^{-1}$.

  a Find the velocity of the particle when $t = 5$.

  b Find the displacement of the particle from 0 when $t = 5$.

  c Comment upon both your answers.

TIP

Distance and displacement are equal only if the direction of motion does not change. Check first to see whether there are values of t when the direction of motion changes, i.e. when $v = 0$.

8 A particle moves in a straight line such that its displacement, s metres, from a fixed point O on the line at time t seconds is given by $s = 5 + 9t^2 - 2t^3$.

  a Find the distance travelled during the first 2 seconds of its motion.

  b Find the distance covered in the first 4 seconds.

  c Find the displacement of the particle from O when $t = 4$.

9 A particle P which is moving in a straight line, is initially at a point O on a line. After t seconds its velocity is $\left(3t^2 - 12t + 9\right)$ ms^{-1}.

a Find the initial velocity.

b Find the time when the acceleration is zero.

c Find the times when the direction of the particle's motion is reversed.

10 A particle moves in a straight line so that the displacement, s metres, from a fixed point O, is given by $s = 12t - 2t^3 - 1$, where t is the time in seconds after passing a point X on the line. Taking displacements to the right of O as positive, and interpreting positive velocities to the right of O:

a Find expressions for the velocity and acceleration of the particle.

b Find the position of the particle relative to O and its velocity when $t = 0$.

c Find the times and positions when the particle reverses direction.

d Find the values of t for which the

   i speed is increasing

   ii velocity is increasing.

16.2 Applications of integration in kinematics

« REMINDER

If a particle moves in a straight line where the acceleration of the particle is a then

$$v = \int a\,dt$$

and

$$s = \int v\,dt$$

In this section you will solve problems that involve both differentiation and integration. The diagram should help you remember when to differentiate and when to integrate.

displacement (s)

$v = \dfrac{ds}{dt}$ $s = \int v\,dt$

velocity (v)

$a = \dfrac{dv}{dt} = \dfrac{d^2 s}{dt^2}$ $v = \int a\,dt$

acceleration (a)

WORKED EXAMPLE 2

A particle moving in a straight line has an initial velocity of $2\,\text{m s}^{-1}$ at a point O on the line.
The particle moves so that its acceleration t seconds later is given by $(2t-6)\,\text{m s}^{-2}$.

Find the

a velocity when $t = 5$

b displacement of the particle from O when $t = 5$.

Answers

a $v = \displaystyle\int a\,\mathrm{d}t$

$v = t^2 - 6t + c$

$v = 2$ when $t = 0$

$2 = 0^2 - 6(0) + c$

$c = 2$

$v = t^2 - 6t + 2$

$t = 5 : v = (5)^2 - 6(5) + 2$

$v = -3\,\text{ms}^{-1}$

The particle is moving at $3\,\text{m s}^{-1}$ towards O.

b $s = \displaystyle\int v\,\mathrm{d}t$

$s = \dfrac{1}{3}t^3 - 3t^2 + 2t + c$ Remember to include the constant term c.

$s = 0$ when $t = 0$:

$0 = \dfrac{1}{3}(0)^3 - 3(0)^2 + 2(0) + c$ Substitute to find c.

$c = 0$

$s = \dfrac{1}{3}t^3 - 3t^2 + 2t$

$t = 5 : s = \dfrac{1}{3}(5)^3 - 3(5)^2 + 2(5)$

$s = -\dfrac{70}{3}\,\text{m}.$

Displacement $= -\dfrac{70}{3}\,\text{m}.$

The particle has changed direction, moving back towards O having passed through O to the opposite side.

Exercise 16.2

1 A particle, moving in a straight line, passes through a fixed point O. Its velocity $v\,\text{ms}^{-1}$, t seconds after passing through O, is given by $v = 12t - t^2$.

    a Find the velocity of the particle when the acceleration is $6\,\text{ms}^{-2}$.

    b Find the time taken before the particle returns to O.

    c Find the distance travelled by the particle in the 2nd second.

    d Find the distance travelled by the particle before it comes to instantaneous rest.

    e Find the distance travelled by the particle in the first 14 seconds.

2 A particle, moving in a straight line, passes through a fixed point O. Its velocity $v\,\text{ms}^{-1}$, t seconds after passing through O, is given by $v = \dfrac{10}{(2t+3)^2}$.

    a Find the acceleration of the particle when $t = 1$.

    b Find an expression for the displacement of the particle from O.

    c Find the distance travelled by the particle in the 3rd second.

3 A particle, moving in a straight line, passes through a fixed point O. Its velocity $v\,\mathrm{ms}^{-1}$, t seconds after passing through O, is given by $v = 3e^{2t} + t$.

   a Find the acceleration of the particle when $t = 1$.

   b Find an expression for the displacement of the particle from O.

   c Find the total distance travelled by the particle in the first 2 seconds of its motion. Give your answer correct to the nearest metre.

4 A particle, moving in a straight line, passes through a fixed point O. Its velocity $v\,\mathrm{ms}^{-1}$, t seconds after passing through O, is given by $v = 2t + 6\cos\left(\dfrac{t}{2}\right)$. Find the displacement of the particle from O when $t = \dfrac{\pi}{3}$ and its acceleration at this instant.

5 A particle starts from rest at a point A and moves along a straight line AB with an acceleration after t seconds given by $a = \left(8 - 2t^2\right)\,\mathrm{ms}^{-2}$. Find:

   a the greatest speed of the particle as it moves along AB

   b the time when the greatest speed occurs

   c the distance travelled in this time.

6 A particle P, starts from rest at a point X and moves in a straight line with an acceleration expressed as $a = 4t$. After 2 seconds, the particle reaches Y and it stops accelerating.

   a Find the velocity of P when it reaches Y.

   b Find the distance XY.

   The particle leaves Y with a velocity $-3\,\mathrm{ms}^{-1}$, and finally comes to rest at point Z.

   c Find the value of t when the particle reaches Z.

   d Find the distance XZ.

7 A particle moves in a straight line so that t seconds after passing through a fixed point O, its acceleration, $a\,\mathrm{ms}^{-2}$, is given by $a = pt + q$, where p and q are constants. The particle passes through O with velocity $3\,\mathrm{ms}^{-1}$ and acceleration $-8\,\mathrm{ms}^{-2}$. The particle first comes to instantaneous rest when $t = 1$.

   a Find the value of p and the value of q.

   b Find an expression, in terms of t, for the displacement of the particle.

   c Find the second value of t for which the particle is at instantaneous rest.

   d Find the distance travelled during the 4th second.

Summary

The relationships between displacement, velocity and acceleration are:

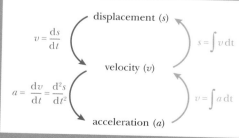

A particle is at instantaneous rest when $v = 0$.

Exercise 16.3

1 A particle starts from rest and moves in a straight line so that t seconds after passing through a fixed point O, its velocity $v\,\text{ms}^{-1}$, is given by $v = 6(1 - e^{-2t})$.
   a Find the velocity of the particle when $t = \ln 5$.
   b State the value which v approaches as t becomes very large.
   c Find the acceleration of the particle when $v = 2$.

2 A particle is moving in a straight line with a velocity given by $v = 2t^2 - 11t + 14$. Initially, the displacement of the body is $50\,\text{m}$ from O.
   a Find the initial velocity of the body.
   b Find the time when the particle first comes to rest.
   c Find the acceleration of the particle when $t = 5$.

3 A particle, moving in a straight line, passes through a fixed point O. Its velocity $v\,\text{ms}^{-1}$, t seconds after passing through O, is given by $v = 3e^{3t} + 4e^{-2t}$.
   a Show that the velocity is never zero.
   b Find the acceleration when $t = \ln 3$.
   c Find, to the nearest metre, the displacement of the particle from O when $t = 3$.

4 A particle, moving in a straight line, passes through a fixed point O. Its velocity $v\,\text{ms}^{-1}$, t seconds after passing through O, is given by $v = \cos 2t + 3\sin 2t$.
   a Find the value of t when the particle is first instantaneously at rest.
   b Find the velocity and acceleration of the particle when $t = \dfrac{\pi}{3}$.

5 A particle moves in a straight line such that its displacement, s metres, from a fixed point O at a time t seconds, is given by $s = t^3 - 3t + 1$. Taking displacements to the right of O as positive, and interpreting positive velocities to the right of O:
   a Find expressions for the particle's velocity (v) and acceleration (a).
   b Describe the motion of the particle when $t = 0$.
   c Describe the motion of the particle at $t = 2$.
   d Find the position of the particle when it changes its direction of motion.

6 The acceleration of a particle P, which is travelling in a straight line is inversely proportional to $(t + 1)^3$. Initially P is at rest at a point O and 3 seconds later it has a speed of $2\,\text{ms}^{-1}$. Find in terms of t the displacement of P from O at any time.

7 A particle moves in a straight line such that its displacement, s metres, from a fixed point O at a time t seconds, is given by:
   $s = 4t + 3$ for $0 \leqslant t \leqslant 4$,
   $s = 3 + 2\ln(t + 5)$ for $t > 4$.
   a Find the initial velocity of the particle.
   b Find the velocity of the particle when **i** $t = 3$ **ii** $t = 5$.
   c Find the acceleration of the particle when **i** $t = 3$ **ii** $t = 5$.
   d Sketch the displacement-time graph for the motion of the particle.
   e Find the distance travelled by the particle in the 8th second.

8 A particle starts from rest and moves in a straight line so that, t seconds after leaving a fixed point O, its velocity, $v\,\text{ms}^{-1}$, is given by $v = 2 + 5\cos 2t$.
   a Find the range of values for the acceleration.
   b Find the distance travelled by the particle before it first comes to instantaneous rest. Give your answer correct to 3 sf.

Answers

Chapter 1

Exercise 1.1

1 one-one   **2** many-one

3 one-one   **4** one-one

5 one-one   **6** one-one

7 one-one   **8** one-many

Exercise 1.2

1 1, 2, 3, 4, 5, 6 and 7

2 a $-11 \leqslant f(x) \leqslant -1$

   b $-2 \leqslant f(x) \leqslant 10$

   c $-3 \leqslant f(x) \leqslant 13$

   d $0 \leqslant f(x) \leqslant 32$

   e $\dfrac{1}{81} \leqslant f(x) \leqslant 27$

   f $\dfrac{-1}{6} \leqslant f(x) \leqslant -1$

3 $g(x) \geqslant -5$

4 $f(x) \leqslant 4$

5 $f(x) \leqslant 3$

6 $f(x) \geqslant -2$

7 $f(x) \leqslant 8$

8 $f(x) \leqslant 3$

9 a $x \in \mathbb{R} \quad x \neq -3$

   b $x \in \mathbb{R} \quad x \neq 2$

   c $x \in \mathbb{R} \quad x \neq -2 \quad x \neq 3$

   d $x \in \mathbb{R} \quad x \neq -2, \quad x \neq 2$

   e $x \in \mathbb{R} \quad x \geqslant 4^{\frac{1}{3}}$

   f $x \in \mathbb{R} \quad x \geqslant -5$

   g $x \in \mathbb{R} \quad x > 2$

   h $x \in \mathbb{R} \quad x < 1$

   i $x \in \mathbb{R}$

Exercise 1.3

1 -4

2 7

3 -2

4 $\dfrac{57}{16}$

5 a fg   **b** gf

6 $x = 1.7$

7 $x = 5\sqrt{2}$

8 $x = 10$

9 $x = \dfrac{1}{3}\left(1 + \sqrt{2}\right)$

10 a fg   **b** gf

   c g^2 **d** f^2

11 a gf   **b** ff

   c fg

12 a domain $x \in \mathbb{R} \quad x \neq -0.5$

     range $g(x) \in \mathbb{R}, \; x \neq 0.5$

   b $x = 5$

   c domain $x \in \mathbb{R} \quad x < -0.5 \; x \geqslant 5$

     range $fg(x) \in \mathbb{R},$

     $0 \leqslant fg(x) \leqslant \dfrac{\sqrt{2}}{2} \; fg(x) > \dfrac{\sqrt{2}}{2}$

Exercise 1.4

1 a $-5, 6$ **b** $-6, 2$

   c $\dfrac{2}{3}, \dfrac{10}{3}$ **d** $-28, 32$

   e $-\dfrac{16}{3}, \dfrac{8}{3}$ **f** $-\dfrac{3}{2}, \dfrac{21}{2}$

   g $15, 21$ **h** $-\dfrac{35}{8}, \dfrac{5}{4}$

   i $2, 6$

2 a $-\dfrac{7}{5}, -17$ **b** $-\dfrac{11}{7}, 7$

   c $-4, -\dfrac{20}{7}$ **d** $\dfrac{3}{5}$

   e $-1, \dfrac{9}{5}$ **f** $\dfrac{8}{5}$

3 a ± 3 **b** $\pm\sqrt{6}$

   c $-4, -2, 3$ **d** $0, 1, 5$

   e $3, 1 + 3\sqrt{6}$ **f** $-1, 1.5$

   g $1, 1.5$ **h** $-1, 3 - \sqrt{6}$

   i no solutions

4 a $(-2, 2); (3, 7)$

   b $(-0.25, 1.25); (0.25, 0.75); (1, 0)$

Exercise 1.5

1 a

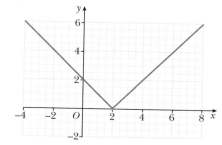

   b

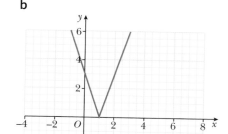

   c

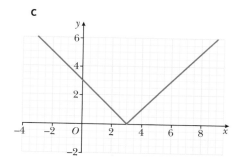

   d

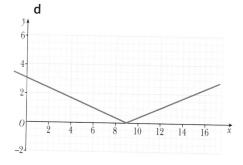

e

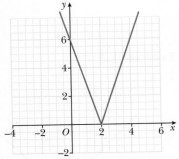

b

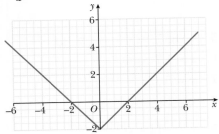

5 a $-8 \leqslant f(x) \leqslant 4$

  b $0 \leqslant f(x) \leqslant 8$

  c $-8 \leqslant f(x) \leqslant 2$

6 a and **b**

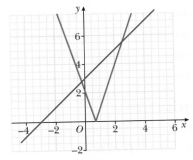

  c $x = -0.25, 2.5$

f

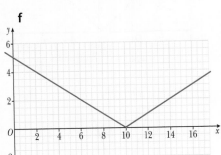

c

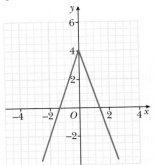

7 a

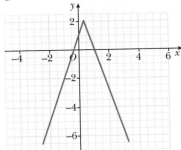

  b $-6 \leqslant f(x) \leqslant 2$

  c $x = \dfrac{5}{3}, -1$

2 a

x	-2	-1	0	1	2	3	4
y	0	1	2	3	2	1	0

b

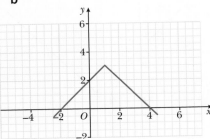

d

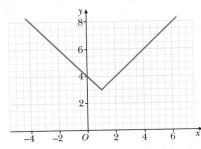

8 a

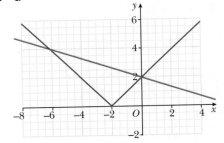

  b $-6 < x < 0$

3 a

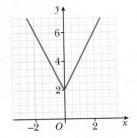

e

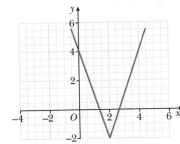

Exercise 1.6

1 $f^{-1}(x) = \sqrt{x+3} - 2$

2 $f^{-1}(x) = \dfrac{2x+5}{x}$

f

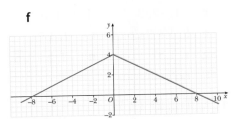

4 a $-6 \leqslant f(x) \leqslant 15$

  b $0 \leqslant f(x) \leqslant 15$

  c $-6 \leqslant f(x) \leqslant 6$

3 $f^{-1}(x) = \dfrac{2 + \sqrt{x-3}}{3}$

4 $f^{-1}(x) = (x-4)^2 + 2$

5 $f^{-1}(x) = \dfrac{x+4}{3}$.

$$g^{-1}(x) = \frac{4x - 4}{x}.$$

6 a $f^{-1}(x) = \sqrt{x-3} + 2$

b $x = 28$

7 a $g^{-1}(x) = \frac{3x+1}{x-3}$. $g(x)$ is a self inverse function

b $x = \frac{19}{3}$

8 a $f^{-1}(x) = 2x + 4$

b $4 \pm 2\sqrt{7}$

9 $\frac{2 - \sqrt{13}}{3}$, $\frac{2 + \sqrt{13}}{3}$

10 $f^{-1}(x) = \sqrt{\frac{4x + 9}{1 - x}}$ $x \neq 1$

11 $x = \frac{1}{25}$

12 $k = -2$

13 a $(3x + 2)^{\frac{1}{3}}$

b $3\sqrt[3]{x} + 2$

14 a $\frac{x-1}{2}$

b $2x - 1$

c $x - 2$

d $x - 1$

e $x - 1$

f $x - 2$

$\left(gf\right)^{-1} = f^{-1}g^{-1}$ $\left(fg\right)^{-1} = g^{-1}f^{-1}$

15 $f(x) = \frac{1}{6}x - \frac{1}{6}$

16 $f(x) = \pm(3x + 1)$

Exercise 1.7

1

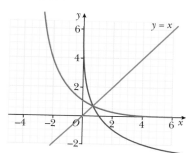

2

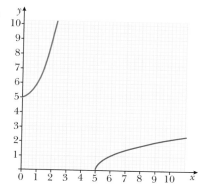

3

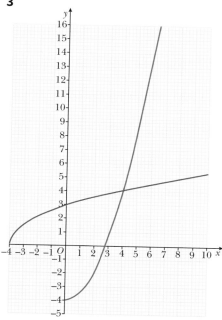

4 a $f^{-1}(x) = \frac{x + 6}{3}$

b

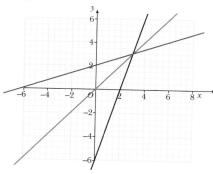

c $(3, 3)$

5 a $f(x)$ is a one to one function, $f^{-1}(x) = 1 + \sqrt{1 + x}$ $x \geqslant -1$

b $f^{-1}(x) \geqslant 1$

c

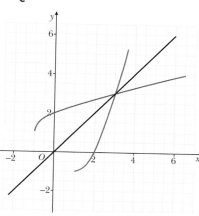

d $(0, 2)$

6 b

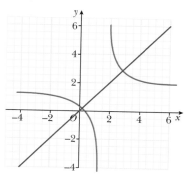

c $\left(0, \frac{1}{3}\right)\left(\frac{1}{3}, 0\right)$

Exercise 1.8

1 a $x = 2$

b $f(x) \geqslant -3$

2 $a = \sqrt{2}$

3 $x = \frac{5}{3}$

4 $1 \pm \frac{1}{\sqrt{2}}$

5 $(-2, 1)$; $(4, 13)$

6 a and **b**

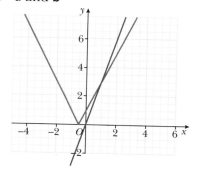

c $x = 1$

7 a 'v' shaped graph, vertex at $(-3, 0)$, y-intercept 3

b $x < 2$

8 $\pm\sqrt{3}$

9 a $\dfrac{x-3}{2}$

b $\dfrac{1}{2x+4}$

c $\dfrac{-1 \pm \sqrt{13}}{2}$

10 a $f^{-1}(x) = \dfrac{1-2x}{x-2}$ $x \neq 2$

b $(1, 1)(-1, -1)$

Chapter 2
Exercise 2.1

1 a $x = -3, y = 2; x = 2, y = 12$

b $x = \dfrac{-1}{3}, y = 3; x = 4, y = 16$

c $x = 2, y = 3; x = 3, y = 2$

d $x = \dfrac{1}{2}, y = \dfrac{-5}{2}; x = 2, y = -1$

e $x = \pm 2, y = \pm 1; x = \pm 1, y = \pm 2$

f $x = -6, y = \dfrac{-1}{3}; x = \dfrac{1}{2}, y = 4$

g $x = -4, y = 11; x = \dfrac{1}{2}, y = 2$

h $x = \dfrac{5\sqrt{2}}{2}, y = -\sqrt{2};$

$x = \dfrac{-5\sqrt{2}}{2}, y = \sqrt{2};$

$x = 1, y = -5;$

$x = -1, y = 5$

2 a $xy = 48, x + y = 16$

b $12\,\text{cm}$ by $4\,\text{cm}$

3 Length 30m, width 10m or length 20m, width 15m

4 17 and 5

5 $(3, 3)$ and $(1, -1)$

6 $(-1, 4), (5, 10); 6\sqrt{2}$

7 $a = -1, b = -4$ $B = (-1, 0)$

8 a $x = 3, y = 4; x = -5, y = 0$

b $4\sqrt{5}$

c $y = -2x$

Exercise 2.2

1 a $(x+3)^2 - 10$

b $(x-1)^2 - 2$

c $\left(x - \dfrac{3}{2}\right)^2 - \dfrac{5}{4}$

d $\left(x - \dfrac{1}{2}\right)^2 - \dfrac{13}{4}$

2 a $2\left(x + \dfrac{3}{2}\right)^2 - \dfrac{5}{2}$

b $2(x+2)^2 - 3$

c $3(x-1)^2 - 2$

d $2\left(x - \dfrac{1}{4}\right)^2 - \dfrac{17}{8}$

3 a $25 - (x-5)^2$

b $36 - (x-6)^2$

c $\dfrac{25}{4} - \left(x - \dfrac{5}{2}\right)^2$

d $\dfrac{49}{4} - \left(x - \dfrac{7}{2}\right)^2$

4 a $9 - (x+2)^2$

b $17 - (x+3)^2$

c $\dfrac{73}{4} - \left(x + \dfrac{5}{2}\right)^2$

d $\dfrac{45}{4} - \left(x + \dfrac{3}{2}\right)^2$

5 a $12 - 3(x+1)^2$

b $5 - 2(x+1)^2$

c $20 - 2(x+2)^2$

d $\dfrac{53}{12} - 15\left(x + \dfrac{1}{6}\right)^2$

6 a $(x-4)^2 + 2$

b $x = 4$

c $(4, 2)$

7 a $-2(x+3)^2 + 25$

b $\cap$ shaped curve, vertex $= (-3, 25)$

c $x = -3$

d 25

8 a $(x-3)^2 + 2$ $a = 1, p = 3, q = 2$

b $(3, 2)$

c minimum

d No

e $\cup$ shaped curve, vertex $= (3, 2)$

9 a $f(x) = 2(x-3)^2 + 5$

b $5, x = 3$

c $f(x) \geq 5$

d $x \geq 3$

10 $a = -20, b = 5, c = -6$

11 $f(x) = 2(x+2)^2 - 3$ $a = 2, p = 2, q = -3$

12 a $f(x) = (x+3)^2 - 10$

b $-3 \pm \sqrt{10}$

13 -0.75

14 a $5\left(x - \dfrac{3}{10}\right)^2 + \dfrac{131}{20}$

b $\left(\dfrac{3}{10}, \dfrac{131}{20}\right)$ minimum

c $\dfrac{131}{20} \leq f(x) \leq 117$

d No, it is not a one-one function.

Exercise 2.3

1 a $y = \left|x^2 - x - 12\right|$

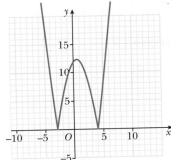

b $y = |x^2 + 3x - 4|$

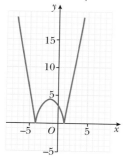

c $y = |2x^2 - 5x - 3|$

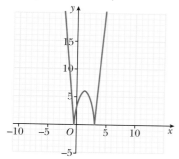

d $y = |x^2 - 2x|$

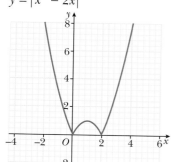

2 a $f(x) = 8 - (x + 2)^2$

b

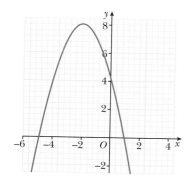

c

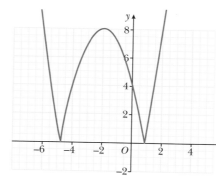

3 a $f(x) = 3(x - 1)^2 - 2$

b

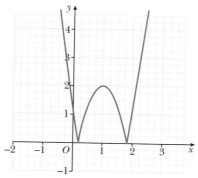

4 $(1, 3), \left((1 + \sqrt{6}), (3 + 2\sqrt{6})\right)$

5 a $(2, 1)$ **b** $k = 0, k > 1$

6 a $(4, 4)$ **b** $k = 4$

7 a $\pm\sqrt{14}$ **b** $\pm\sqrt{3}$

  c $-1, 2$

  d $-3, -1, -2 - \sqrt{7}, -2 + \sqrt{7}$

  e $1 - \sqrt{\dfrac{7}{2}}, \ 1 + \sqrt{\dfrac{7}{2}}$

  f $1 - \sqrt{10}, \ 1 + \sqrt{10}$

8 a $y = |x^2 - 12|$

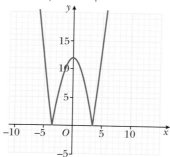

  b $x < 3 \quad x > 4$

9 a $x = 5, y = 11; x = \sqrt{3},$
     $y = 1 + 2\sqrt{3}$

  b $x = -2, y = 5; x = 0, y = 3;$
     $x = 3, y = 0$

  c $x = -7, y = 9; x = -5, y = 7;$
     $x = 2, y = 0$

Exercise 2.4

1 a $x < -6, \quad x > 3$

  b $-6 < x < 0$

  c $x \leqslant -4, \quad x \geqslant \dfrac{1}{3}$

  d $x \leqslant -\dfrac{1}{2}, \quad x \geqslant \dfrac{3}{2}$

  e $0 \leqslant x \leqslant \dfrac{3}{4}$

  f $x \leqslant 7 - \sqrt{46}, \quad x \geqslant 7 + \sqrt{46}$

2 a $-\dfrac{3}{2} < x < 2$

  b $x \leqslant -\dfrac{1}{2}, \quad x \geqslant 4$

  c $-3 \leqslant x \leqslant \dfrac{4}{3}$

  d $x < -6, \quad x > 1$

  e $\dfrac{1}{2} \leqslant x \leqslant \dfrac{3}{2}$

  f $2 \leqslant x \leqslant 7$

3 a $-3 - \sqrt{10} < x < -3 + \sqrt{10}$

  b $x \leqslant \dfrac{1}{2}(1 - \sqrt{5}),$
     $x \geqslant \dfrac{1}{2}(1 + \sqrt{5})$

  c $\dfrac{1}{2}(1 - \sqrt{13}) < x < \dfrac{1}{2}(1 + \sqrt{13})$

  d $\dfrac{1}{2}(3 - \sqrt{5}) < x < \dfrac{1}{2}(3 + \sqrt{5})$

4 a $-3 \leqslant x \leqslant -1$

  b $x \leqslant -3, x \geqslant 5$

  c $2.5 < x < 3$

  d $-3 < x < 4$

5 a $-2 < x < -1, 2 < x < 3$

  b $x \leqslant 0, x \geqslant 6$

  c $3 - \sqrt{17} < x < 2,$
     $4 < x < 3 + \sqrt{17}$

6 a $p = 4, q = 5$

193

b $5, x = -4$

c $\dfrac{1}{5}$

Exercise 2.5

1 a no roots

  b two distinct roots

  c two equal roots

  d no roots

  e two distinct roots

  f two distinct roots

  g two equal roots

  h no roots

  i two equal roots

2 a $-6 < k < 6$

  b $k > \dfrac{9}{20}$

  c $k > \dfrac{25}{28}$

3 a $k \leqslant \dfrac{9}{4}$

  b $k \geqslant -\dfrac{1}{7}$

  c $k \leqslant -4\sqrt{3}, \quad k \geqslant 4\sqrt{3}$

4 $k = \pm 24$

5 $b^2 = 4a$

6 $k = \dfrac{1}{3}$

7 $k = 0, k = 3$

8 $a = -2$, roots are 0, 2; $a = 6$, roots are $-4, -2$

Exercise 2.6

2 a $\left(2 - \sqrt{2},\ 0\right), \left(2 + \sqrt{2}, 0\right)$

  b $k = -7$

3 $k = -4, k = 0$

4 $c = \pm 4$

5 $k < 2 - 2\sqrt{2}\ , k > 2 + 2\sqrt{2}$

6 a $k = \pm 4$

  b $\left(\dfrac{3}{2}, \dfrac{-5}{2}\right) \qquad \left(-\dfrac{3}{2}, \dfrac{5}{2}\right)$

7 $k > -5$

8 $-11 < x < 1$

9 $m = -5, -1$

Exercise 2.7

1 a $\dfrac{-5}{3} < x < \dfrac{3}{2}$

  b $x < -1 \quad x > 4$

2 $-13 \leqslant x \leqslant -2$

3 a $f(x) = 2(x + 2)^2 - 6$

    $A = 2, B = 2, C = -6$

  b -6

  c $-2 \pm \sqrt{3}$

4 a 2

  b $f(x) \geqslant -4$

  c $f^{-1}(x) = 2 + \sqrt{x + 4}$

5 $A(2, 21), B(7, 16)$

6 $k < -1, k > \dfrac{5}{4}$

7 a $18 - (x - 3)^2$

  b 18

  c $\left(3 - 3\sqrt{2}, 0\right) \quad \left(3 + 3\sqrt{2}, 0\right)$

  d

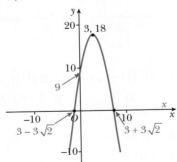

8 $x < -3 \quad x > 2$

9 a $4\left(x + \dfrac{3}{4}\right)^2 + \dfrac{19}{4}$;

    $a = 4,\ b = \dfrac{3}{4},\ c = \dfrac{19}{4}$

  b $x = -\dfrac{3}{4}, \dfrac{19}{4}$

  c $-2.5 < x < 1$

10 $x < 1 - \sqrt{13} \quad x > 1 + \sqrt{13}$

11 $p = -7, q = -2$

12 a $k \leqslant 4, k \geqslant 12$

  b $k = 4$

  c $x = 0.5$

13 a $f(x) = (x - 1)^2 - 2$

  b $-2 \leqslant f(x) \leqslant 14$

  c $f(x)$ is not a one-to-one function

14 a $f(x) = 22 - (x - 4)^2$ $a = 22$, $b = 4$, $(4, 22)$

  b

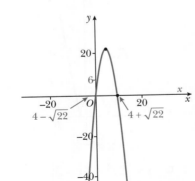

Chapter 3

Exercise 3.1

1 a x^9

  b x^{28}

  c $16x^{12}$

  d x^4

  e x^2

  f $3x^3$

  g x^{-10}

  h x^{15}

  i $6x^{-2}$

  j $\dfrac{x^9}{8}$

  k $36x^{-6}$

  l $\dfrac{2}{5}x^{-1}$

  m $2x^{\frac{1}{2}}$

  n $\dfrac{2}{9}x^{-\frac{5}{3}}$

  o $\dfrac{y^3}{2}$

  p $\dfrac{1}{64}a^{-12}b^{-6}$

  q $2x^5$

  r $\dfrac{2}{3}x^4y^{12}$

  s $2(1 + 2x)^{\frac{1}{2}}\left(1 + 2x + 2x^2\right)$

  t $\dfrac{1}{16}x^{-4}$

  u $\dfrac{8}{3}x^2y^{-8}$

2 $a = 3, b = 6$

3 $a = -3, b = \dfrac{3}{2}$

4 $x = 5, y = 8$

5 $2(1 + x)(1 + 2x)^{-\frac{1}{2}}$

Exercise 3.2

1 a $x = 1$

  b $y = \dfrac{5}{3}$

  c $x = -1$

  d $x = 2, x = -1$

2 a $x = -3$

  b $x = \dfrac{9}{4}$

  c $n = 6$

  d $x = 8$

e $x = \dfrac{3}{4}$ f $x = \dfrac{1}{5}$

g $y = \dfrac{3}{2}$ h $x = 8$

i $x = 2, x = 0$ j $x = 2, x = 0$

k $x = \pm\dfrac{1}{3}$ l $x = 81$

m $x = 9$ n $x = -3 \pm \sqrt{17}$

o $y = \dfrac{13}{4}$ p $t = 3$

3 a $x = \dfrac{2}{13}$ b $x = \dfrac{6}{5}$

c $y = -1$

4 a $x = 2$ b $y = 3$

c $x = -1$

5 a $x = 1, y = 3$ b $x = 1, y = 2$

6 a $y = 4, y = -2$ b $x = 16$

7 a $y = 5, y = 3$ b $x = 25, x = 9$

8 a $x = 5, x = -2$ b $x = \pm 5$

Exercise 3.3

1 a $6\sqrt{3}$ b $2\sqrt{3} - \sqrt{2}$

c $2 - 6\sqrt{2}$

2 $6 + 7\sqrt{5}$

3 $8\sqrt{2} - \sqrt{3} - 5$.

4 aC, bE, cB, dD, eA

5 $a = 22 - 3\sqrt{2}$ $b = 10 + \sqrt{2}$

$c = 12 - 4\sqrt{2}$ $d = 8 + 2\sqrt{2}$

$e = 2 - 2\sqrt{2}$

$f = -2 - 10\sqrt{2}$

Exercise 3.4

1 a 5 b 3

c $2\sqrt{2}$ d $\sqrt{35}$

e 6 f $12\sqrt{6}$

g 12 h 40

i $40\sqrt{5}$ j $81\sqrt{3}$

2 a $\sqrt{6}$ b 2

c $\sqrt{7}$ d $\sqrt{2}$

e $\sqrt{5}$ f 3

g $\dfrac{1}{2}$ h 4

i $\dfrac{16}{7}$ j $\dfrac{1}{3}$

k $3\sqrt{3}$

m 6

o $5\sqrt{14}$

3 a $2\sqrt{6}$ b $2\sqrt{10}$

c $4\sqrt{3}$ d $3\sqrt{5}$

e $6\sqrt{2}$ f $3\sqrt{3}$

g $4\sqrt{5}$ h $2\sqrt{17}$

i $10\sqrt{5}$ j $9\sqrt{2}$

k $\sqrt{2}$ l $\dfrac{9}{2}$

m $3\sqrt{2}$ n $3\sqrt{2}$

o $\dfrac{8}{3}$ p $12\sqrt{3}$

q $4\sqrt{10}$ r $2\sqrt{11}$

s 2

4 a $5\sqrt{2}$ b $2\sqrt{3}$

c $8\sqrt{5}$ d $3\sqrt{3} + 3\sqrt{2}$

e $2\sqrt{7} - 2\sqrt{3}$ f $2\sqrt{3}$

g $13\sqrt{3}$ h $2\sqrt{3}$

i $9\sqrt{3}$ j $18\sqrt{5}$

k $\sqrt{15}$ l $-\sqrt{5}$

m $-12\sqrt{5}$ n $-6\sqrt{2}$

o $7\sqrt{15}$

5 a $2 - 3\sqrt{2}$ b $6 - \sqrt{15}$

c $12 - 4\sqrt{6}$ d 42

e $10\sqrt{3}$ f $\sqrt{30} + 5\sqrt{3}$

g $4 - 2\sqrt{3}$ h 2

i 1 j $19 - 3\sqrt{35}$

k $17 - \sqrt{3}$ l $20 - 10\sqrt{3}$

m $5\sqrt{6} - 11$ n $28 + 18\sqrt{2}$

o $3\sqrt{10} - 8$

6 a $14 - 6\sqrt{5}$ b $29 + 12\sqrt{5}$

c $12\sqrt{3} - 16$

7 a $\dfrac{17}{2}$ cm² b $\sqrt{66}$ cm

8 $\sqrt{39}$ cm

l 6

n $3\sqrt{5}$

Exercise 3.5

1 a $\dfrac{2\sqrt{3}}{3}$ b $\dfrac{5\sqrt{2}}{2}$

c $\dfrac{\sqrt{3}}{2}$ d $3\sqrt{2}$

e $\dfrac{\sqrt{6}}{6}$ f $\dfrac{1}{8}$

g $2\sqrt{3}$ h $\dfrac{3 + \sqrt{3}}{3}$

i $\dfrac{2 - 5\sqrt{2}}{2}$ j $\dfrac{2 + 5\sqrt{2}}{2}$

k $4\sqrt{3}$ l $\dfrac{8}{3}$

m $-3 - 2\sqrt{2}$ n $\dfrac{2 + 3\sqrt{2}}{7}$

o $17 - 9\sqrt{3}$ p $\dfrac{49 + 17\sqrt{7}}{36}$

2 $\dfrac{21}{5}$

3 $\sin 60° = \dfrac{\sqrt{3}}{2}$

$\cos 60° = \dfrac{1}{2}$

$\tan 60° = \sqrt{3}$

$\sin 30° = \dfrac{1}{2}$

$\cos 30° = \dfrac{\sqrt{3}}{2}$

$\tan 30° = \dfrac{\sqrt{3}}{3}$

4 $\dfrac{1}{2}$

5 $7 + \sqrt{13}$

6 $-14 + 8\sqrt{3}$

7 a $1 + \sqrt{3}$

b $4\sqrt{5} - 2\sqrt{3}$

8 a $\dfrac{\sqrt{10}}{5}$

b $\dfrac{\sqrt{15}}{5}$

9 $22 + 6\sqrt{5}$

Exercise 3.6

1. a $\dfrac{10 + 13\sqrt{2}}{14}$

   b $4\sqrt{2} - 6, \quad 4\sqrt{2} + 6$

   c $\dfrac{23 + 3\sqrt{5}}{2}$

   d $\dfrac{31}{13}$

   e 11

   f $\dfrac{4\left(3 + \sqrt{2}\right)}{5}$

   g $3 - \sqrt{2}$

2. $13 + 4\sqrt{3}$

3. $x = 1, y = 3$

4. $x = 2\sqrt{3}, \quad y = 2\sqrt{2}$

5. $\dfrac{1 - \sqrt{3}}{2}, \quad \dfrac{1 + \sqrt{3}}{2}$

Exercise 3.7

1. a $512x^9$ b $25a^2 b$

   c $2b^{-2}$

2. $a = -1, \; b = \dfrac{29}{3}$

3. a $x = -3$ b $x = \dfrac{1}{10}$

   c $x = 8$

4. $x = 1, y = 2$

5. a $y = 4, y = -1$ b $x = -1, x = 64$

6. $4\sqrt{3} + 6\sqrt{2}$

7. $\left(4 + \dfrac{\sqrt{2}}{2}, 1\right)$

8. 15

9. a $7\sqrt{2}$ b $\dfrac{24 - 8\sqrt{2}}{7}$

10. $\dfrac{29}{2}$

11. $4\sqrt{2}$

12. $x = 49$

Chapter 4
Exercise 4.1

1. a $x^3 + x^2 - x - 1$

   b $x^3 - 6x^2 + 11x - 6$

   c $x^3 + 8x^2 + 21x + 18$

   d $4x^4 + 8x^3 - 4x + 1$

   e $3x^4 - 10x^3 + 3x^2 + 12x - 4$

   f $8x^3 - 36x^2 + 54x - 27$

2. a $4x^3 - 2x^2 + 3x - 6$

   b $5x^3 - 4x^2 - 3x + 9$

   c $3x^6 - 2x^5 + 9x^4 - 26x^3$
   $+ 14x^2 + 3x - 7$

3. a $4x^2 + 6x + 4$

   b $6x^3 + 6x^2 + 4x - 5$

   c $-6x^5 + 7x^3 - 5x^2 - x - 7$

Exercise 4.2

1. a $x^2 - x + 2$

   b $x^2 + x - 2$

   c $x^2 + 6x + 2$

   d $6x^2 + 13x - 2$

   e $4x^2 + 8x + 3$

   f $x^2 + x + 1$

   g $6x^2 + 5x + 1$

   h $4x^2 - 4x + 1$

   i $3x^2 + 10x + 3$

   j $2x^2 + x - 1$

2. a $x^3 + x^2 + 4x + 1$

   b $2x^3 + 5x + 7$

   c $x^3 - x^2 - 4x + 4$

3. a $x^2 - 2x + 4$

   b $4x^2 + 8x + 3$

Exercise 4.3

2. a $a = -20$ b $a = 16$

   c $a = 29$

3. $b = -20 - 5a$

4. a $a = 3, b = -27$

   b $a = -20, b = 18$

5. $a = 5, b = -9$

6. $p = -20, q = 3$

Exercise 4.4

1. a $(x + 1)(x + 5)(x - 3)$

   b $(2x - 1)(x + 1)(x + 3)$

   c $\left(x^2 + 1\right)(3x - 1)$

   d $(5x - 1)(x + 1)(x + 2)$

   e $(x - 1)(3x - 1)(x + 2)$

2. a $-4, 1, 2$ b 2

   c $-2, -1, 3$ d $-1, 2$

   e $-0.2, 1, 6$

3. a $-2, -3 - \sqrt{10}, \sqrt{10} - 3$

   b $3, \dfrac{1}{2}\left(7 - \sqrt{13}\right), \; \dfrac{1}{2}\left(7 + \sqrt{13}\right)$

   c $1, \dfrac{1}{2}(-3 - \sqrt{29}),$
   $\dfrac{1}{2}(-3 + \sqrt{29})$

4. $(x + 2)\left(x^2 + x + 1\right)$

5. $(x - 1)(x + 1)^2$

6. $a = 2, b = 0, c = 3$

7. $x = -1, x = 2$

Exercise 4.5

1. a 0 b 55

   c $-91/8$

2. a 5 b -4

   c 6

3. 4

4. 8

5. -5

6. a $a = -8, b = 12$

   b $(x + 3)(x - 2)^2$

Exercise 4.6

1. a $a = 3, b = -4$

   b $2, -2, -3$

2. a 0

   b $a = -1, b = -4$

3. a $b = 2a + 32$

   b $a = -13, b = 6$

   c $(2x - 1)(x + 3)(x - 2)$

4. a $k = -3, r = -12$

   b $(x - 5)\left(x^2 + 2x + 3\right)$

5. a 10

   b 50

   c $x = -3, \; -2 - \sqrt{6}, -2 + \sqrt{6}$

6. a $-21, (x - 1)$

   b $a = -1, b = -2, c = -1$

   c $x = 1, \quad 1 + \sqrt{2}, \; 1 - \sqrt{2}$

7. $8x^2 - 32x + 64, -80$

8. $5x^2 - 4x + 2, -13$

9. a -6

10 a $a = 3, b = -2, c = 60$

  b $x < -5, 3 < x < 4$

Chapter 5
Exercise 5.1

1 a $4, \dfrac{2}{3}$ **b** $-2, -8$

  c $-4, 1\dfrac{3}{7}$ **d** $-2, \dfrac{1}{2}$

  e $-1, 1$ **f** $-\dfrac{3}{2}, 0$

  g $-\dfrac{8}{5}, 4$ **h** $\dfrac{2}{3}$

  i $-4, \dfrac{8}{7}$

2 $x = 1, y = 1$ $x = \dfrac{4}{3}, y = \dfrac{1}{3}$

3 $-\dfrac{2}{3}, -\dfrac{1}{3}$

4 a

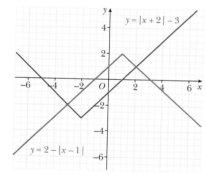

  b $(2, 1), (-3, -2)$

5 $2 \pm \sqrt{7}, \pm \sqrt{5}$

6 $0.5, 2.5$

7 a $4, 8$ **b** $2, 2^{\frac{2}{3}}$

8 $-5, -\dfrac{1}{2}, 3$

Exercise 5.2

1 $-0.5 < x < 0.75.$

2 a

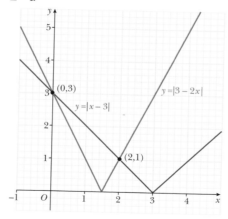

  b $x \geq 2, x \leq 0$

3 a $x < -\dfrac{2}{3}, x > 2$ **b** $-1 \leq x \leq 5$

  c $\dfrac{7}{2} < x < \dfrac{13}{2}$ **d** $x < -5, x > 1$

  e $x < -\dfrac{13}{5}, x > \dfrac{11}{5}$

  f $1 \leq x \leq 3$

4 a $\dfrac{4}{3} \leq x \leq 6$ **b** $x > -2$

  c $x \geq \dfrac{1}{2}$

5 a $\dfrac{1}{5} \leq x \leq 1$ **b** $x > -1$

  c $x < -\dfrac{3}{2}, x > \dfrac{1}{2}$

  d $-\dfrac{5}{3} < x < -1$ **e** $1 \leq x \leq \dfrac{5}{3}$

  f $-\dfrac{2}{3} < x < 4$

6 a $\dfrac{1}{3} < x < 7$

  b $-3 \leq x \leq -\dfrac{7}{3}$

  c $x \leq -4, x \geq -\dfrac{3}{2}$

  d $x \leq \dfrac{1}{2}$ **e** $-6 < x < 3$

  f $x \leq -\dfrac{12}{5}, x \geq 36$

7 a $-\dfrac{3}{2} < x < 3$

  b $x < -13, x > \dfrac{1}{3}$

  c $x \leq -32, x \geq 4$

8 $a = 10$

9 no solutions exist

10 $0 \leq x \leq \dfrac{8}{5}$

Exercise 5.3

1 $A(-2, 0), B(4, 0), C(5, 0), D(0, 40)$

2 a ⌢⌣ shaped curve, axis intercepts $(-2, 0)$, $(1, 0)$, $(4, 0)$, $(0, 8)$

  b ⌣⌢ shaped curve, axis intercepts $(-3, 0)$, $(-2, 0)$, $(4, 0)$, $(0, 24)$

  c ⌢⌣ shaped curve, axis intercepts $(-3, 0)$, $\left(\dfrac{3}{2}, 0\right)$, $(3, 0)$, $(0, 27)$

  d ⌣⌢ shaped curve, axis intercepts $(-2, 0)$, $\left(\dfrac{1}{2}, 0\right)$, $(2, 0)$, $(0, -4)$

3 $A\left(\dfrac{1}{2}, 0\right), B(0, 18)$

4 a ⌢⌣ shaped curve, axis intercepts $(2, 0)$ and $(0, 0)$ where $(2, 0)$ is a minimum point

  b ⌣⌢ shaped curve, axis intercepts $(2, 0)$ and $(0, 0)$ where $(0, 0)$ is a minimum point

  c ⌢⌣ shaped curve, axis intercepts $(-3, 0)$, $(-1, 0)$, $(0, 9)$ where $(-3, 0)$ is a maximum point

  d ⌣⌢ shaped curve, axis intercepts $(1, 0)$, $(0, 1)$ where $(1, 0)$ is a minimum point

5 a

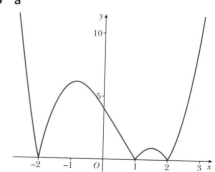

b

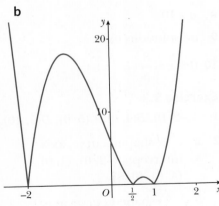

c

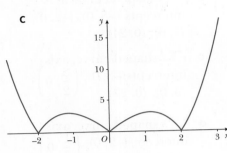

d

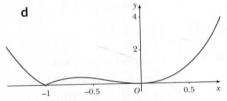

6 a $\wedge\!\!\vee$ shaped curve, axis intercepts $(-2, 0)$, $(0, 0)$, $(2, 0)$ $x(2 - x)(x + 2)$

b $\vee\!\!\wedge$ shaped curve, axis intercepts $(-2, 0)$, $(2, 0)$, $(1, 0)$, $(0, -4)$ $(1 - x)(x - 2)(x + 2)$

c $\wedge\!\!\vee$ shaped curve, axis intercepts $(-1, 0)$, $\left(-\dfrac{1}{2}, 0\right)$, $(2, 0)$, $(0, -2)$ $(2x + 1)(x + 1)(x - 2)$

d $\wedge\!\!\vee$ shaped curve, axis intercepts $(0, 0)$, $(2, 0)$ $3x(x - 2)^2$

7 a

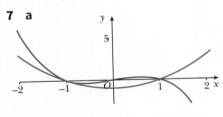

b $(-1, 0)$, $(1, 0)$

8 a

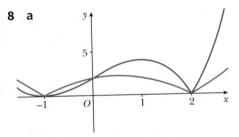

b $(-1, 0)$, $(2, 0)$, $(0, 2)$ $(-2, 4)$

9 $a = 1$, $b = 2$ and $k = -2$

10 a

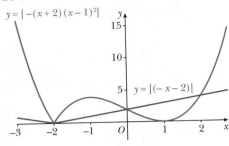

b $(-2, 0)$, $(0, 2)$, $(2, 4)$

Exercise 5.4

1 a $x \leqslant -2, 0 \leqslant x \leqslant 1$

  b $-1.8 \leqslant x \leqslant -0.4$, $x \geqslant 1.2$

  c $x \leqslant -2.3$

2 a $x \leqslant 3$

  b $0.5 \leqslant x \leqslant 1.6$, $x \geqslant 2.9$

  c $x \geqslant 3.2$

3 a $x < -1, 0 < x < 1$

  b $x \leqslant -0.9$, $-0.2 \leqslant x \leqslant 1.1$

  c $x > -1.3$

Exercise 5.5

1 a $\pm\sqrt{5}, \pm\sqrt{6}$ **b** $\pm\sqrt{2}, \pm 2$

  c $\pm\dfrac{3}{2}, \pm 2$ **d** $\pm\dfrac{\sqrt{6}}{6}$

  e $\pm\sqrt{\dfrac{2}{3}}$ **f** $\pm\sqrt{\dfrac{3}{2}}, \pm\dfrac{\sqrt{3}}{3}$

  g $\pm 2, \pm 3$ **h** $27, -8$

  i $\pm\sqrt{3}$

2 a $\pm 2, \pm\sqrt{1.41}$ **b** ± 1.73

  c ± 0.702 **d** $1, 2$

  e $1.59, -1.26$ **f** $\pm 1, \pm 2$

3 $x = -3, 2$

4 a $\dfrac{1}{4}$ **b** $4, 9$

  c $1, 25$ **d** $9, 25$

  e $25, 49$ **f** 9

  g $1, 9$ **h** 36

  i $4, 6.25$

5 81

6 a $7 - \sqrt{x} = \dfrac{10}{\sqrt{x}}$

  b $(4, 5)$, $(25, 2)$

7 a $2, 3$ **b** 2

  c $1, 3$ **d** $-\dfrac{1}{2}, \dfrac{1}{2}$

  e $-2, 0$ **f** $-1, 2$

8 $-2, 1$

9 b Length $8.47\,\text{cm}$, Width $5.31\,\text{cm}$.

10 $-4, -3, 1, 2$

Exercise 5.6

1 $x = -\dfrac{2}{3}, x = \dfrac{4}{5}$

2 $-\dfrac{7}{3} < x < 3$

3 $2 < x < 3$

4 $\dfrac{1}{5} < x < 1$

5 $x \geqslant -\dfrac{2}{5}, x \leqslant -4$

6 $x < -\dfrac{12}{5}, x > 24$

7 a

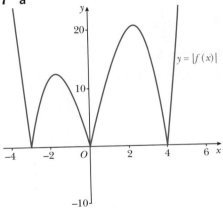

b

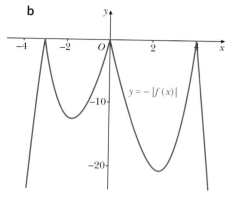

$y = -|f(x)|$

8 $x > 4k$, $x < -\dfrac{2}{3}k$

9

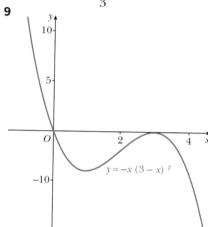

$y = -x(3-x)^2$

10 a

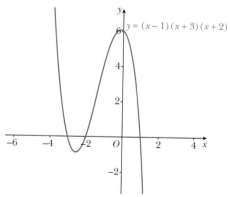

$y = (x-1)(x+3)(x+2)$

b

$y = |(x-1)(x+3)(x+2)|$

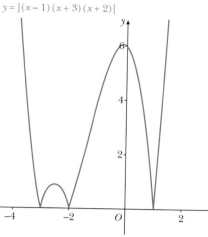

11 a $x(x-2)(x+1)$

b

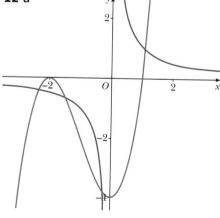

$y = (x-1)(2-x)$

$y = x^3 - x^2 - 2x$

12 a

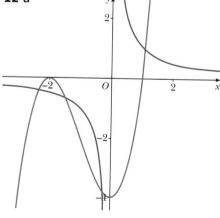

b 4

Chapter 6
Exercise 6.1
1 a $\lg 10\,000 = 4$ **b** $x = \lg 80$
   c $x = \lg 0.002$
2 a 1.34 **b** 2.34
   c −0.658

3 a $10^3 = 1000$ **b** $10^{-2} = \left(\dfrac{1}{100}\right)$
   c $x = 10^6$ **d** $x = 10^{-0.5}$
4 a 1260 **b** 0.794
   c 1.33
5 a −1 **b** 0.2
   c 3.5 **d** 1.25
   e 2.5 **f** −1.2

Exercise 6.2
1 a $\log_4 16 = 2$
   b $\log_4 \dfrac{1}{16} = -2$
   c $\log_a b = 3$
   d $\log_y 6 = x$
2 a $3^3 = 27$ **b** $4^3 = 64$
   c $25^{0.5} = 5$ **d** $16^{\frac{1}{4}} = 2$
3 a 64 **b** 25
   c $\sqrt{5}$ **d** 5
   e 15.5 **f** −3.5
4 a 0.5 **b** 0.5
   c −3 **d** 4.5
   e $\dfrac{1}{3}$ **f** $\dfrac{1}{2}$

Exercise 6.3
1 a $\lg 15$ **b** $\log 45$
   c $\log_4 3$ **d** 2
   e $\log_7 20$ **f** $\log_4 \left(\dfrac{1}{4}\right)$
   g 2 **h** 2
   i $\lg 4$ **j** $\log_4 \left(\dfrac{1}{8}\right)$
   k 1 **l** $\log_3 5$
2 a 3 **b** 2
   c $\dfrac{2}{3}$ **d** −1
   e $\dfrac{-1}{4}$
3 a $\log_a 10$ **b** $\log_a 3$
   c $\log_a 2$
4 a 0.4 **b** 0.6
   c 1.4 **d** 1.5
   e −0.3
5 $\log p + 2\log q + \dfrac{1}{2}\log r$

6 $\log \dfrac{p^3 q^n}{r^4}$

7 a $2\log p + \log q$

  b $\log p - \log q - \log r$

  c $\dfrac{1}{2}\log q - \dfrac{1}{2}\log r$

  d $-2 - 2\log p$

  e $n\log p + m\log q$

Exercise 6.4

1 a 3   **b** −1

  c $\dfrac{1}{35}$ **d** 15

  e 56   **f** 6

  g 0.3   **h** 5

  i 4   **j** 3

  k 500   **l** 14

2 a $x = \dfrac{10}{3}$, $y = \dfrac{1}{3}$

  b $x = 1000$, $y = 100$

  c $x = 8, y = 2$ $x = \dfrac{1}{2}, y = \dfrac{1}{2}$

  d $x = \dfrac{1}{2}, y = 1$

Exercise 6.5

1 a 0.646   **b** 0.792

  c 2.77   **d** 1.87

  e −0.774   **f** 1.22

2 a 0.408   **b** 1.22

  c −0.576   **d** −0.0792

  e −3.54   **f** 0.877

3 a 1.58   **b** 0, 2

  c 1, 3   **d** 0.5, 0.792

  e −1, 2.32   **f** 2.32

Exercise 6.6

1 a 1.09   **b** 1.16

  c 1.43

3 9

4 a 16   **b** 1.71

5 $x = 5, y = 40$

Exercise 6.7

1 a 20.1   **b** 12.2

  c 1.35   **d** 0.0183

2 a 1.61   **b** 1.13

  c −0.288   **d** 0.329

3 a 2   **b** 3

  c $\dfrac{2}{5}$ **d** 5

  e −1

4 a 5   **b** 12

  c 2   **d** 0.25

5 a 3.53   **b** 1.84

  c 2.04   **d** 1.47

6 a $\ln 5$ **b** $\ln 8$

  c $\dfrac{1}{2}(\ln 24 + 3)$

7 a 54.6   **b** 0.00248

  c 2980   **d** 6.19

8 a −3.64   **b** 207

  c 2.39   **d** 1.48

9 a $x = \dfrac{1}{2}\left(1 + e^4\right)$

  b $\dfrac{1}{2}(1 - \ln 5)$

  c $2\ln 2, \quad \ln 3 - \ln 2$

10 a 0.301

  b −2.64, 4.25

11 a 0.333, 5.29

  b $x = 2.30, y = 1.30$

Exercise 6.8

1 137

2 16 days

3 a 4 g   **b** 0.0579

  c 18 days

4 a $15000   **b** $1360

  c 14 months

Exercise 6.9

  a Graph 6   **b** Graph 3

  c Graph 2   **d** Graph 4

  e Graph 5   **f** Graph 1

Exercise 6.10

1 a asymptote: $y = -3$,

    y-intercept: $(0, -1)$

    x-intercept: $\left(\ln\dfrac{3}{2}, 0\right)$

  b asymptote: $y = 3$,

    y-intercept: $(0, 1)$

    x-intercept: $\left(\ln\dfrac{3}{2}, 0\right)$

  c asymptote: $y = -3$,

    y-intercept: $(0, -1)$

    x-intercept: $\left(-\ln\dfrac{3}{2}, 0\right)$

  d asymptote: $y = 3$,

    y-intercept: $(0, 1)$

    x-intercept: $\left(-\ln\dfrac{3}{2}, 0\right)$

  e asymptote: $y = 3$,

    y-intercept: $(0, 5)$

  f asymptote: $y = -3$,

    y-intercept: $(0, -5)$

  g asymptote: $y = 3$,

    y-intercept: $(0, 5)$

  h asymptote: $y = -3$,

    y-intercept: $(0, -5)$

2 a asymptote: $y = -2$,

    y-intercept: $(0, \ln 4)$

    x-intercept: $\left(-\dfrac{3}{2}, 0\right)$

  b asymptote: $y = -2$,

    y-intercept: $(0, -\ln 4)$

    x-intercept: $\left(-\dfrac{3}{2}, 0\right)$

  c asymptote: $y = -2$,

    y-intercept: $(0, 2\ln 4)$

    x-intercept: $\left(-\dfrac{3}{2}, 0\right)$

  d asymptote: $y = -2$,

    y-intercept: $(0, -2\ln 4)$

    x-intercept: $\left(-\dfrac{3}{2}, 0\right)$

Exercise 6.11

1 a $f^{-1}(x) = \ln(x - 3), x > 3$

  b $f^{-1}(x) = \ln\left(\dfrac{x + 1}{3}\right), x > -1$

  c $f^{-1}(x) = \dfrac{1}{2}\ln\dfrac{x - 1}{4}, x > 1$

  d $f^{-1}(x) = \dfrac{-1}{2}\ln\dfrac{x - 4}{5}, x > 4$

e $f^{-1}(x) = -\ln\dfrac{2-x}{3}, \; x < 2$

f $f^{-1}(x) = \dfrac{-1}{2}\ln\dfrac{6-x}{3}, \; x < 6$

2 a $f^{-1}(x) = e^x - 2$

b $f^{-1}(x) = e^{\frac{x}{2}} - 3$

c $f^{-1}(x) = \dfrac{1}{2}\left(e^{\frac{x}{2}} - 3\right)$

d $f^{-1}(x) = \dfrac{1}{3}\left(1 + e^{\frac{-x}{4}}\right)$

3 a $f(x) > 1$

b $f^{-1}(x) = \dfrac{1}{3}\ln(x-1) \; x > 1$

c $x > 1$

d x

e f and f^{-1} are reflections of each other in the line $y = x$

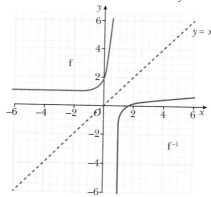

4 a i x^6 **ii** 729

b 1.65

Exercise 6.12

1 a 4

b 5, 125

2 a $x = \dfrac{7}{2}, \; y = \dfrac{3}{2}$

b $x = 4, y = 2; \; x = 9, y = 3$

3 −1.89

4 a $(x-1)(x-3)(x-9)$

b 0, 1, 2

5 a $(4x-1)(x-2)(x-5)$

b $-1, \dfrac{1}{2}, 1.16$

6 c 1.58

7 18.7

8 $a = 20.6, \; n = 2.49$

9 a $60°C$

b $27.0°C$

c 9 minutes

10 a i $16x^2$ **ii** $2x + \ln 4$

b 16

Chapter 7

Exercise 7.1

1 a 5   **b** 13

c 10   **d** 17

e 20   **f** $4\sqrt{2}$

g $\sqrt{29}$ **h** 10

4 15 units²

5 −3, or 7

6 $x = 1, x = -8$

7 $(9, -1)$

8 $(3p, 3q)$

Exercise 7.2

1 a 2   **b** 3

c 0.5   **d** 0.75

e −0.25   **f** $\dfrac{4}{7}$

2 $\dfrac{p-3}{q-1}$

3 a $-\dfrac{1}{4}$ **b** $\dfrac{3}{2}$

c $-3\dfrac{1}{2}$ **d** $-\dfrac{4}{11}$

e $\dfrac{2}{7}$

6 d Rectangle

8 a A, B, D

b 7 units

9 P, R, S

Exercise 7.3

1 a $y = 2x - 7$

b $y = -2x + 9$

2 a $y = 4x + 4$

b $y + 12x = 43$

c $y = 9$

3 a $y = 3x - 9$

b $y + 2x = 7$

c $3y = 4x + 33$

4 $y = x + 3$

5 a $y + 2x = 12$

b $2y + x + 3 = 0$

c $y = 7x + 2 = 0$

6 a $\dfrac{b-q}{a-p}$

b $b = 7a, \; q = 7p$

c 7

7 $(2, 2)$

8 a $3x + 2y = 2, \; 4x + y + 1 = 0$

b $\left(\dfrac{-4}{5}, \dfrac{11}{5}\right)$

Exercise 7.4

1 a 14 units²   **b** 66 units²

2 a 61.5 units²   **b** 33 units²

3 $k = 5$

4 a $8y = x + 15, \; 2y + x + 5 = 0$

b $(-7, 1)$ **d** 30 units²

e $\dfrac{6\sqrt{65}}{13}$ units

5 5 units²

6 a $y = 3x + 22$

b i $Q(0, 2), R(-7, 1)$

iii 10 units²

7 a $P(7, 0)$

b $y + 2x + 6 = 0$

c $R(-3, 0)$

e 20 units²

Exercise 7.5

1 a $y = ax^3 + b, \; Y = y, \; X = x^3,$
     $m = a, \; c = b$

b $yx^2 = ax^3 + b, \; Y = x^2 y,$
     $X = x^3, \; m = a, \; c = b$

c $y = a + b\sqrt{x}, \; Y = y, \; X = \sqrt{x},$
     $m = b, \; c = a$

d $y = \dfrac{a}{x} + b$
     $Y = y, \; X = \dfrac{1}{x}, \; m = a, \; c = b$

e $y = ax + bx^2$

$Y = \dfrac{x}{y}$, $X = y$, $m = b$, $c = a$

f $x^2 - \dfrac{1}{y} = (a + b)x - ab$,

$Y = x^2 - \dfrac{1}{y}$, $X = x$,

$m = a + b$, $c = -ab$

g $y^2 = ax - b$
$Y = y^2$, $X = x$, $m = a$, $c = -b$

h $y = a + \dfrac{by}{x}$

$Y = y$, $X = \dfrac{x}{y}$, $m = b$, $c = a$

2 a $\lg y = a\lg(x) - \lg(b)$, $Y = \lg y$,
$X = \lg(x)$, $m = a$, $c = -\lg(b)$

b $x = a\ln(y) - k$, $Y = x$,
$X = \ln(y)$, $m = a$, $c = -k$

c $\lg y = (n + 2)\lg x + \lg a$,
$Y = \lg y$, $X = \lg x$, $m = n + 2$,
$c = \lg a$

d $x = a\dfrac{e^y}{x} + b$

$Y = x$, $X = \dfrac{e^y}{x}$, $m = a$, $c = b$

e $\ln y = b\ln x + a$, $Y = \ln y$,
$X = \ln x$, $m = b$, $c = a$

f $\ln y = b\ln x + a$ $Y = \ln y$,
$X = \ln x$, $m = b$, $c = a$

Exercise 7.6

1 a $y = 3x$

b $y = 4x^2 + 1$

c $y = \dfrac{1}{2}\sqrt[3]{x} + 1$

d $y = -\dfrac{3}{x} + 10$

e $y = -3 \times 2^x + 7$

f $y = -\dfrac{3}{4} \times \ln x + 4$

2 a i $y = \dfrac{1}{2x - 3}$

ii $y = \dfrac{1}{5}$

b i $y = x(x + 3)$

ii $y = 28$

c i $y = \dfrac{-5\sqrt{x} + 18}{x}$

ii $y = 2$

d i $y = (9 - x)^2$

ii $y = 25$

3 $y = -3x^{\frac{5}{2}} + 22x^2$

4 a $y = \left(-2\left(3^x\right) + 15\right)^{\frac{1}{2}}$

b $x = 1$

5 a $e^y = 2\sqrt{x} - 4$

b $y = \ln\left(2\sqrt{x} - 4\right)$

6 a $\lg y = 3x - 14$

b $y = 10^{-14} \times 10^{3x}$

7 a $y = 1.5 \times x^{1.5}$

b $x = 4$

8 a $\ln y = 3\ln x - 2$

b $y = e^{-2}x^3$

Exercise 7.7

1 a

x	1	2	3	4	5
x^2	1	4	9	16	25

c $y = 0.5x^2 + 12$

d $x = \sqrt{6}$

2 a

x	1	2	3	4	5
$\dfrac{y}{x}$	74	63	54	43	35

c $y = -10x^2 + 84x$

d $x = 1.5$

3 b $y = \dfrac{2x}{x - 2}$

c $y = \dfrac{10}{3}$

4 $p = 2$, $q = 34$

5 $a = 27$, $b = 1.6$

6 b $p = 0.02d^4$

7 b $k = 95.5$, $a = 0.93$

Exercise 7.8

2 $a = 1$ or 11

3 $a = 3$ or 11

4 $3x - 10y = 3$

6 a $3x + 2y = 5$

b $(3, -2)$

7 a $\dfrac{2}{3}$

b $OP = 5\dfrac{1}{2}$ units,

$OQ = 7\dfrac{1}{3}$ units

c $20\dfrac{1}{6}$ units²

8 $a = 1, 3$

9 a $\dfrac{1}{y} = -\dfrac{1}{x} + \dfrac{1}{a}$

$Y = \dfrac{1}{y}$, $X = \dfrac{1}{x}$, $m = -1$, $c = \dfrac{1}{a}$

b $x = a\ln(y) - k$, $Y = x$,
$X = \ln(y)$, $m = a$, $c = -k$

10 a $y = 3x^{\frac{1}{2}} - x^{-\frac{1}{2}}$

b $y = 5.5$

11 a $y = \dfrac{4}{x} - 5x$

b $x = \dfrac{2}{3}$, $y = \dfrac{8}{3}$; $x = -\dfrac{2}{3}$, $y = -\dfrac{8}{3}$

12 a $\ln y = 2e^x - 2$

b $\ln y = 6$

c $x = \ln 5$

13 b $a = 950$, $k = -0.3$

14 a $b = 0.25$, $c = 9$

b $y = \dfrac{\sqrt{95}}{4}$

Chapter 8
Exercise 8.1

1 a $\dfrac{\pi}{6}$ **b** $\dfrac{\pi}{3}$

c $\dfrac{7\pi}{9}$ **d** $\dfrac{25\pi}{18}$

e $\dfrac{7\pi}{4}$ **f** 3π

g 5π **h** $\dfrac{25\pi}{6}$

i $\dfrac{\pi}{36}$ **j** $\dfrac{35\pi}{18}$

2 a 270°   **b** 150°
  c 105°   **d** 40°
  e 300°   **f** 108°
  g 162°   **h** 84°
  i 81°   **j** 216°

3 a 0.471   **b** 0.838
  c 1.54   **d** 1.97
  e 4.63

4 a 85.9°   **b** 126.1°
  c 60.7°   **d** 110.6°
  e 39.0°

5 a 0.932   **b** 0.697
  c 2.57   **d** 0.866
  e 0.809   **f** −1

Exercise 8.2

1 a 4π cm   **b** $\dfrac{10\pi}{9}$ cm

  c $\dfrac{15\pi}{2}$ cm   **d** $\dfrac{15\pi}{2}$ cm

2 a 12 cm   **b** 1.5 cm

3 a 1.6 rad   **b** 1.33 rad

4 a 10.5 cm   **b** 28.8 cm
  c 20.8 cm

5 4 cm

6 a 7.81 cm   **b** 1.75 rad
  c 29.3 cm

7 34.0 cm

Exercise 8.3

1 a $\dfrac{9\pi}{2}$ cm²   **b** $\dfrac{135\pi}{4}$ cm²

  c $\dfrac{175\pi}{3}$ cm²   **d** $\dfrac{135\pi}{2}$ cm²

2 a 16.3 cm   **b** 9.22 cm

3 a 1.56 rad   **b** 2 rad

4 a 0.75 rad   **b** 54 cm²

5 $60r - r^2$

7 a 1.55 rad   **b** 1.19 rad
  c 7.66 cm²

8 a 0.723 rad   **b** 7.78 cm
  c 5.78 cm²   **d** 3.63 cm²

9 a $9\sqrt{3}$ cm²   **b** 6π cm²
  c $\left(18\pi - 27\sqrt{3}\right)$ cm²

Exercise 8.4

1 8 cm

2 a 33.7 cm   **b** 114 cm

3 $\dfrac{40\pi}{3}$ cm

4 4.44 rad

5 24.6 cm

6 a 1.25 rad   **b** 2.41 cm²

7 12.3 cm²

Chapter 9

Exercise 9.1

1 a $\dfrac{1}{\sqrt{10}}$ **b** $\dfrac{3}{\sqrt{10}}$

  c $\dfrac{1}{10}$ **d** 1

  e $\dfrac{7 + \sqrt{10}}{9}$

2 a $\dfrac{\sqrt{7}}{3}$ **b** $\sqrt{\dfrac{2}{7}}$

  c $\dfrac{2}{9}$ **d** $\dfrac{\sqrt{7} + \sqrt{2}}{3}$

  e $\dfrac{7\sqrt{2} - 2\sqrt{7}}{6}$

3 a $\dfrac{2\sqrt{2}}{3}$ **b** $2\sqrt{2}$

  c $\dfrac{2\sqrt{2}}{3}$ **d** 1

  e $\dfrac{3 - 18\sqrt{2}}{8}$

4 a $\dfrac{1}{2}$ **b** $\dfrac{1}{3}$

  c $2\sqrt{3}$ **d** $\dfrac{\sqrt{3} + 1}{2}$

  e $\dfrac{-1 + \sqrt{3}}{4}$ **f** $\dfrac{-6 + 4\sqrt{3}}{15}$

5 a $\dfrac{\sqrt{6}}{4}$ **b** $\dfrac{3}{4}$

  c $2\sqrt{3}$ **d** 0

  e $\dfrac{-6 + 2\sqrt{3}}{3}$ **f** $\dfrac{2}{3}$

Exercise 9.2

1

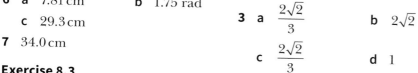

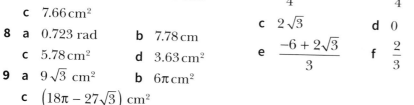

2 a second   **b** fourth
  c third   **d** third
  e fourth   **f** second
  g first   **h** first
  i first   **j** second

Exercise 9.3

1 a $-\sin 40$ **b** $-\cos 20$
  c $\tan 10$ **d** $-\cos 85$
  e $-\tan 40$ **f** $\sin 72$
  g $-\tan 60$ **h** $-\cos 30$
  i $-\tan 72$ **j** $-\sin 45$

2 a $\dfrac{3}{4}$ **b** $-\dfrac{4}{5}$

3 a $\dfrac{1}{2}$ **b** $-\dfrac{\sqrt{3}}{3}$

4 a $-\dfrac{5}{13}$ **b** $-\dfrac{12}{5}$

5 a $-\dfrac{3}{5}$ **b** $-\dfrac{4}{5}$

6 a $-\dfrac{3}{5}$ **b** $-\dfrac{4}{5}$

c $-\dfrac{1}{2}$ **d** $\sqrt{3}$

7 a $\dfrac{3}{5}$ **b** $-\dfrac{4}{3}$

c $-\dfrac{12}{13}$ **d** $-\dfrac{12}{5}$

Exercise 9.4

1 a i amplitude = 3,
period = 360°, (90°, 3), (270°, −3)

ii amplitude = 3,
period = 180°, (0°, 3),
(90°, −3), (180°, 3),
(270°, −3), (360°, 3)

iii amplitude = 2,
period = 120°, (30°, 2),
(90°, −2), (150°, 2),
(210°, −2), (270°, 2),
(330°, −2)

iv amplitude = 4,
period = 1080°, (0°, 4),
(540°, −4), (1080°, 4)

v amplitude = 4,
period = 360°, (90°, 6),
(270°, −2)

vi amplitude = 5,
period = 180°, (0°, 3),
(90°, −7), (180°, 3),
(270°, −7), (360°, 3)

2 a i amplitude = 3,
period = 2π,
(0, 3), (π, −3), (2π, 3)

ii amplitude = 1, period = π,
$\left(\dfrac{\pi}{4}, 1\right), \left(\dfrac{3\pi}{4}, -1\right),$
$\left(\dfrac{5\pi}{4}, 1\right), \left(\dfrac{7\pi}{4}, -1\right)$

iii amplitude = 3, period = π,
$(0, 3), \left(\dfrac{\pi}{2}, -3\right), (\pi, 3),$
$\left(\dfrac{3\pi}{2}, -3\right), (2\pi, 3)$

iv amplitude = 4,
period = 4π, (π, 4)

v amplitude = 1,
period = π,
$(0, 5), \left(\dfrac{\pi}{2}, 3\right), (\pi, 5),$
$\left(\dfrac{3\pi}{2}, 3,\right), (2\pi, 5)$

vi amplitude = 2,
period = $\dfrac{2\pi}{3}$,
$\left(\dfrac{\pi}{6}, 0\right), \left(\dfrac{\pi}{2}, -4\right),$
$\left(\dfrac{5\pi}{6}, 0\right), \left(\dfrac{7\pi}{6}, -4\right),$
$\left(\dfrac{3\pi}{2}, 0\right), \left(\dfrac{11\pi}{6}, -4\right)$

3 $a = 3, b = 2, c = 1$

4 $a = 3, b = 2, c = 1$

5 $a = 1, b = 2, c = 3$

6 a i period = 60°, x = 30°,
x = 90°, x = 150°, x = 210°,
x = 270°, x = 330°

ii period = 540°, x = 270°

iii period = 90°, x = 45°,
x = 135°, x = 225°, x = 315°

7 a i period = 2π, x = π

ii period = 3π, x = $\dfrac{3\pi}{2}$

iii period = $\dfrac{\pi}{2}$, x = $\dfrac{\pi}{4}$,
x = $\dfrac{3\pi}{4}$, x = $\dfrac{5\pi}{4}$,
x = $\dfrac{7\pi}{4}$

8 $A = 3, B = 1, C = 2$

9 $a = 3, b = 4, c = 2$

10 a $A = 4, B = 3$
b Amplitude = 4

11 $A = -1, B = 5, C = 2$

12 b 1

13 b 1

14 b 6

Exercise 9.5

1 a $f(x) \geqslant 0$ **b** $0 \leqslant f(x) \leqslant 1$
c $0 \leqslant f(x) \leqslant 2$ **d** $0 \leqslant f(x) \leqslant 1$
e $0 \leqslant f(x) \leqslant 3$ **f** $0 \leqslant f(x) \leqslant 2$
g $0 \leqslant f(x) \leqslant 2$ **h** $0 \leqslant f(x) \leqslant 5$
i $0 \leqslant f(x) \leqslant 3$

2 c 4
3 c 2
4 c 3
5 b 5
6 b 4
7 b 4
8 b 6
9 $1 < k < 3$
10 $a = 1, b = 2, c = 2$

Exercise 9.6

1 a 23.6°, 156° **b** 72.5°, 287°
c 71.6°, 252° **d** 204°, 336°
e 106°, 286° **f** 244°, 296°
g 36.9°, 143 **h** 109°, 251°

2 a $\dfrac{\pi}{6}, \dfrac{5\pi}{6}$ **b** 0.381, 3.52
c $\dfrac{\pi}{3}, \dfrac{2\pi}{3}$ **d** $\dfrac{2\pi}{3}, \dfrac{5\pi}{3}$
e no solutions **f** 2.28, 4.01
g 0.201, 2.94 **h** 3.99, 5.44

3 a 17.7°, 42.3°, 138°, 162°
b 77.1°, 103°
c 21.1°, 81.1°, 141°
d 72.3°, 108°
e 0°, 180°
f 67.9°, 112°
g 73.2°, 163°
h no solutions

4 a $\dfrac{\pi}{2}, \dfrac{7\pi}{6}$ **b** 76.6°
c $\dfrac{5\pi}{12}, \dfrac{13\pi}{12}$ **d** 115°, 175°
e 33.8°
f 0.29, 1.86, 3.43, 5.00

5 a 51.3°, 231° **b** 55.9°, 146°
c 45°, 135°, 225°, 315°
d 60°, 180°, 300°, 360°

6 29.4°, 89.4°, 149.4°

7 a 0°, 30°, 180°, 210°, 360°

  b 0°, 38.7°, 180°, 218.7°, 360°

  c 70.5°, 90°, 270°, 289.5°

  d 0°, 135°, 180°, 315°, 360°

  e 11.5°, 90°, 168.5°, 270°

  f 0°, 45°, 180°, 225°, 360°

8 a 60°, 120°, 240°, 300°

  b 26.6°, 153°, 207°, 333°

9 a 45°, 63.4°, 225°, 243°

  b 25.7°, 154°, 230°, 310°

  c 0°, 48.2°, 120°, 240°, 312°, 360°

  d 65.5°, 295°

  e 0°, 48.6°, 131°, 180°, 360°

  f 0°, 180°, 360°

  g 36.9°, 143°, 199°, 341°

  h 0°, 75.5°, 180°, 284°, 360°

  i 34.5°, 146°

10 1.74, 4.55

Exercise 9.8

1 a 101°, 281°   **b** 109°, 251°

  c 14.5°, 166°   **d** 180°

2 a 3.48, 5.94   **b** 1.11, 4.25

  c 1.74, 4.54   **d** 0.588, 3.73

3 a 15°, 75°, 135°   **b** 60°, 120°

  c 45°, 135°   **d** 65.7°, 114°

4 a 0°, 120°, 360°   **b** 30°, 90°

  c $\dfrac{\pi}{24}, \dfrac{13\pi}{24}$ **d** 1.28, 2.00

5 a 30°, 150°, 210°, 330

  b 36.9°, 143°, 217°, 323°

  c 60°, 120°, 240°, 300°

6 a 41.9°, 138°, 194°, 346°

  b 70.5°, 180°, 289°

  c 14.4°, 63.4°, 194°, 243°

  d 45°, 105°, 165°, 225°, 285°, 345°

  e 60°, 120, 240°, 300°

  f 51.3°, 90°, 231°, 270°

  g 60°, 300°

  h 45°, 166°, 225°, 346°

Exercise 9.10

1 a $f(x) = 2\cos 2x$

  b $f(x) = \cos\left(\dfrac{x}{2}\right) + 2$

  c $f(x) = 3\cos\left(\dfrac{\pi x}{4}\right)$

2 a $\dfrac{4\pi}{9}$

  b $0, \dfrac{\pi}{2}, 2\pi$

  c $\dfrac{\pi}{3}, \dfrac{5\pi}{9}, \pi, \dfrac{11\pi}{9}, \dfrac{5\pi}{3}, \dfrac{17\pi}{9}$

  d $\dfrac{\pi}{4}, \dfrac{3\pi}{4}, \dfrac{5\pi}{4}, \dfrac{7\pi}{4}$

3 a $\dfrac{10}{9}$

  b $3 + 2\sqrt{3}$

  c $\pm\dfrac{1}{2}\sqrt{5}$

4 a $a = 3, b = 2, c = 1$

  b period $= \pi$, amplitude $= 3$

5 b $\dfrac{3\pi}{2}$

6 i and ii

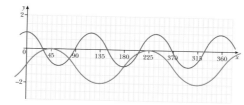

  iii 4 solutions

7 a $2 - 2\sin^2 x + \sin x$

  b $0, \dfrac{\pi}{6}, \dfrac{5\pi}{6}, \pi$

8 a $\dfrac{5}{4}$

  b $\dfrac{4}{3}$

  c $-\dfrac{\sqrt{3}}{3}$

  d $\dfrac{2\sqrt{3}}{3}$

10 a 60°, 180°, 300°

  b $0, \dfrac{3\pi}{2}, 2\pi$

Chapter 10

Exercise 10.1

1 a 720   **b** 132

  c 28   **d** ¾

  e 120

2 a 3!   **b** $\dfrac{11!}{9!}$

  c $\dfrac{8!}{5!3!}$ **d** $\dfrac{5!}{2!3!}$

  e $\dfrac{39!}{37!2!}$ **f** $\dfrac{(n+2)!}{n!}$

  g $\dfrac{(n+1)!}{(n-2)!}$ **h** $\dfrac{n!}{(n-3)!3!}$

  j $\dfrac{(n-1)!}{(n-5)!4!}$

Exercise 10.2

1 120

2 a 120   **b** 720

  c 5040

3 a 120   **b** 12

4 a 24   **b** 6

5 a 120   **b** 48

  c 72

6 720   **7** 36

8 120960   **9** 12

Exercise 10.3

1 a 2520   **b** 720

  c 1814400   **d** 120

2 210   **3** 151200

4 120   **5** 60480

6 5040   **7** 6720

8 20

9 a 360   **b** 1800

10 30240

Example 10.4

1 a 6   **b** 10

  c 1   **d** 35

  e 1   **f** 28

2 $\dfrac{7!}{3!4!} = \dfrac{7!}{4!3!}$

3 a 462   **b** 210

    c 31 824

4 84   **5** 20

6 350   **7** 180

8 210

9 a 525   **b** 756

10 70   **11** 126

12 64   **13** 200

14 2156

Exercise 10.5

1 21 600   **2** 7200

3 1152

4 a 288   **b** 576

5 1 693 440

6 a 70   **b** 65

    c 15

7 a 90   **b** 40

8 8

9 a 3 628 800   **b** 5184

10 21 624

11 64 800

12 7200

13 a 40 320   **b** 1152

    c 52

14 a 495   **b** 210

15 a 720   **b** 240

16 a 1176   **b** 12

17 a 40 320   **b** 576

    c 36   **d** 108

18 240

Chapter 11

Exercise 11.1

1 a $x^4 + 4x^3 + 6x^2 + 4x + 1$

    b $x^3 + 9x^2 + 27x + 27$

    c $x^4 + 4x^3 y + 6x^2 y^2 + 4xy^3 + y^4$

    d $-x^5 + 5x^4 - 10x^3 + 10x^2$
      $-5x + 1$

    e $x^6 + 6x^5 y + 15x^4 y^2 + 20x^3 y^3$
      $+15x^2 y^4 + 6xy^5 + y^6$

    f $y^4 + 12y^3 + 54y^2 + 108y + 81$

    g $a^4 - 4a^3 b + 6a^2 b^2 - 4ab^3 + b^4$

    h $x^4 + 12x^3 y + 54x^2 y^2 + 108xy^3$
      $+81y^4$

    i $x^4 - 12x^3 y + 54x^2 y^2 - 108xy^3$
      $+81y^4$

    j $81x^4 - 324x^3 + 486x^2 - 324x$
      $+81$

    k $x^3 + \dfrac{27}{x^3} + 9x + \dfrac{27}{x}$

    l $x^9 - \dfrac{1}{8x^6} - \dfrac{3x^4}{2} + \dfrac{3}{4x}$

2 a 8   **b** 12

    c -8 **d** -8

    e -12 **f** -32

    g 2430   **h** $\dfrac{-16}{27}$

3 a $1 + 3x + 3x^2 + x^3$

    b $1 + 5x + 9x^2 + 7x^3 + 2x^4$

4 a $10 + 3\sqrt{3} + \left(\sqrt{3}\right)^3$

    b $10 - 3\sqrt{3} - \left(\sqrt{3}\right)^3$

    c 20

5 24

6 20 000

7 a $1 + 5x + 10x^2 + 10x^3 + 5x^4 + x^5$

    b 45

8 $a = \dfrac{-1}{6} \quad b = \dfrac{1}{2} \quad c = \dfrac{-1}{2} \quad d = \dfrac{1}{6}$

9 3.75

10 $-8x^4 - 4x^3 + 6x^2 + 5x + 1$

Exercise 11.2

1 a row 2 $\,_2C_0 \,_2C_1 \,_2C_2$

    b row 6 $\,_6C_0 \,_6C_1 \,_6C_2 \,_6C_3$
      $\,_6C_4 \,_6C_5 \,_6C_6$

    c row 7 $\,_7C_0 \,_7C_1 \,_7C_2 \,_7C_3 \,_7C_4$
      $\,_7C_5 \,_7C_6 \,_7C_7$

2 a $x^3 + 3x^2 + 3x + 1$

    b $x^4 - 4x^3 + 6x^2 - 4x + 1$

    c $-8x^3 + 12x^2 - 6x + 1$

    d $x^4 + 12x^3 + 54x^2 + 108x + 81$

    e $16y^4 - 32y^3 + 24y^2 - 8y + 1$

    f $x^5 + 10x^4 + 40x^3 + 80x^2$
      $+80x + 32$

    g $a^4 - 12a^3 b + 54a^2 b^2$
      $-108\,ab^3 + 81b^4$

    h $16x^4 + 160x^3 y + 600x^2 y^2$
      $+1000xy^3 + 625y^4$

    i $0.0625x^4 - 2x^3 + 24x^2 - 128x$
      $+256$

    j $-0.00001x^5 + 0.001x^4$
      $-0.04x^3 + 0.8x^2 - 8x + 32$

    k $x^4 + \dfrac{81}{x^4} - 12x^2 - \dfrac{108}{x^2} + 54$

    l $x^{10} - \dfrac{1}{32x^{10}} - \dfrac{5x^6}{2} + \dfrac{5}{16x^6} +$
      $\dfrac{5x^2}{2} - \dfrac{5}{4x^2}$

3 a $90x^3$ **b** $435\,456\,x^3$

    c $540x^3$ **d** $1080x^3$

    e $20x^3$ **f** $-61236y^3$

    g $2\,800\,000x^3$

    h $-53\,084\,160x^3$

4 a $1024x^{10} + 5120x^9 + 11520x^8$

    b $256x^8 - 1024x^7 + 1792x^6$

    c $-16384x^7 + 28\,672x^6 - 21504x^5$

    d $729x^6 + 4374x^5 + 10\,935x^4$

    e $x^8 - 24x^7 + 252x^6$

    f $\dfrac{x^8}{65\,536} + \dfrac{x^7}{1024} + \dfrac{7x^6}{256}$

    g $x^{16} - 24x^{14} + 252x^{12}$

    h $512\,x^9 - 11\,520\,x^8 y$
      $+115\,200x^7 y^2$

5 a $1 + 18x + 135x^2 + 540x^3$

    b 495

6 a $1 + 3x + \dfrac{33x^2}{8} + \dfrac{55x^3}{16}$

    b $\dfrac{187}{16}$

7 a $1 - 40x + 700x^2 - 7000x^3$

    b $-9800x^3$

8 a $729 + 2916x + 4860x^2$

    b 3402

9 -280

10 $\dfrac{70}{81}$

Exercise 11.3

1 $a + 6d, \ a + 11d$

2 a 288   **b** 0

   c -620 **d** $96x$

3 a $5 + 2n$ **b** $25 - 8n$

4 23, 2

5 a $86, -7$ **b** 50

6 2160

7 2

8 a 15, 2   **b** 4440

9 6480

10 41583

11 2, 5, 8, 11, 14

12 14, 4

13 0.5, 200

14 2, 364

15 270

16 3, 152

17 16000

18 a $p = 1.7$ $q = 0.1$

   b $\dfrac{n+8}{5}$, 0.2

19 -12, 4

20 13

Exercise 11.4

1 a 3, 4374   **b** No

   c No   **d** $\dfrac{1}{2}, \dfrac{1}{128}$

   e No   **f** a, a^7

2 -4, 3

3 3

4 ± 1.5

5 $\left(\dfrac{3}{4}\right)2^{n-1}$

6 14

7 6, 13.5

8 6.75

9 $\dfrac{5}{2}, -\dfrac{1}{3}$

10 b 6, 0.5   **c** 0.375

11 18th

12 1.5, 2, 24

13 a -728

   b $53\dfrac{25}{27}$

   c $\dfrac{182}{729}$

d $2 - \left(\dfrac{1}{2}\right)^n$

14 7

15 31

16 189000

17 $\pm\dfrac{2\sqrt{3}}{3}$

18 The 11th term $\left(\dfrac{8}{19683}\right)$

19 24575.25

20 $5 + 15 + 45 + 135 + 405$

Exercise 11.5

1 a 64   **b** $\dfrac{8}{3}$

   c $\dfrac{5}{9}$ **d** 56

2 12

3 $\dfrac{9}{10}$

4 $\dfrac{1}{7}$, 6

5 a

$0.4\dot{5} = \dfrac{45}{100} + \dfrac{45}{10000} + \dfrac{45}{1000000} + \ldots$

6 $-\dfrac{1}{2}, -9$

7 $\dfrac{2}{3}, \dfrac{1}{3}$, 18, 6, 2   or 9, 6, 4

8 a $\dfrac{8192}{3}\left(\dfrac{1}{2}\right)^{1-n}$

   b $\dfrac{16384}{3}$

9 53

10 a $\dfrac{2}{3}$

   b 81

11 a 16

   b $\dfrac{5}{2}$

   c The progression does not converge since r is not in the range $-1 < r < 1$.

12 a $-\dfrac{1}{4}, \dfrac{5}{4}$ **b** 51.2

13 a 2.37   **b** 34.6   **c** 36

14 a $\dfrac{1}{3}\left[1 - \left(\dfrac{1}{10}\right)^n\right]$ $\dfrac{1}{3}$

   b $\dfrac{32}{3}\left[1 - \left(-\dfrac{1}{2}\right)^n\right]$ $\dfrac{32}{3}$

   c $\dfrac{16}{5}\left[1 - \left(-\dfrac{3}{2}\right)^n\right]$ does not converge

15 $-\dfrac{2}{5}$ 5.00

16 $\$20441700$

Exercise 11.6

1 2, 3

2 a 1, $\dfrac{1}{2}$ **b** 2

3 3

4 $\dfrac{4}{3}, -1, \dfrac{3}{4}$ or $\dfrac{3}{4}, -1, \dfrac{4}{3}$

5 5, 10, 20 or 20, 10, 5

6 2.32

Exercise 11.7

1 -108864

2 $4x\left(27 + 4x^2\right)$

3 a $1 + 24x + 252x^2 + 1512x^3 + \ldots$

4 a $16 + 96x + 216x^2 + 216x^3 + 81x^4$

   b 124

5 a $1 - 24x + 264x^2$

   b 192

6 4375

7 -672

8 $\ldots + 216x^2y^2 + 96xy^3 + 16y^4$

9 a $1 + 6kx + 15k^2x^2 + 20k^3x^3$

   b 0.4

10 3:5

11 a 5

   b $2 + 69x + 1015x^2$

12 a $1 + 4x + 6x^2 + 4x^3 + x^4$

   b $577 - 408\sqrt{2}$

13 $x = -5, y = 25$ or $x = 4, y = 16$

14 a $x = -\dfrac{1}{2}$ $y = -\dfrac{1}{8}$

   b $-\dfrac{1}{3}$

   c 272.5

15 $243\sqrt{6}$ 1410

16 90m

17 $\dfrac{1}{3}$

18 1

209

19 $2 \pm \sqrt{2}$, $\frac{1}{4}(2 \pm \sqrt{2})$

20 a $3, 12, 48$ $\quad 3 \times 4^{n-1}$

21 0.375 m east of its starting point,
1.5 m

Chapter 12
Exercise 12.1

1 a $7x^6$ **b** $9x^8$

  c $-2x^{-3}$ **d** $-x^{-2}$

  e $-3x^{-2}$ **f** $\frac{-5}{2}x^{-6}$

  g $\frac{2}{3}x^{-\frac{1}{3}}$ **h** $\frac{3}{2}x^{\frac{1}{2}}$

  i $-\frac{1}{2}x^{-\frac{3}{2}}$ **j** $-\frac{2}{3}x^{-\frac{5}{3}}$

  k $\frac{4}{3}x^{\frac{1}{3}}$ **l** $-\frac{1}{4}x^{-\frac{3}{2}}$

  m 0 **n** $x^{-\frac{1}{2}}$

  o $4x$ **p** $16x^7$

  q $\frac{1}{4}x^{-\frac{1}{2}}$ **r** $\frac{3}{2}$

  s $\frac{3}{4}x^{\frac{1}{2}}$ **t** $-\frac{1}{2}x^{-\frac{3}{2}}$

2 a $12x^2 - 6$

  b $8x^3 - 9x^2 - 2$

  c $3x^{-2} + 1$

  d $6x - 2x^{-2} + 3x^{-4}$

  e $4 + 2x^{-3} + \frac{1}{4}x^{-\frac{3}{2}}$

  f $\frac{1}{2}x^{-\frac{1}{2}} + \frac{15}{4}x^{\frac{1}{2}}$

  g $\frac{3}{2} + \frac{3}{2}x^{-2}$

  h $-3x^{-2} + \frac{5}{2}x^{-\frac{7}{2}}$

  i $5x^{\frac{3}{2}} - x^{-\frac{1}{2}} + 2x^{-\frac{3}{2}}$

  j $16x^3 + 18x^2$

  k $-2x^{-3} + \frac{15}{2}x^{-4}$

  l $\frac{5}{2}x^{\frac{3}{2}} - x^{-\frac{1}{2}}$

  m $8x - 4$

  n $16x^3 - 8x$

  o $12x - 5$

3 a -8 **b** 22

  c $1, -1$ **d** -1

  e -4

4 $(0,3), \left(\frac{2}{3}, \frac{77}{27}\right)$

5 $\frac{1}{3}$

6 -1

7 $0, 8$

8 $1, 5$

9 $(4, -5)$

10 $\left(\frac{3}{4}, \frac{3}{16}\right)$

11 $p = \frac{3}{4}, q = -5$

12 a -9

  b $a = -\frac{19}{3}, 3$

13 a $x^2 - x - 6$

  b $x > 3, x < -2$

Exercise 12.2

1 a $12(3x + 2)^3$

  b $10(2x - 3)^4$

  c $-28(1 - 4x)^6$

  d $2\left(\frac{1}{3}x - 3\right)^5$.

  e $\frac{3}{2}(3x + 1)^2$

  f $60(x - 1)^4$

  g $-24(3 - 2x)^2$

  h $-12(2x - 5)^3$

  i $18x(3x^2 + 2)^2$

  j $\frac{42x^2}{(1 - 2x^3)^8}$

  k $6(x - 2)^2(x - 1)x^2$

  l $\frac{6(x^3 - 2)(x^3 + 4)^2}{x^4}$

2 a $-\frac{1}{(x - 5)^2}$

  b $-\frac{8}{(2x + 1)^2}$

  c $\frac{6}{(1 - 2x)^2}$

  d $-\frac{72x}{(3x^2 - 2)^2}$

  e $\frac{-1}{2\sqrt{x}(1 + \sqrt{x})^2}$

  f $-\frac{3}{(x - 4)^4}$

  g $-\frac{15}{2(5x - 2)^{\frac{3}{2}}}$

  h $\frac{2}{(3 - 2x)^3}$

3 a $\frac{1}{\sqrt{2x + 2}}$

  b $-\frac{5}{2\sqrt{1 - 5x}}$

  c $\frac{2x}{\sqrt{2x^2 + 1}}$

  d $\frac{3x^2 - 4}{2\sqrt{x^3 - 4x}}$

  e $\frac{1}{(3x - 2)^{\frac{2}{3}}}$

  f $\frac{4}{\sqrt{2x + 5}}$

  g $\frac{1}{(2x + 1)^{\frac{3}{2}}}$

  h $\frac{4}{(3x - 1)(1 - 3x)^{\frac{1}{3}}}$

4 576

5 0

6 $\frac{5}{2}, 10$

7 $\frac{3}{8}$

9 $-\frac{21}{125}$

Exercise 12.3

1 **a** $4x + 3$

b $4x - 10$

c $2(x+1)^2(4x+1)$

d $-3x(1-x)^2(5x-2)$

e $\dfrac{x}{2}(x+3)^{-\frac{1}{2}}(5x+12)$

f $\dfrac{3x+4}{2\sqrt{x+1}}$

g $2x(2x-3)^{-\frac{1}{2}}(5x-6)$

h $\dfrac{9x^4 - 10x^2 + 1}{\sqrt{x}}$

i $9x^2 + 4x - 3$

j $2(x+3)^2(4x-3)$

k $4x(x^2 - 1)$

l $54x^2 - 30x - 16$

2 9

3 20

4 16 and 0

5 $x = 0.5, -2, -1$

6 $x = \dfrac{17}{3}$

7 $k = \dfrac{9}{2}(x-1)$

8 **a** $\dfrac{(3-x)(3-5x)}{2\sqrt{x}}$

b $x = 3$ or 0.6

Exercise 12.4

1 **a** $-\dfrac{16}{(x+5)^2}$ **b** $\dfrac{16}{(2x+5)^2}$

c $\dfrac{4}{(x+2)^2}$

d $\dfrac{(x+1)(x+5)}{(x+3)^2}$

e $-\dfrac{6x}{(x^2-2)^2}$

f $\dfrac{-x-4}{2\sqrt{x}(x-4)^2}$

g $\dfrac{-3x-4}{2x^3\sqrt{x+1}}$

h $\dfrac{2(x^2+x+4)}{(2x+1)^2}$

2 -1

3 $-2 \pm \sqrt{11}$

4 $\dfrac{10}{3}$

5 $\dfrac{5}{18}$

6 $\dfrac{1}{2}$

7 $\left(-1, -\dfrac{1}{2}\right), \left(3, \dfrac{1}{6}\right)$

8 $\left(-4, \dfrac{4}{3}\right), \left(2, \dfrac{2}{3}\right)$

Exercise 12.5

1 **a** $y = 11 - 7x$

b $y = \dfrac{1}{4}x + 2$

c $y = -2x - 2$

d $y = -5x - 9$

e $y = 80x - 64$

f $y = \dfrac{4}{9}(x-1)$

2 **a** $y = \dfrac{1}{7}(26 - x)$

b $y = \dfrac{1}{8}(42 - x)$

c $y = \dfrac{1}{2}(x+1)$

d $\dfrac{1}{3}(x+11)$

e $x = 2$

f $y = 7x - 20$

3 $(4, -31)$

4 $y = -6, y = 21$

5 $\left(\dfrac{1}{2}, 2\sqrt{2}\right)$

6 **a** $y = 10x - 11$ **b** $(2, 1)$

7 $p = \dfrac{5}{2}, q = -\dfrac{3}{2}$

8 $y = -2x$

9 $p = -4, q = 1$

Exercise 12.6

1 $\dfrac{97}{1350}$

2 0.03

3 $900p$

4 $-\dfrac{7p}{81}$

5 $10\pi\,\text{cm}^3$

6 $\dfrac{9\pi}{4}$

7 **a** $y = \dfrac{560\sqrt{3}}{x^2}$,

b $-71.8p$, decrease.

Exercise 12.7

1 $\dfrac{2}{27}$

2 10

3 $-\dfrac{16}{5}$

4 48

5 $\dfrac{8}{175}$

6 -0.06

7 $0.995\,\text{cm}\,\text{s}^{-1}$

8 $0.0212\,\text{cm}\,\text{s}^{-1}$

9 **a** $120\,\text{cm}^2\,\text{s}^{-1}$ **b** $600\,\text{cm}^3\,\text{s}^{-1}$

10 $503\,\text{cm}^2\text{s}^{-1}$

11 $-0.00637\,\text{cm}^3\text{min}^{-1}$

12 $30\,\text{cm}^3\text{s}^{-1}$

Exercise 12.8

1 **a** $36x^2$ **b** $\dfrac{36}{x^5} + 6x^2$

c $\dfrac{-x^{\frac{3}{2}} - 6}{x^3}$ **d** $500(1-5x)^3$

e $-\dfrac{25}{4(5x-2)^{\frac{3}{2}}}$ **f** $\dfrac{15}{(2x+4)^{\frac{5}{2}}}$

2 **a** $-24(x^2 - 6x + 8)$

b $\dfrac{3(x+1)}{4x^{\frac{5}{2}}}$ **c** $\dfrac{6}{(3x+1)^3}$

d $\dfrac{2(2x+7)}{(x-1)^4}$ **e** $\dfrac{2(x+3)}{x^4}$

f $\dfrac{-4}{(4x+3)^{\frac{3}{2}}}$

3 **a** 2 **b** -2

c -6

4 $x = -0.5, 1.5$

5 $-\dfrac{2}{125}$

6 24

7 a $\dfrac{dy}{dx} = 12x^2 - 12x - 9$

   b 24, −24

Exercise 12.9

1 a (1, 4) minimum

   b $\left(-\dfrac{5}{4}, -\dfrac{147}{8}\right)$ minimum

   c (1, −4) minimum, (3, 0) maximum

   d (5, 0) minimum

   e (−5, −97) minimum, (1, 11) maximum

   f $\left(\dfrac{1}{2}, \dfrac{13}{4}\right)$ maximum

2 a $\left(2, 2\sqrt{2}\right)$ minimum

   b (2, 12) minimum

   c $\left(6, \dfrac{1}{12}\right)$ maximum

   d $\left(-\dfrac{1}{2}, -16\right)$ minimum,

     $\left(\dfrac{1}{2}, 16\right)$ maximum

   e $\left(1, \dfrac{1}{2}\right)$ maximum,

     $\left(-1, -\dfrac{1}{2}\right)$ minimum

   f (1, 3) maximum

3 $\dfrac{10}{(x+3)^2}$ the numerator

   of $\dfrac{dy}{dx}$ is never zero

4 $a = 9$

5 a $a = -12, b = -13$

   b maximum

   c (2, −29) minimum

Exercise 12.10

1 a $(40 - 2x)\left(25x - 2x^2\right)$

   b $4(3x - 50)(x - 5)$

   c $x = 5\,\text{cm}$

2 b $L = 28.3\,\text{m}$ when $x = 7.07\,\text{m}$

---

3 c $x = 63.7\,\text{m} \; y = 0\,\text{m}$

4 b $108\sqrt{2}\ \text{cm}^2$

5 b $a = 9$

6 125 barrels, \$312 500

7 a $y = \dfrac{4500}{x^2}$

   c $A = 3740\,\text{cm}^3 \; x = 10\sqrt[3]{3}$ cm

8 b $38\,400\,\text{cm}^3$

Exercise 12.11

1 a $54 - 6x^2$

   b $x > 3, \; x < -3$

2 $24y + x + 386 = 0, \; 24y + x - 484 = 0$

3 $a = 64$

4 $\dfrac{19p}{2}$

5 0.02

6 $0.0477\ \text{cm s}^{-1}$

7 a $a = 2, b = 1$

   b minimum

8 $x = 100$, Profit $= \$10\,000$

9 b $x = 42.4\,\text{m}, A = 1800\,\text{cm}^2$

10 b $A = 200x - 2x^2 - \dfrac{1}{2}\pi x^2$

   c $56.0\,\text{cm}, 28.0\,\text{cm}$

Chapter 13
Exercise 13.1

1 a $2\mathbf{j}$ **b** $3\mathbf{i}$

   c $4\mathbf{i} + \mathbf{j}$ **d** $2\mathbf{i} + 2\mathbf{j}$

   e $2\mathbf{i}$ **f** $-2\mathbf{i} + \mathbf{j}$

   g $-2\mathbf{i} - 2\mathbf{j}$ **h** $-4\mathbf{i} + \mathbf{j}$

   i $-\mathbf{i} - \mathbf{j}$

2 a 3   **b** 10

   c 26   **d** 5

   e $\sqrt{53}$ **f** $\sqrt{89}$

   g $3\sqrt{2}$ **h** $3\sqrt{5}$

3 $18\mathbf{i} + 24\mathbf{j}$

4 $20\mathbf{i} - 48\mathbf{j}$

5 a $\dfrac{1}{5}(3\mathbf{i} + 4\mathbf{j})$

   b $\dfrac{1}{13}(5\mathbf{i} + 12\mathbf{j})$

   c $\dfrac{1}{5}(-3\mathbf{i} - 4\mathbf{j})$

---

   d $\dfrac{\sqrt{89}}{89}(8\mathbf{i} - 5\mathbf{j})$

   e $\dfrac{\sqrt{2}}{2}(\mathbf{i} + \mathbf{j})$

6 a $-6\mathbf{i} + 4\mathbf{j}$ **b** $5\mathbf{i} - 4\mathbf{j}$

   c $-13\mathbf{i} - 1.5\mathbf{j}$ **d** $1.5\mathbf{i} + \mathbf{j}$

7 a A and D, B and C, B and E, A and F

   b D and F, C and E

8 a $\dfrac{\pm\sqrt{3}}{2}$

   b 0   **c** $\dfrac{\pm 2\sqrt{2}}{3}$

Exercise 13.2

1 a $\begin{pmatrix} 0 \\ 11 \end{pmatrix}$ **b** $\begin{pmatrix} 2 \\ -2 \end{pmatrix}$

   c $\begin{pmatrix} 10 \\ -1 \end{pmatrix}$

2 $\begin{pmatrix} -5 \\ 4 \end{pmatrix}$

3 $\begin{pmatrix} 1 \\ 2 \end{pmatrix}$

4 $2\mathbf{i} + 2\mathbf{j}$

5 $\mathbf{i} + \mathbf{j}$

6 $\dfrac{13}{7}\mathbf{i} + \dfrac{18}{7}\mathbf{j}$

8 $\lambda = \dfrac{3}{2}, \mu = 7$

9 a $\begin{pmatrix} -8 \\ -4 \end{pmatrix}$ **b** $4\sqrt{5}$

   c $\begin{pmatrix} -1 \\ 4 \end{pmatrix}$

10 $\begin{pmatrix} 5 \\ 11 \end{pmatrix}$

11 Answer is **a**.

Exercise 13.3

1 a $c - b, \dfrac{1}{2}(c - b)$

2 a $q - p, \dfrac{1}{5}(q - p), \dfrac{1}{5}(q - 4p)$

Exercise 13.4

1 a $(2\mathbf{i} + 3\mathbf{j})\,\text{ms}^{-1}$

 b $(15\mathbf{i} - 25\mathbf{j})\,\text{m}$

 c $10\,\text{h}$

2 $(16.25\mathbf{i} + 11.5\mathbf{j})\,\text{ms}^{-1}$

3 $230\mathbf{i}$

4 a $8\mathbf{i} + 8\mathbf{j}\,\text{kmh}^{-1}$

 b $20\sqrt{3}\,\mathbf{i} + 20\mathbf{j}\,\text{kmh}^{-1}$

 c $-40\sqrt{3}\,\mathbf{i} + 40\mathbf{j}\,\text{ms}^{-1}$

5 a $26\,\text{ms}^{-1}$

 b i $60\mathbf{i} - 36\mathbf{j}$

  ii $70\mathbf{i} - 12\mathbf{j}$

  iii $80\mathbf{i} + 12\mathbf{j}$

 c $\mathbf{r} = \begin{pmatrix} 50 \\ -60 \end{pmatrix} + t\begin{pmatrix} 10 \\ 24 \end{pmatrix}$

6 a $10\,\text{kmh}^{-1}$

 b $-4\mathbf{i} + 6\mathbf{j}$

 c $\mathbf{r} = \begin{pmatrix} -20 \\ 18 \end{pmatrix} + t\begin{pmatrix} 8 \\ -6 \end{pmatrix}$

 d 5pm

7 a $15\mathbf{i} - 5\sqrt{3}\,\mathbf{j}\,\text{kmh}^{-1}$

 b i $40\mathbf{i} + (6 - 10\sqrt{3})\mathbf{j}$

  ii $17.5\mathbf{i} + (6 - 2.5\sqrt{3})\mathbf{j}$

 c $\mathbf{r} = \begin{pmatrix} 10 \\ 6 \end{pmatrix} + t\begin{pmatrix} 15 \\ -5\sqrt{3} \end{pmatrix}$

8 a $7\mathbf{i} + 5\mathbf{j}$

 b $6\mathbf{i} - 8\mathbf{j}\,\text{ms}^{-1}$

 c $10\,\text{ms}^{-1}$

9 $\mathbf{r} = \begin{pmatrix} -5 \\ 0 \end{pmatrix} + t\begin{pmatrix} 2 \\ 1 \end{pmatrix}$

10 $\mathbf{r} = \begin{pmatrix} 5 \\ -1 \end{pmatrix} + t\begin{pmatrix} 1 \\ -1 \end{pmatrix}$

Exercise 13.5

1 a 10 **b** $\sqrt{274}$

2 $6\mathbf{i} - 3\mathbf{j}$

3 $\sqrt{5}$

4 a $\mathbf{p} + \mathbf{q}$

 b $\dfrac{3}{2}\mathbf{p} + \dfrac{1}{2}\mathbf{q}$

5 a $\sqrt{65}$ **b** $\dfrac{3}{2}\mathbf{i} + \mathbf{j}$

 c $\dfrac{5}{4}\mathbf{i} - \mathbf{j}$

6 a $\begin{pmatrix} 6 \\ 2 \end{pmatrix}$ **b** $\begin{pmatrix} \frac{14}{3} \\ 3 \end{pmatrix}$

 c $\begin{pmatrix} 34 \\ -19 \end{pmatrix}$ **d** $\begin{pmatrix} 5.2 \\ 2.6 \end{pmatrix}$

7 a $\dfrac{1}{2}(a - b),\ \dfrac{1}{2}a - b$

 b $\dfrac{1}{3}b - \dfrac{1}{6}a$

8 a $5\,\text{km.h}^{-1}$ **b** $14\mathbf{i} + 11\mathbf{j}$

9 a $(5 + 3t)\mathbf{i} + (10 - t)\mathbf{j}$

 b $14\mathbf{i} + 7\mathbf{j}$

 c 10 minutes after the start

10 $-60\mathbf{i} + 80\mathbf{j}\,\text{kmh}^{-1}$

11 a $\mathbf{r} = \begin{pmatrix} -3 \\ -2 \end{pmatrix} + t\begin{pmatrix} 2 \\ 4 \end{pmatrix}$

 b $2\mathbf{i} + 8\mathbf{j}$

 c $t = 1.5$ seconds

12 a $301°$

 b $243\,\text{kmh}^{-1}$

13 $8.81\,\text{ms}^{-1},\ 027.3°$

14 a $10.5\,\text{ms}^{-1}$ **b** $082.7°$

15 a $11.1\,\text{kmh}^{-1},\ 015.7°$

 b 113 minutes

16 a $10\mathbf{i} + t(12\mathbf{i} + 5\mathbf{j})$

 b $20\mathbf{i} - 4\mathbf{j} + t(3\mathbf{i} + 10\mathbf{j})$

 c $-10\mathbf{i} + 4\mathbf{j} + t(15\mathbf{i} - 5\mathbf{j})$

 d $12:40\text{pm}$

Chapter 14
Exercise 14.1

1 a $2e^{2x}$ **b** $8e^{8x}$

 c $8e^{4x}$ **d** $-6e^{-2x}$

 e $-3e^{-\frac{x}{3}}$ **f** $2e^{2x+4}$

 g $3x^2 e^{x^3+3}$ **h** $6 + \dfrac{e^{\sqrt{x}}}{\sqrt{x}}$

 i $-2e^{-2x}$ **j** $-9e^{3x}$

 k $\dfrac{2}{3}e^x + \dfrac{1}{3}e^{-x}$ **l** $16x + 12x^2 e^{x^3}$

2 a $4e^x(x + 1)$

 b $x^2 e^{4x}(4x + 3)$

 c $e^{-2x}(4 - 8x)$

 d $\dfrac{e^{2x}(4x + 1)}{2\sqrt{x}}$

 e $\dfrac{e^{3x}(3x - 2)}{x^3}$

 f $\dfrac{e^{3x}(6x - 1)}{4x^{\frac{3}{2}}}$

 g $e^{2x} - \dfrac{e^{-x}}{2}$

 h $\dfrac{2 - 4e^{2x}(x + 2)}{(e^{2x} + 1)^2}$

3 a i $y = 2ex - e$

  ii $y = -\dfrac{x}{2e} + e + \dfrac{1}{2e}$

 b i $y = 3x - 1$

  ii $y = -\dfrac{x}{3} - 1$

 c i $y = 4x + 2$

  ii $y = 2 - \dfrac{x}{4}$

 d i $y = -\dfrac{x}{2} + \dfrac{1}{4} + \dfrac{\ln 2}{2}$

  ii $y = 2x + \dfrac{1}{4} - \ln 4$

4 $(0, 0),\ (2, 4e^{-2})$

5 a $\left(3, \dfrac{e^3}{27}\right)$ minimum

 b $\left(-1, \dfrac{4}{e}\right)$ maximum,

  $(1, 0)$ minimum

 c $(0, 1)$ maximum

Exercise 14.2

1 a $\dfrac{1}{x}$ **b** $\dfrac{1}{x}$

 c $\dfrac{3}{3x - 2}$ **d** $2 + \dfrac{4x}{2x^2 - 1}$

 e $\dfrac{12}{4x + 1}$ **f** $\dfrac{1}{2x + 1}$

 g $\dfrac{9}{3x - 2}$ **h** $3 + \dfrac{1}{x}$

 i $\dfrac{2}{2x - 1}$ **j** $\dfrac{1}{x \ln 2x}$

 k $\dfrac{3}{2(x + \sqrt{x})}$

 l $\dfrac{3x^3 + 1}{x^4 + x \ln 2x}$

2 a $\ln(2x) + 1$

b $3x^2(3\ln x + 1)$

c $x - \dfrac{1}{x} + 2x\ln 2x$

d $3\ln(2x^2) + 2$

e $x^2\left[3\ln(\ln 2x) + \dfrac{1}{\ln 2x}\right]$

f $-\dfrac{2[\ln(2x) - 1]}{3x^2}$

g $\dfrac{2(\ln x) - 2}{\sqrt{x}(\ln x)^2}$

h $\dfrac{3x}{3x - 1} + \ln\left(\dfrac{1 - 3x}{4}\right)$

i $\dfrac{3[\ln(1 - 3x) - 1]}{(1 - 3x)^2}$

3 $6\ln 2 + 2,\ 12\ln 2 + 10$

4 a $\dfrac{1}{2x - 1}$

b $\dfrac{2}{3 - 2x}$

c $\dfrac{4x + 1}{x^2 + x}$

d $\dfrac{2}{3x^2 + 4x + 1}$

e $\dfrac{6(x - 1)}{x(3x - 2)}$

f $\dfrac{x^2 - 4x + 2}{x^3 - 3x^2 + 2x}$

g $\dfrac{-3x^2 + 4x - 3}{3x^3 - 2x^2 - 3x + 2}$

h $\dfrac{1 - 3x}{(x - 3)(x + 1)}$

i $\dfrac{-x^2 + 6x + 3}{x(x - 1)(x + 1)(x + 3)}$

5 a $\dfrac{1}{x\ln 4}$

b $\dfrac{3}{x\ln 3}$

c $\dfrac{-2}{\ln 2 - x\ln 4}$

6 a $\dfrac{6x^2}{2x^3 - 1}$

b $\dfrac{5 - 8x^{\frac{3}{2}}}{10x - 4x^{\frac{5}{2}}}$

c $\dfrac{1 - 2x}{-x^2 + x + 20}$

Exercise 14.3

1 a $3\sec^2(3x)$

b $-3\cos x - 3\sec^2 x$

c $-4\sin 2x - 2\cos 2x$

d $24\cos 3x$

e $6\sec^2(3x)$

f $-\sin\dfrac{1}{2}x - \dfrac{1}{2}\cos\dfrac{1}{2}x$

2 a $4\sin x\cos\ x$

b $16\sin 4x\cos 4x$

c $2\sin x\cos x(2 + 3\cos x)$

d $3(1 - \sin x)(x + \cos x)^2$

e $24\sin\left(4x + \dfrac{\pi}{3}\right)\cos\left(4x + \dfrac{\pi}{3}\right)$

f $-16\sin x\cos^3 x$
$+18\tan^2 2x\sec^2 2x$

3 a $\cos x - x\sin x$

b $3\cos 3x\cos x - \sin x\sin 3x$

c $6x^2\tan x + 2x^3\sec^2 x$

d $\dfrac{3}{2}\tan^2\left(\dfrac{x}{3}\right) + \dfrac{1}{2}\sec^2\left(\dfrac{x}{3}\right)$
$+\dfrac{4}{3}x\tan\left(\dfrac{x}{3}\right)\sec^2\left(\dfrac{x}{3}\right) - \dfrac{1}{2}$

e $-10\cot 2x\,\text{cosec}\,2x$

f $\dfrac{2}{3}\sec x + \dfrac{2}{3}x\tan x\sec x$

g $\dfrac{2x\tan x\sec^2 x - \tan^2 x}{2x^2}$

h $\dfrac{3(\sin 2x + \cos 2x + 3)}{2(\cos x - \sin x)^3}$

i $\dfrac{2x(2x + 1)\cos x^2 - 2\sin x^2}{(2x + 1)^2}$

j $4\tan(2x)\sec^2(2x)$

k $\dfrac{\sec^2 x}{2}$

l $\dfrac{2}{(\sin x + \cos x)^2}$

4 a $e^{\sin x}\cos x$

b $-3\sin 3x e^{\cos 3x}$

c $2e^{\tan 2x}\sec^2 2x$

d $e^{(\sin x - \cos x)}(\sin x + \cos x)$

e $e^x\cos 2x - 2e^x\sin 2x$

f $2e^{2x}\cos\dfrac{1}{3}x - \dfrac{1}{3}e^{2x}\sin\dfrac{1}{3}x$

g $-e^x(\sin x + 2\sin 2x$
$+\cos x - \cos 2x)$

h $3x^2 e^{-\sin x} - x^3 e^{-\sin x}\cos x$

i $2\cot 2x$

j $3x^2\ln(\cos x) - x^3\tan x$

k $e^{x-1}(\sin 2x + 2\cos 2x)$

l $\dfrac{(-3x\sin x + \sin x + x\cos x)}{e^{3x}}$

5 a $\dfrac{\pi}{6} - \dfrac{\pi^2\sqrt{3}}{36}$

b $-\dfrac{4(1 + \sqrt{3})}{49}$

6 b $(0, 0), \left(\dfrac{2\pi}{3}, \dfrac{3\sqrt{3}}{4}\right)$

7 a $\dfrac{2}{\sin 2x\cos 2x}$

b $2\cot 4x$

Exercise 14.4

1 a $\dfrac{dy}{dx} = e^{-x}(\cos x - \sin x)$

b $(-\dfrac{3\pi}{4}, -\dfrac{1}{\sqrt{2}}e^{\frac{3\pi}{4}})$
minimum, $(\dfrac{\pi}{4}, \dfrac{1}{\sqrt{2}}e^{-\frac{\pi}{4}})$
maximum

2 $P = \left(\dfrac{2}{3}, 0\right)$ $Q = (0, -3e)$

3 $-\dfrac{3}{2}\sqrt{3}$

4 a $\dfrac{4x(\cos 3x) + 6x^2\sin 3x}{\cos^2(3x)}$

b $-\dfrac{4\pi}{3}$

5 a The graph cuts the axes at $(0, 0)$

b maximum point at $(1, \dfrac{1}{e})$

c $y = e^2 x + 2e^{-2} - 2e^2$

214

6 20

7 $a = \dfrac{1}{2}e^{\frac{1}{2}}$, $b = -\dfrac{1}{8}$

8 $y = \dfrac{\pi - 2x}{9} + \dfrac{3\sqrt{3}}{2}$

9 $-2\sqrt{3}\,p$

10 c 7.02 metres

11 a $\left(\dfrac{\pi}{4}, \sqrt{2}\right)$ maximum,

$\left(\dfrac{5\pi}{4}, -\sqrt{2}\right)$ minimum

b (0, 2) maximum,
$(\pi, -2)$ minimum
$(2\pi, 2)$ maximum

c $\left(\dfrac{\pi}{18}, 1\right)$ maximum,

$\left(\dfrac{7\pi}{18}, -1\right)$ minimum,

$\left(\dfrac{13\pi}{18}, 1\right)$ maximum

d $(-1, -2e)$ minimum,

e $(16, -4 + 8\ln 2)$ maximum

12 a $y = 8\ln 2 - 4x$

b $y = x + 3$

c $p = \dfrac{8}{5}$, $q = -\dfrac{3}{5}$

Exercise 14.5

1 $y = -\sqrt{3}x + \dfrac{\pi}{2\sqrt{3}} + \dfrac{1}{2}$

2 $y = 3 - x$

3 a $\dfrac{e^x}{e^x + 3}$

b $\dfrac{-2(1 - x)(x + 2)^2}{x^2}$

c $\dfrac{3\left(x^2 - 1\right)}{x\left(x^2 - 3\right)}$

4 a $\ln(\sin x) + \dfrac{x\cos x}{\sin x}$

b $\dfrac{\left(e^{\tan x}\right)^{-\frac{1}{2}}\left(e^{\tan x}\right)}{2\cos^2 x}$

5 $-\dfrac{1}{6}$

6 $5p$

7 a $y = x - 1$ **b** (0, 0)

c $\ln 2 - 1$

8 b 109°

9 c 30°

Chapter 15
Exercise 15.1

1 a $y = \dfrac{5}{7}x^7 + c$

b $y = \dfrac{3}{5}x^5 + c$

c $y = \dfrac{4}{5}x^5 + c$

d $y = -\dfrac{2}{3x^3} + c$

e $y = \dfrac{1}{3x} + c$

f $y = 4\sqrt{x} + c$

2 a $y = x^5 + \dfrac{3}{5}x^5 - x + c$

b $y = x^6 - x^3 + x^2 + c$

c $y = -\dfrac{3}{x^2} + \dfrac{1}{2x^4} + x^2 + c$

d $y = -\dfrac{1}{4x^4} - \dfrac{11}{8x^2} - 6x + c$

3 a $y = 2x^3 - 2x^2 + c$

b $y = \dfrac{x^6}{3} - \dfrac{x^4}{4} + c$

c $y = 3x^3 - \dfrac{12x^{\frac{5}{2}}}{5} + \dfrac{x^2}{2} + c$

d $y = \dfrac{3x^4}{2} + x^3 - \dfrac{3x^2}{2} + c$

e $y = \dfrac{x^2}{6} - \dfrac{2}{3x} + c$

f $y = -2x - \dfrac{2}{x} + c$

g $y = \dfrac{x^4}{6} - \dfrac{x}{3} - \dfrac{2}{3x} + c$

h $y = 12\sqrt{x} - \dfrac{4x^{\frac{3}{2}}}{3} + c$

4 $y = \dfrac{x^4}{4} - \dfrac{2x^3}{3} + 3x + 2$

5 $y = x^3 + x^2 - 7$

6 $y = 4x^{\frac{5}{2}} + 4x^{\frac{3}{2}} - 4x + 5$

7 $y = \dfrac{x^3}{3} - \dfrac{16x}{3} + 5$

Exercise 15.2

1 a $x^8 + c$ **b** $\dfrac{x^6}{3} + c$

c $-\dfrac{2}{3x^3} + c$ **d** $-\dfrac{1}{x^4} + c$

e $\dfrac{3\sqrt{x}}{2} + c$ **f** $-\dfrac{2}{5x^{\frac{5}{2}}} + c$

2 a $\dfrac{x^3}{3} - \dfrac{7x^2}{2} + 10x + c$

b $2x^3 + \dfrac{3x^2}{2} - 3x + c$

c $\dfrac{16x^3}{3} - 20x^2 + 25x + c$

d $\dfrac{2x^{\frac{5}{2}}}{5} + 2x^{\frac{3}{2}} + \dfrac{3x^2}{2} + x + c$

e $2x^4 + 16x^3 + 36x^2 + c$

f $\dfrac{6x^{\frac{7}{3}}}{7} - \dfrac{3x^{\frac{4}{3}}}{4} + c$

3 a $\dfrac{1}{x^2} + x + c$

b $\dfrac{x^3}{12} - \dfrac{2}{x} + c$

c $\dfrac{x^5}{20} - \dfrac{x^4}{8} + \dfrac{x^3}{12} + c$

d $x + \dfrac{4}{\sqrt{x}} + c$

e $\dfrac{2x^{\frac{3}{2}}}{3} - \dfrac{2}{5x^{\frac{5}{2}}} + c$

f $2x^2 + \dfrac{6}{x^2} - \dfrac{3}{2x^6} + c$

Exercise 15.3

1 a $\dfrac{1}{4}(x+3)^4 + c$

b $\dfrac{1}{10}(2x-1)^5 + c$

c $\dfrac{1}{7}(2x+5)^7 + c$

d $-\dfrac{1}{5}(3-2x)^5 + c$

e $\dfrac{1}{5}(3x+2)^{\frac{5}{3}} + c$

f $\dfrac{1}{5}(2x+1)^{\frac{5}{2}} + c$

g $-4\sqrt{x+1} + c$

h $-\dfrac{25}{9x+6} + c$

i $\dfrac{1}{18(1-3x)^4} + c$

2 $y = 2x^{\frac{3}{2}} - 4x^{\frac{1}{2}} - 1$

3 $y = 4x^{\frac{5}{2}} - 4x^{\frac{1}{2}} + 7$

4 a $k = -8$

b $y = x^3 - 4x^2 + 9$

Exercise 15.4

1 a $\dfrac{e^{6x}}{6} + c$

b $-\dfrac{e^{-3x}}{3} + c$

c $3e^{\frac{1}{3}x} + c$

d $-\dfrac{e^{-4x}}{4} + c$ **e** $\dfrac{2e^{3x}}{3} + c$

f $6e^{4x} + c$ **g** $\dfrac{e^{x+1}}{2} + c$

h $-e^{5-3x} + c$ **i** $\dfrac{e^{4x-1}}{16} + c$

2 a $2e^x - \dfrac{e^{4x}}{4} + c$

b $9x + 2e^{3x} + \dfrac{e^{6x}}{6} + c$

c $9x - \dfrac{e^{-3x}}{3} + 9e^{3x} + \dfrac{9e^{6x}}{2} + c$

d $\dfrac{e^{-x}\left(e^{3x}-2\right)}{2} + c$

e $\dfrac{e^{4x}}{4} - \dfrac{e^{3x}}{9} + c$

f $\dfrac{1}{3}e^{-3x} - \dfrac{1}{2}e^{-2x} + c$

3 a $2e^{2x} - 4\sqrt{x} + c$

b $\dfrac{x^4}{4} - \dfrac{2e^{3x+1}}{3} + c$

4 $y = e^x + 2\sqrt{x} - 1 - e$

5 $y = \dfrac{e^x}{2} - \dfrac{3x^2}{2} + 5$

6 $y = 5e^{-3x} + 18$

Exercise 15.5

1 a $-\dfrac{1}{6}\cos 6x + c$

b $\dfrac{1}{4}\sin 4x + c$

c $-4\cos\dfrac{x}{4} + c$

d $\sin 3x + c$

e $-\dfrac{5}{2}\cos 2x + c$

f $\dfrac{4}{3}\sin(3x+2) + c$

g $\dfrac{2}{5}\cos(1-5x) + c$

h $2\sin(3x+1) + c$

i $4\cos\left(3 - \dfrac{1}{2}x\right) + c$

2 a $3x + 2\cos x + c$

b $\dfrac{2x^{\frac{3}{2}}}{3} + \dfrac{3\sin 2x}{2}$

c $\dfrac{\sin 4x}{2} - \dfrac{3\pi}{4}\cos\dfrac{4x}{3} + c$

d $\dfrac{-1}{x^2} - \dfrac{3}{2}\sin\dfrac{2x}{3} + c$

e $\dfrac{3\cos 4x}{4} - e^{-x} + c$

f $-6\sqrt{x} - \dfrac{4}{3}\cos\dfrac{3x}{4} + c$

3 $y = \dfrac{x^3}{3} - 4\sin x + 3$

4 $y = 2\sin x + 3\cos x - 2\sqrt{2}$

5 $y = \dfrac{2x^{\frac{3}{2}}}{3} + 18\cos\dfrac{1}{3}x + 2$

6 $y = -\dfrac{15}{4}\cos 2x - \dfrac{1}{9}\sin 3x + \dfrac{2x}{3} + 3$

Exercise 15.6

1 a $7\ln x + c$ **b** $12\ln x + c$

c $\dfrac{1}{3}\ln x + c$ **d** $\dfrac{4}{3}\ln x + c$

e $\dfrac{1}{2}\ln(x+1) + c$

f $-\dfrac{1}{7}\ln(1-7x) + c$

g $\dfrac{3}{4}\ln(4x-1) + c$

h $-5\ln(2-x) + c$

i $-\dfrac{2}{15}\ln(1-3x) + c$

2 a $x^2 + 3\ln x + c$

b $16x - \dfrac{1}{x} + 8\ln x + c$

c $x - \dfrac{4}{x} - 4\ln x + c$

d $2x + \ln x + c$

e $-\dfrac{1}{9x^3} - \dfrac{2}{3}\ln x + c$

f $\dfrac{x^3}{3} - \dfrac{3}{x^3} - 6\ln x + c$

g $2\ln x - \dfrac{6}{\sqrt{x}} + c$

h $\dfrac{2}{3}x^{\frac{3}{2}} - 2\ln x + c$

i $\dfrac{e^{2x}}{4} - \ln x + c$

3 $y = \dfrac{1}{2}\log(4x-1) + 3$

4 $y = 4\ln x - 3x + 8$

5 $y = -\dfrac{1}{e^x} + 2\ln(x+1) + \dfrac{1}{e}$

Exercise 15.7

1 b $\dfrac{\sqrt{x-4}}{2x^2} + c$

2 a $16x\left(2x^2+2\right)^3$

  b $\dfrac{1}{2}\left(2x^2+2\right)^4 + c$

3 a $\dfrac{2\ln x}{x}$

  b $\dfrac{1}{2}(\ln x)^2 + c$

4 a $y = 8(x+2)\left(x^2+4x-1\right)^3$

  b $\dfrac{1}{8}\left(x^2+4x-1\right)^4 + c$

5 a $4x^3 e^{x^4}$

  b $\dfrac{1}{4}e^{x^4} + c$

6 a $4\cos 2x\left(\sin 2x + 3\right)$

  b $6\cos 2x\left(\sin 2x + 3\right)^3 + c$

7 a $5\sin^4 x \cos x$

  b $\dfrac{1}{5}\sin^5 x + c$

8 a $\dfrac{9x^2}{2}\left(x^3+5\right)^{0.5}$

  b $\dfrac{2}{9}\left(x^3+5\right)^{\frac{3}{2}} + c$

9 a $\dfrac{x}{\sqrt{x^2+3}}$

  b $\left(x^2+3\right)^{\frac{1}{2}} + c$

10 a $k = -2$

  b $-\dfrac{3}{\left(x^2+3\right)^2} + c$

Exercise 15.8

1 a $\dfrac{381}{7}$ **b** $\dfrac{52}{81}$

  c 44 **d** $\dfrac{140}{3}$

  e 3 **f** $\dfrac{13}{2}$

  g $\dfrac{321}{16}$ **h** $\dfrac{242}{81}$

  i $-\dfrac{103}{2}$ **j** $\dfrac{442}{15}$

  k 5.77 **l** $\dfrac{38}{3}$

Exercise 15.9

1 a $12x^3\left(x^4+4\right)^2$ **b** 51167

2 a 56 **b** 14

  c 413 **d** $\dfrac{220}{441}$

  e $\dfrac{2}{15}$ **f** 8.99

3 a $\dfrac{1}{3}\left(e^6-1\right)$ **b** $\dfrac{1}{2}\left(\sqrt{e}-1\right)$

  c $\dfrac{7}{3}\left(1-\dfrac{1}{e^9}\right)$ **d** $\dfrac{1}{4}\left(e^2-1\right)$

  e $\dfrac{2e^6-2}{3e^4}$

  f $\dfrac{1}{12}\left(7+18e^6+9e^{12}+2e^{18}\right)$

  g $\dfrac{1}{12}\left(-43+24e^2+16e^3+3e^4\right)$

  h $\dfrac{-31}{8}-\dfrac{1}{8e^2}+2e^2$

  i $-\dfrac{2}{3}-\dfrac{1}{3e^4}+e^4$

4 a 1 **b** $\dfrac{1}{6}(2+9\pi)$

  c $-\dfrac{\sqrt{2}}{6}$ **d** $\dfrac{3}{2}$

  e $\dfrac{1}{6}\left(2+3\pi^2\right)$ **f** $\dfrac{1}{6}\left(\sqrt{2}-1\right)$

5 a $\dfrac{3}{2}\ln\dfrac{11}{3}$ **b** $\dfrac{\ln 17}{4}$

  c $\dfrac{\ln 5}{2}$ **d** $\dfrac{3\ln 7}{2}$

  e $\ln 7$ **f** $\dfrac{2}{3}\ln\dfrac{11}{5}$

6 a $6+\dfrac{3}{2}\ln 7$ **b** $\ln\dfrac{4}{7}$

  c $\dfrac{\ln 3}{2}-\dfrac{3}{2}$

7 5

8 a $x+2+\dfrac{2}{x+2}$

  b $\dfrac{27}{2}+\ln 8$

9 a $3x+1,\ -1$

10 $2\ln 5 - 4$

2 a $4e^x\left(1+e^x\right)^3$ **b** 1190

3 a $\dfrac{4x^2+1}{\sqrt{2x^2+1}}$ **b** 6

4 b 0.835

5 a $\dfrac{2x+3}{5+3x+x^2}$ **b** $\ln 9$

Exercise 15.10

1 a $64/3$ **b** $16/3$

  c $2/3$ **d** 4.49

  e 0.300 **f** 4

2 a $9/2$ **b** 0.159

  c $2\ln 5$ **d** 2.77

3 a $\dfrac{32}{3}$ **b** $\dfrac{937}{12}$

  c $\dfrac{81}{2}$ **d** $\dfrac{253}{12}$

  e $\dfrac{2368}{3}$ **f** $\dfrac{27}{2}$

4 $\dfrac{1}{6}$

5 $2\sqrt{2}-2$

6 1.31

7 0.959

8 $k = \dfrac{1}{3}\left(e^2+2\right)$

Exercise 15.11

1 3

2 a $\dfrac{32}{3}$ **b** $\dfrac{125}{6}$

  c $\dfrac{125}{6}$ **d** $\dfrac{32}{3}$

  e $\dfrac{9}{2}$ **f** $\dfrac{32}{3}$

3 a 32 **b** $\dfrac{64}{3}$

4 $\dfrac{11}{6}$

5 a $P = (0, 8),\ Q = (4, 8)$

  b $\dfrac{64}{3}$

6 a $A = (-2, 2),\ B = (2, 2)$

  b $\dfrac{128}{3}$

7 $\dfrac{8}{3}$

Exercise 15.12

1 $y = x^4 - 2x^2 - x - 6$

2 $p = \dfrac{1}{3}$

3 $y = x^3 - 2x^2 - x + 8$

4 a $y = \dfrac{x^3}{12} + \dfrac{e^x}{4} + \dfrac{2}{3}$

b $y = \dfrac{x}{4} + \dfrac{11}{12}$

5 a $k = -8$

b $y = 4\cos 2x - 4x + 1$

6 a $y = \dfrac{2}{3}\sin\left(3x - \dfrac{\pi}{3}\right)$

b $y + x = \dfrac{\pi}{3} + \dfrac{\sqrt{3}}{3}$

7 a $-\sin x\, e^{\cos x}$ **b** $-3e^{\cos x}$

8 a $-3x\left(1 - x^2\right)^{\frac{1}{2}}$

b $-\dfrac{1}{3}x\sqrt{1 - x^2}$

9 a $\dfrac{3x^2}{\left(1 + x^3\right)}$ **b** 0.785

10 a $-3\sin x\cos^2 x$ **b** $\dfrac{1}{3} - \dfrac{\sqrt{3}}{8}$

11 $p = 0$

12 $k = \dfrac{4}{3}$

13 $\dfrac{8}{3}$

14 a $\left(-\dfrac{1}{2}, 0\right)$ **b** $\left(\dfrac{45}{4}\right)$

15 $\dfrac{2\sqrt{3}}{3} - 1$

16 a $x = 1, x = 3.5$

b $\dfrac{45}{4} - 7\ln\dfrac{7}{2}$

17 a $(2, 2)$

b $\dfrac{7}{2} - 4\ln 2$

Chapter 16

Exercise 16.1

1 a $6\,\text{m s}^{-1}$ **b** $85\,\text{m s}^{-2}$

2 a $6\,\text{m s}^{-1}$ **b** $10\,\text{m s}^{-2}$

3 a $4\,\text{s}$ **b** $4\,\text{m s}^{-1}$

4 a $9.6\,\text{m s}^{-1}$ **b** $\ln\dfrac{17}{12}\,\text{m}$

c $-\dfrac{25}{144}\,\text{m s}^{-2}$

5 a $\dfrac{\pi}{2}\,\text{s}$

b $3.03\,\text{m s}^{-2}$

6 a $28\,\text{m s}^{-1}$

b $v = 3\left(t + \dfrac{1}{3}\right)^2 + \dfrac{35}{3}$ is always positive

7 a $-3\,\text{m s}^{-1}$

b $-\dfrac{70}{3}\,\text{m}$

c When $t = 5$, P has changed direction and is moving back towards O and passes through O to the opposite side.

8 a $20\,\text{m}$ **b** $38\,\text{m}$

c $21\,\text{m}$

9 a $9\,\text{m s}^{-1}$ **b** $2\,\text{s}$

c $1 < t < 3$

10 a $v = 12 - 6t^2$, $a = -12t$

b $s = -1$, $v = 12$, $a = 0$. The particle started to the left of O and was travelling to the right at a constant speed $12\,\text{m s}^{-1}$

c $t = \sqrt{2}$, $s = 10.3\,\text{m}$

d i $t \geqslant \sqrt{2}$ **ii** never

Exercise 16.2

1 a $27\,\text{m s}^{-1}$ **b** $18\,\text{s}$

c $\dfrac{47}{3}\,\text{m}$ **d** $288\,\text{m}$

e $\dfrac{944}{3}\,\text{m}$

2 a $-\dfrac{40}{125}\,\text{m s}^{-2}$ **b** $\dfrac{10t}{3(2t + 3)}$

c $\dfrac{10}{63}\,\text{m}$

3 a $\left(6e^2 + 1\right)\,\text{m s}^{-2}$

b $\dfrac{1}{2}\left(3e^{2t} + t^2 - 3\right)$

c $82\,\text{m}$

4 $\left(6 + \dfrac{\pi^2}{9}\right)\,\text{m}$, $0.5\,\text{m s}^{-2}$

5 a $\dfrac{32}{3}\,\text{m s}^{-1}$ **b** $t = 2$

c $\dfrac{40}{3}\,\text{m}$

6 a $8\,\text{m s}^{-1}$ **b** $\dfrac{16}{3}\,\text{m}$

c 3.06 **d** $9.85\,\text{m}$

7 a $p = 10$, $q = -8$

b $s = \dfrac{5}{3}t^3 - 4t^2 + 3t$

c $\dfrac{3}{5}\,\text{s}$ **d** $\dfrac{110}{3}\,\text{m}$

Exercise 16.3

1 a $5.76\,\text{m s}^{-1}$ **b** $6\,\text{m s}^{-1}$

c $8\,\text{m s}^{-2}$

2 a $14\,\text{m s}^{-1}$ **b** $2\,\text{s}$

c $9\,\text{m s}^{-2}$

3 b $242\,\text{m s}^{-2}$ **c** $8104\,\text{m}$

4 a $1.41\,\text{s}$

b $\dfrac{-1 + 3\sqrt{3}}{2}\,\text{m s}^{-1}$, $-3 - \sqrt{3}\,\text{m s}^{-2}$

5 a $v = 3t^2 - 3$, $a = 6t$

b The particle is $1\,\text{m}$ from O and moving to the right of O with a velocity $-3\,\text{m s}^{-1}$

c The particle is $3\,\text{m}$ from O and moving to the left of O with a velocity $9\,\text{m s}^{-1}$

d The change in direction is when $t = 1$ when it is $1\,\text{m}$ to the left of O.

6 $s = \dfrac{32t^2}{15t + 15}$

7 a $4\,\text{m s}^{-1}$

b i $4\,\text{m s}^{-1}$ **ii** $\dfrac{1}{5}\,\text{m s}^{-1}$

c i $0\,\text{m s}^{-2}$ **ii** $-\dfrac{1}{50}\,\text{m s}^{-2}$

d

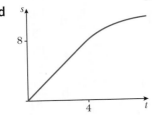

e $0.16\,\text{m}$

8 a $-10 \leqslant a \leqslant 10$

b $4.27\,\text{m}$